1970

P9-CBH-239

Schiller in Russian literature

3 0301 00035336 3

This book may be kept

FOURTEEN DAYS

A fine will be charged for each day the book is kept overtime.

DE 14 '71			
GAYLORD 142			PRINTED IN U.S.A.

Schiller in Russian Literature

University of Pennsylvania Studies
in Germanic Languages and Literatures

Edited by

ANDRÉ VON GRONICKA : OTTO SPRINGER

With the cooperation of

Adolph C. Gorr
Adolph D. Klarmann
Albert L. Lloyd
Heinz Moenkemeyer
Alfred Senn

Schiller in Russian Literature

By

Edmund K. Kostka

Philadelphia

University of Pennsylvania Press

LIBRARY
College of St. Francis
JOLIET, ILL.

© 1965 by the Trustees of the University of Pennsylvania

Published in Great Britain, India, and Pakistan
by the Oxford University Press
London, Bombay, and Karachi

Library of Congress Catalogue Card Number: 63–7865

7391

Printed in the United States of America

891.7
K864

To my Parents, with Gratitude

52510

Acknowledgments

I WISH TO EXPRESS GRATITUDE TO PROFESSOR ANDRÉ VON Gronicka for his assistance in the preparation of this study, an earlier version of which was a dissertation presented at Columbia University. Thanks are extended not only for his helpful suggestions and stimulating criticism, but also for his great interest in the project and the constant encouragement given throughout. Thanks are due, furthermore, to Professors Leon Stilman and Susanne H. Nobbe for their suggestions and enlightening criticism. I wish also to thank Professors N. Oulianoff and Chandler B. Beall for valuable bibliographical and topical hints regarding the chapters on Ogarev and Dostoyevsky. For advice on matters of style I am indebted to Professor Edgar R. Lorch.

E. K.

Contents

List of Abbreviations

ASEER—The American Slavic and East European Review.

GR—Germanic Review.

PMLA—Publications of the Modern Language Association of America.

PQ—Philological Quarterly.

SEEJ—The Slavic and East European Journal.

SEER—Slavonic and East European Review.

SEES—Slavic and East-European Studies.

Schiller in Russian Literature

Introduction

THE INFLUENCE OF SCHILLER LOOMS LARGE AT THE BEGINNING of modern Russian literature. As early as 1782 the author of *Die Räuber* became known to the students of Moscow University through the lectures of Professor J. G. Schwarz who was Schiller's first literary standard bearer in that city. On September 19, 1787, upon the recommendation of F. M. Klinger, the actors of the Petersburg Court Theatre performed the first act of Schiller's *Don Carlos* on the amateur stage at Gatchina Castle.[1] The Russian première of the whole drama followed on November 9 of the same year in Riga. In 1788 Ivan Sokolov, a Moscow University student, translated the drama *Kabale und Liebe,* and in 1792 Nikolay Sandunov, the brother of the famous comedian, Sila Sandunov, produced a Russian version of *Die Räuber.*

In the following year N. M. Karamzin wrote a poem entitled, "Song of the World" which is a rather free elaboration of Schiller's dithyrambic ode, "An die Freude." Schiller's dramas, especially *Die Räuber* and *Kabale und Liebe,* were a favorite theme of discussion in the "Friendly Literary Society" (founded 1801), one of the first literary circles in Russia dedicated to the "transplanting of the poetry of Wieland, Schiller, and Goethe on to Russian soil."[2]

The first critical essay on Schiller in Russia appeared in 1805

[1] The Gatchina Castle, near St. Petersburg, was the residence of the then heir, later Emperor Paul I.

[2] I. I. Zamotin, *Romantizm dvadtsatykh godov XIX stoletia v russkoy literature* (St. Petersburg–Moskva, 1913), II, 104. N.B.: All translations are mine unless otherwise indicated. The transliteration of Russian words is based on the system adopted by the American Council of Learned Societies.

in the Moscow periodical *Avrora*. Written by De-Sanglet, one of the magazine's editors, it contained "an aesthetical and 'philosophical' characterization of Schiller's works."[3] This article, together with the subsequent translations of Schiller's dramas in the Twenties and Thirties, contributed much to the development and refinement of literary taste in Russia. From an aesthetic point of view, Schiller proved a real revelation to the educated classes. But Schiller's idealism appealed above all to the restless imagination of the younger generation. His enthusiasm for justice and freedom, for the good and the beautiful, for brotherhood and universal love, kindled the hearts of those Russian intellectuals who dreamed of a better order of things for the long-suffering Russian people. Some of them tried to put into practice Schiller's aesthetic and humanitarian concepts. Referring to these sociopolitical reformers, a critic remarks:

> Von ihnen hat zuerst der erwähnte "russische Posa" Karasin[4] den Versuch unternommen, Russland auf der Grundlage von Schiller's ästhetischem Staat aufzubauen. Der Versuch misslang. Erst Alexander Herzen schuf unmittelbar aus dem Geist seines "Lehrers Schiller" die Grundlagen für sein Reformwerk, das später von Tschernyschewski und Michalowski weiterausgebaut wurde.[5]

Schiller, the poet of freedom, assumed a special significance for the Russian people in those times of political reaction. It was during the periods of police terror and ruthless oppression that Schiller's spirit helped to keep alive the spark of hope, the will to resistance among intimidated liberals and exiled revolutionaries. To these Russians struggling against despotism and degradation, Schiller was far more than just another foreign writer—

---

[3] *Schiller*, ed. S. A. Vengerov (St. Petersburg, 1900), IV, 535.

[4] Vasily Nazarovich Karazin (1773–1842). Cp. Alexander Herzen's essay "Emperor Alexander I and V. N. Karazin," A. I. Gertsen, *Poln. sobr. soch. i pisem* (St. Petersburg, 1919), XV, 141 ff.

[5] Otto P. Peterson, *Schiller in Russland* (New York, 1934), p. 325.

to them he was a dear friend and comrade-in-arms. As a Russian critic attests :

He [Schiller] has been for us one of those friends and writers we shall always remember with a sentiment of profound gratitude. Although he is a poet from a foreign land, a representative of a foreign literature who addresses an altogether different society, he has, nonetheless, in the course of time become more familiar and intelligible to the Russian reading public than other men of letters who though "related to us by blood," who even though writing in Russian, yet do not respond to the most burning spiritual needs of our society, who offer stones instead of bread.[6]

Among the many who helped to make Schiller "more familiar and intelligible" to the Russians the name of V. A. Zhukovsky stands out in a special way. A gifted poet and translator of genius, he succeeded in making Schiller almost a national Russian bard. However, he conceived of Schiller as a romantic poet *par excellence* and had little understanding for his philosophical and aesthetic writings. Commenting on Zhukovsky's peculiar concept of romanticism, a German scholar observes : "Wenn der Begriff der Romantik in Russland immer anders verstanden wurde als in Deutschland selbst, so liegt es zum grossen Teile gerade an dem Einfluss von Shukowski."[7] Belinsky was quick to recognize the great achievement of Zhukovsky as interpreter and translator

[6] Yury Veselovsky, "Schiller kak vdokhnovitel Russkikh Pisateley," *Russkaya Mysl,* II (Moskva, 1906), 1. Cp. also Rudolf Fischer : "Die Dekabristen wie die revolutionären Demokraten und alle Nachfolger, die bewusst für ihre Ideen fielen, handelten eben im Sinne Schillers : in der Freiheit der Entscheidung für das als Recht erkannte. Solche Opfer sind unsterblich und mahnen in Ewigkeit." "Schillers Widerhall in der Russischen Literatur," *Berichte über die Verhandlungen der Sächsischen Akademie der Wissenschaften zu Leipzig* (Berlin, 1958), Bd. 103, Heft 5, p. 26.

[7] Maximilian Braun, *Russische Dichtung im neunzehnten Jahrhundert* (Heidelberg, 1953), p. 37. The Soviet critic Yu. Tynyanov says in this connection : "By 'romanticism' one understood sometimes in Russia the German or English influence in general which had taken the place of the

of Schiller and repeatedly paid tribute to him in his articles.
If Schiller's poetry has become a national poetry in Russia,
and if every Russian can understand it easily, then, according
to this critic, they have Zhukovsky to thank for it : "Through
Zhukovsky we come to understand and love Schiller already
in childhood, as if he were our national poet who speaks to us
in Russian sounds, in the Russian language."[8] And another Russian critic goes even so far as to declare that Schiller's "Greek"
ballads, owing to Zhukovsky, are possibly more "classical" in
Russia than in Germany.[9]

Zhukovsky made an excellent translation of *Die Jungfrau von
Orleans*. But his fame rests principally on his masterly renderings
of Schiller's poems, which at once found their way into the hearts
of the Russian people and of Russian school children in the most
distant corners of the country. It was only through Zhukovsky
that Schiller came to be known in Russia also for his lyric poetry;
the merit of these masterly translations is heightened by the fact
that this work of popularizing Schiller was, as had been the case
with Goethe, accomplished by Zhukovsky single-handed.[10]

An interesting detail of Schiller's influence on Zhukovsky deserves to be mentioned in this connection. Profoundly impressed
by the humanitarian content of Schiller's tragedies which he saw
performed during his trip through Europe (1820–21), he resolved
to buy back his former serfs, whom he had sold before his departure, and made written arrangements for their immediate release.
"In a case like this," observes a Russian critic, "it is superfluous
to make any comment on the humane and noble influence of

French influence; thus, Schiller, Goethe, and even Lessing were ranked as
'romanticists.' " *Pushkin v mirovoy literature* (Leningrad, 1926), p. 215.
    [8] Belinsky, *Sochinenia* (Kiev, 1911), III, 394.
    [9] D. S. Mirsky, *History of Russian Literature* (London, 1927), p. 100.
    [10] Cp. C. E. Passage, "The Influence of Schiller in Russia," *ASEER* (May
1946), p. 135.

Schiller's poetry."[11] Many other details of Schiller's influence on Zhukovsky could be adduced but as this area has been sufficiently explored we may limit ourselves to referring the reader to the works in question.[12]

An important contribution to Schiller's fame in Russia was made by the periodicals *Moskovsky Vestnik, Moskovsky Telegraf, Teleskop,* and *Syn Otechestva.* M. P. Pogodin, the editor of *Moskovsky Vestnik,* played the leading role in this popularization of the German poet, publishing excerpts from *Wallensteins Lager, Maria Stuart, Wallensteins Tod,* and many others. Equally important was the influence of the Russian theatres. As early as 1810 *Maria Stuart* had triumphed on the stage of the St. Petersburg theatre, and *Die Räuber* followed successfully in 1814. In the 1820's the trend towards romanticism and toward Schiller increased greatly. The first performance of *Don Carlos* in St. Petersburg, in February, 1829, became a tremendous success and the theatre critic of the magazine *Syn Otechestva* declared enthusiastically that he could think of "the future of the Russian drama and the Russian theatre only in terms of an imitation of Schiller and other great and original creators of the European drama."[13]

The government officials and Tsar Nicholas I, by contrast, showed no enthusiasm at all for the rebellious author of *Die Räuber* and the liberalizing author of *Don Carlos,* and it is reported that the Tsar expressed himself very severely concerning the "harmful influence" of Schiller's dramas upon the minds of the younger generation.[14]

[11] Yury Veselovsky, *op. cit.,* p. 4.
[12] Cp. M. Ehrhard, *Joukovski et le pré-romantisme Russe* (Paris, 1938); Matthew Volm, *W. A. Zhukovskij als Übersetzer* (Ann Arbor, Michigan, 1945). In Part I of his work Volm gives a detailed analysis of Zhukovsky's relationship to Schiller.
[13] Zamotin, *op. cit., II,* 96.
[14] Zamotin, *op. cit., II,* 116. The reference is probably to Schiller's "harm-

Nevertheless, the vogue of Schiller in Russia continued in the 1830's and 1840's with unabated force. The best minds of the progressive intelligentsia all fell under the influence of the German poet at one time or other. Stankevich, Botkin, Bakunin, Granovsky, Belinsky, and many others went in their development through a phase of ardent enthusiasm for Schiller's lofty idealism and poetic genius. In the words of a Russian critic, Schiller was "the leader of our most eminent and progressive men, of the true educators of our society in the Forties, and his great importance in the history of the development of our Russian society is beyond any doubt."[15] Moreover, surprising as it may seem, Schiller's admirers did not come only from the "progressive" literary or political camp. Men of widely divergent, or downright hostile views, bowed in reverence before the author of *Don Carlos*. Thus, the Westerners and their implacable foes, the Slavophils, both idolized Schiller and rivaled each other in poring over his poetry and translating his works.

In the wake of the general enthusiasm for Schiller, some of the most original and most indigenously Russian poets came under his spell and willingly paid tribute to his genius. Pushkin, it is true, "did not read German and, due to the peculiarities of his nature, did not fully sympathize with Schiller; nonetheless, the *Oeuvres dramatiques de Schiller* were the first books he insistently demanded from his brother while planning his *Boris Godunov*."[16] Incomparably more powerful was Schiller's impact on Lermontov who, at the age of fifteen, became an ardent Schiller enthusiast when he saw a performance of *Die Räuber* in the Moscow

ful influence" upon the minds of the Decembrist revolutionaries who organized an unsuccessful uprising against Nicholas I in December 1825.

[15] F. F. Nelidov, *Ocherki po istorii noveyshey Russkoy Literatury* (Moskva, 1907), p. 82.

[16] *Schiller*, ed. Vengerov, I, i. See also Rudolf Fischer, "Schiller und Puschkin," *Wissenschaftliche Zeitschrift der Karl Marx-Universität Leipzig,* IX (Leipzig, 1959/1960), Heft 1, pp. 73–76.

theatre. Under the impression of this performance he translated several of Schiller's poems into Russian and wrote a series of "Storm and Stress" tragedies which overflow with Schillerean rhetoric and passion.

Schiller's influence and popularity in Russia continued through the second half of the nineteenth century with undiminished force. There is hardly a famous writer in that period who cannot be connected with Schiller in one way or another. Thus, Schiller was admired, studied, translated, and imitated by Gogol, Herzen, Ogarev, Tyutchev, Turgenev, Chernyshevsky, Dostoyevsky, V. Ivanov, Bely, Blok, and many others. Enthusiasm for a poetry which glorified the struggle against oppression and despotism was the starting point of Ogarev's career as a political writer and social revolutionary. Under the auspices of Karl Moor and Marquis Posa there grew and flourished his memorable friendship with Alexander Herzen which culminated in the cofounding and editorship of the famous periodical *Kolokol* (1857).

Like his friend Ogarev, Herzen preserved for Schiller a profound sentiment of veneration, to the last days of his life calling him affectionately "my old teacher, Schiller."[17] Faithful to their youthful oath on the Vorobyovy Hills, taken under the direct influence of Schiller's *Don Carlos,* both Ogarev and Herzen had dedicated their lives to the cause of freedom and the welfare of humanity.

Probably not many realize how closely the life and works of Dostoyevsky are intertwined with the author of *Don Carlos,* and that the Russian novelist owes more to Schiller than to any other writer. Schiller was the main source of his youthful exaltation, the poet about whom he raved and dreamed in his school years. In his last novel, *The Brothers Karamazov* (1880), and in his

---

[17] Gertsen, *Poln. sobr. soch. i pisem,* XXI, 486. "To the Other Side," (1869), written one year before his death.

address on Pushkin a short time before his death, Dostoyevsky paid glowing tribute to the genius of Schiller, ranking him with Cervantes and Shakespeare. The Russian symbolists also had an unusually high esteem for the German poet and one of them, Vyacheslav Ivanov, looked up to Schiller with reverence, venerating him as a forefather of modern symbolism both in aesthetics and in poetry.

Schiller's fame in Russia suffered no decline with the beginning of the twentieth century. In 1900 an edition of Schiller's collected works in a Russian translation was published in Petersburg and the editor, S. A. Vengerov, declared in the foreword that in Russia "Schiller had become one of the most popular, if not the most popular of the great Western writers." And another Russian critic makes the following observation on Schiller's influence on the contemporary Russian generation :

In fact, who does not know F. Schiller, "the pride and glory of German literature, the great poet of all humanity"? His ballads we know by heart by the time we are twelve years old; we learn the German language from his *Geschichte des Dreissigjährigen Krieges,* and his *Jungfrau von Orleans* has been seen on the stage by every inhabitant of Moscow in his school days.[18]

Nothing, it appears, has been able to impair Schiller's amazing popularity in Russia, neither the great world wars nor the great revolutions. Indeed, his impact on the Russian mind may be said to have been greater than that of any other Western European writer :

Kaum einer der westeuropäischen Dichter wurde in Russland mit solcher Begeisterung und solchem Enthusiasmus gelesen, wie Schiller. Die Geschichte des russischen "Schillerianismus" ist noch nicht geschrieben. Aber man darf ja ohne weiteres sagen—eine "Schillersche" Periode haben fast alle grossen russischen Dichter

---

[18] A. E. Gruzinsky, *Literaturnoye ocherki* (Moskva, 1902), p. 25.

und Denker erlebt. Die Dramen und die Lyrik Schillers haben aber nicht nur auf das ästhetische Empfinden gewirkt. Der Ideengehalt der Schillerschen Werke riss einen russischen Leser stärker und mächtiger hin, als die künstlerischen Schönheiten.[19]

Before the first world war, the Academy of Sciences at St. Petersburg conceived the plan of publishing a monumental work on Schiller's influence in Russia. The outbreak of the war and the subsequent revolutions prevented the realization of this project. It was only in 1934 that Otto P. Peterson took a first step in the direction of exploring Schiller's impact on Russian literature and civilization. But his book, written "to give future scholars a basis for the further cultivation of this virgin ground in Schiller philology,"[20] covers only the years from 1785 to 1805. A second volume which was to deal with Schiller's influence on the principal writers of the nineteenth century has never materialized.

The present study will attempt to fill this gap in Schiller scholarship by analyzing and interpreting Schiller's influence on Russian literature from Stankevich to Vyacheslav Ivanov. In view of the great number of authors who were under the influence of the German poet at one time or another, in one form or another, the project will have to be carried out on a modest scale. To write exhaustively on Schiller's influence in Russia would be a monumental, multi-volume enterprise requiring the

[19] D. Cyzevskyj, "Schiller und die Brüder Karamasow," *Zeitschrift für Slawische Philologie,* VI (Leipzig, 1929), 3. Lenin also fell under the spell of Schiller. As O. B. Lepeshinskaya reports he liked to read poetry when an exile in Siberia : "Lenin loved poetry, especially classical poetry : Pushkin, Byron, Schiller, Shakespeare. . . ." V. I. Lenin, *O Literature i iskusstve* (Moskva, 1957), p. 569.

[20] Peterson, *Schiller in Russland,* Vorwort. Peterson's book was criticized as "inaccurate" and "exaggerated." Cp. Ju. M. Lotman, "Neue Materialien über die Anfänge der Beschäftigung mit Schiller in der Russischen Literatur," *Wissenschaftliche Zeitschrift der Ernst-Moritz-Arndt-Universität Greifswald* (Greifswald, 1958/59), VIII, 5/6, p. 419.

combined and coordinated efforts of a team of scholars over a prolonged period of time.

To be sure, a general survey of Schiller's influence on Russian writers including all the important names would have been feasible, but such an approach, superficial by its very nature, seemed incompatible with the character of a study which demands search, detailed analysis, and critical evaluation. Under these circumstances, the selective approach has been adopted and the number of authors advisedly restricted to relatively few who, however, may be considered as characteristic or representative of the development of Russian thought and literature.

Considerable attention has been given to the Stankevich circle which was instrumental in the introduction of German idealist philosophy in Russia and in the stimulation of a native romantic idealism which flourished in the Twenties and early Thirties. Out of the Stankevich circle emerged the Russian Westerners, including Botkin, Belinsky, Bakunin, and Granovsky. Lermontov, who marks the transition from romanticism to realism, was also connected with the Stankevich circle. Lermontov's place in Russian literature is firmly established and if he is second to anyone, then it is only to Pushkin.

In the mid-nineteenth century Herzen became one of the most influential leaders of Russian thought and literature. In the late Fifties, though an emigrant, Herzen was, through his periodical *Kolokol,* the principal political force in Russia. Intertwined with and inseparable from Herzen's life are the life and activity of his friend and political ally, Ogarev.

The following decades see the rise of Dostoyevsky, the creator of the modern psychological novel, who has had an enormous influence on contemporary literature in all parts of the civilized world. Strongly influenced by Dostoyevsky were Vyacheslav Ivanov and almost the entire Symbolist movement in Russia. In the years before the first world war Vyacheslav Ivanov was the recognized leader of the Symbolist poets in St. Petersburg.

It will be one of the goals of this study to throw into relief the salient elements in each author's appreciation of Schiller, his dependence on him for guidance and inspiration or, as the case may be, his struggle with Schiller and his rebellion against Schiller's philosophy. The purpose of this work will not be the complete gathering of all references to Schiller but rather an incisive analysis of Schiller's importance to each author and a clear representation of Schiller's meaning to him. It is hoped that the critical elucidation of the Russian writers' reactions to the German poet and their evaluation of him will prove informative and useful to scholars concerned with German, Russian, and comparative literature.

Every effort has been made to obtain the vital material from the primary Russian sources. Sometimes, however, because of the unavailability of the original source, secondary sources have been used insofar as they contributed characteristic or interesting details of an author's idiosyncrasy in regard to Schiller.

In general, each author's biography has served as the basis and framework for his view of the German poet. But no attempt has been made to adhere rigidly to the chronology of an author's life if a deviation from the chronology sheds light on a broader, more general line of development in his attitude toward Schiller, or if that author's views of the German poet can thus be made more coherent, concise, and forceful. In conclusion to these explanatory remarks it may be added that I focus on Schiller, but that also other writers had an influence on Russian literature. The bird's-eye view of Schiller-in-Russia, contained in this Introduction, is offered as background information for the detailed study that is to follow.

I

Stankevich

IN THE EARLY 1830's THE UNIVERSITY OF MOSCOW HARBORED among its students an exceptional set of able young men who met almost daily and eventually constituted the two renowned circles of Stankevich and Herzen. The circle of Stankevich "which faithfully continued the tradition of Prince Odoevski's Philosophical Society of the Twenties"[1] dedicated itself to the study of German literature and philosophy. Herzen's circle concentrated on social and political questions and was the first in Russia to assimilate and propagate the teachings of the Utopian socialism of Saint-Simon and Fourier. From these two remarkable circles there originated the so-called Westerners who played such an outstanding part in the development of Russian thought and literature. The movement of the Westerners crystallized about 1840 "when the philosophical idealists of the circle of Stankevich and the socialist idealists of the circle of Herzen became united in one movement, equally opposed to official Russia and to Slavophilism,"[2]

Nikolay Vladimirovich Stankevich (1813–40) is one of the most fascinating men in the intellectual history of nineteenth-century Russia. In the memory of his contemporaries and in the legend woven by posterity "his face is surrounded with a halo of almost sacred purity."[3] Harmonious strength, depth of soul, vivid

[1] Herbert E. Bowman, *Vissarion Belinski* (Cambridge, Mass., 1954), p. 40.
[2] D. S. Mirsky, *A History of Russian Literature* (London, 1927), p. 210.
[3] V. A. Astrov. *Ne nashli puti* (St. Petersburg, 1914), p. 36.

24

spiritual passion, singular complexity and versatility together with unusual simplicity and directness are the chief characteristics of his personality. His sensitive soul was like a concave mirror which reflected and gathered the most burning and most vital problems of his time—pointing the way to the solution of many of them. Rightfully he has been called "the Father of Occidentophilism,"[4] for on most of the later Westerners he deeply impressed the stamp of his spirit.

His many-sided nature was equally responsive to thought and creative production, poetry and art; he was "endowed with the faculty not to subject, not to rule but to inspire, educate, develop —and although not creative himself, to live in the thoughts and creations of those whom he enlightened."[5] In this respect Stankevich may well be compared to Herder whose role in German literature it was to act as stimulator and inspirer of a spiritual revolution.

Stankevich was seventeen when he entered Moscow University. He lived in the house of the philosopher, Professor Pavlov. "There Stankevich immersed himself completely in the world of German romanticism. Schiller's aesthetic world-view impressed him particularly. 'Art is becoming a God for me,' he wrote at this time."[6] The elite of Russian youth came to be associated with his group which was formed in 1831. Belinsky, Botkin, Granovsky, Neverov, and Bakunin were its most active members. But also Lermontov, Krasov, Klushnikov, Katkov, Kudryavtsev, K. Aksakov, and I. S. Turgenev experienced the influence of Stankevich at one time or another. Among the members of the circle proper it was Belinsky who felt the impact of Stankevich's genius most

[4] *Ibid.*, p. 45.
[5] A. Veselovsky, *Zapadnove vlianie v novoy Russkoy Literature* (Moskva, 1916), p. 216.
[6] Vasily Zenkovsky, *A History of Russian Philosophy* (New York, 1953), I, 240.

LIBRARY
College of St. Francis
JOLIET, ILL.

5 2510

deeply and most enduringly.[7] Belinsky's early articles bear the mark of Stankevich's genius :

Stankevich's views on art, on poetry and its relationship to life developed in the articles of Belinsky into that new powerful criticism, into that new *Weltanschauung,* into that philosophy of life which fascinated all thoughtful persons in Russia and caused all pedants and doctrinaires to recoil from Belinsky with a shudder.[8]

For himself and for his friends Stankevich knew only one goal. This goal was moral self-education and elaboration of a philosophy of life as a personal preparation for the difficult school of life. Four chief elements participated in this process of self-development : philosophy, literature, religion, and history. "It goes without saying that real life did not cease to give its instructive lessons. Schelling, Kant, Fichte, and Hegel made their contributions."[9] In poetry the attention of the circle was centered upon Goethe, Schiller, Hoffmann, and Shakespeare.[10] In the philosophical field Stankevich acted as a pioneer among his countrymen. The methodical and organized study of philosophy hardly existed in Russia before he initiated his program of earnest intellectual research.

During his first two years at the University of Moscow (1830–32) Stankevich "thoroughly mastered the German language and thoroughly acquainted himself with the poets of Germany."[11] That he had an excellent knowledge of German is also vouched for by his friend, I. S. Turgenev : "He [Stankevich] spoke French

[7] Cp. Bowman, *Vissarion Belinsky,* p. 44 : "That Belinsky's first serious introduction to philosophical idealism was made in a student circle which revolved around Stankevich is perhaps the major fact of Belinsky's early intellectual life."

[8] Alexander I. Gertsen, *Byloye i dumy* (Leningrad, 1946), p. 230.

[9] P. Sakulin, "Istoriko–literaturnye besedy," *Vestnik Yevropy,* II (Petrograd, 1915), 247.

[10] Cp. N. O. Lossky, *History of Russian Philosophy* (New York, 1951), p. 51.

[11] I. L. "N. V. Stankevich," *Biblioteka dla chtenia* (St. Petersburg, March–April 1858), p. 11.

pretty well but German better; he knew the German language very well."[12] Since Belinsky did not know German, Stankevich and the other members of the circle had to lend a helping hand : they translated, made excerpts and interpreted the difficult German treatises to Belinsky "to enable him to keep abreast of the great intellectual currents."[13] In addition, to facilitate their common systematic study of German philosophy and literature, Stankevich opened his library, well stocked with foreign works, to all his friends. Thus, under Stankevich's inspired and unchallenged leadership, the circle became "one of those few in which the Russia of the future was being born."[14]

Stankevich generously put his material and spiritual resources at the disposal of his friends but his own literary production remained surprisingly small. All we have from him is an immature quasi-historical drama entitled *Skopin–Shuysky,* a poor novel, thirty mediocre poems, a few philosophical fragments, and a very remarkable correspondence, full of brilliant ideas and striking definitions. For this very reason his correspondence has been treasured by posterity :

It permits us to listen to the genuine timbre of his voice, to experience the overflowing of his feelings and cherished dreams, to vibrate with the many-stringed chords of his heart; Stankevich's volume of letters in its unvarnished frankness is by itself a wonderful poem about a Russian idealist prematurely carried away by death.[15]

[12] L. N. Maykov, "Zapiska I. S. Turgeneva," *Vestnik Yevropy* (St. Petersburg, January 1899), p. 15.

[13] A. Veselovsky, *op. cit.,* p. 216.

[14] N. P. Sidorov, "N. V. Stankevich," *Golos Minuvshago* (St. Petersburg, September 1913), p. 2.

[15] Sidorov, "N. V. Stankevich," p. 5. Cp. also L. N. Tolstoy's letter to his grandmother of August 1858 : "Have you . . . ever read the correspondence of Stankevich? If not, for heaven's sake do read it ! Never has any other book made such an impression on me." *Tolstovsky muzey* (St. Petersburg, 1911), I, 114.

Herder, Goethe, and Schiller were his favorites among the German poets. Herder's *Ideen zur Philosophie der Geschichte der Menschheit* must have stirred him profoundly for in many of his letters recurs the telling phrase : "Es herrscht eine allweise Güte über die Welt."[16] This is undoubtedly parallel to Herder's expression : "Es waltet eine weise Güte im Schicksal der Menschen." With still greater emotion and awe Stankevich looked up to Goethe and Schiller. The reason for his admiring attitude toward the two German poets can be found in his spiritual affinity with the philosophical aspects of their poetry. An enthusiastic follower of Schelling, he valued the works of Goethe and Schiller as a confirmation, on a poetic level, of Schelling's idealistic philosophy of nature.[17]

Stankevich venerated Goethe and Schiller as sublime geniuses and preceptors of humanity, as models and leaders toward the lofty goal of moral self-education and universal happiness. Besides the philosophical it was, above all, the didactic element in the writings of the two German poets which seemed to him of the greatest importance. The flaming verses of Goethe and Schiller were used by him "as a weapon for the fight with one's own and others' selfish passions and as such were transmitted to others."[18] But the influence of Goethe and Schiller and of German literature in general was not limited to this alone : it also broadened Stankevich's mind and aroused the dormant forces of his genius to full activity.

Stankevich who "found in Schiller both moral support and

[16] *N. V. Stankevich-Perepiska,* ed. Aleksey Stankevich (Moskva, 1914), pp. 217, 237, 303, 317, 543.

[17] Cp. V. K. Yarmerstedt : "The philosophical poetry, especially of Schiller and Goethe, on which Stankevich was brought up, harmonized in its character with the poetical philosophy of nature expounded by Schelling." "Mirosozertsanie kruzhka Stankevicha i poeziya Koltsova," *Voprosy Filosofii i Psikhologii* (Moskva, March, 1894), p. 175.

[18] I. L., "N. V. Stankevich," p. 12.

consolation"[19] did not miss the chance to let his friends participate in the uplifting effects of the poetry of Schiller. Thus, in 1832, seeing off a young candidate to St. Petersburg and to a life of struggle, Stankevich exhorted him with the following verses of Schiller :[20]

> Festen Mut in schwerem Leiden,
> Hilfe, wo die Unschuld weint,
> Ewigkeit geschwornen Eiden,
> Wahrheit gegen Freund und Feind,
> Männerstolz vor Königsthronen,–
> Brüder, gält es Gut und Blut–
> Dem Verdienste seine Kronen,
> Untergang der Lügenbrut!

The choice of these lines from the poem "An die Freude" is certainly indicative of Stankevich's frame of mind and philosophy of life in the early Thirties. Schiller's humanism, his love of truth and faith in man, his profound belief in the ultimate triumph of good over evil—all this together with his apotheosis of joy and friendship harmonized in a high degree with Stankevich's ideals of moral self-education and universal happiness. Schiller's enthusiastic call to all mankind : "Seid umschlungen Millionen!" found a resounding echo in the heart of the young Russian idealist and, through him, among the members of his circle.

Stankevich's glowing sympathy for Schiller is documented by his letters which make it abundantly clear that he valued the German poet "chiefly as an idealistic thinker. He was fascinated by the principal theses of his philosophy of life, quoting repeatedly excerpts from his works in his correspondence, and ecstatically admiring his individual heroes."[21] Thus, in the spring

[19] F. F. Nelidov, *Ocherki po istorii noveyshey Russkoy Literatury* (Moskva, 1907), p. 81.

[20] N. S. Tikhonravov, *Sochinenia* (Moskva, 1898), III¹, 601–602.

[21] Yury Veselovsky, "Schiller kak vdokhnovitel Russkikh Pisateley," *Russkaya Mysl,* II (Moskva, 1906), 10.

of 1833, Stankevich eagerly looked forward to seeing the great actor Mochalov in the role of Ferdinand on the stage of the Moscow theatre. In a letter of May 2, 1833, he writes to his friend Yanuary Neverov : "It would be fascinating for me to see *Kabale und Liebe* about which we have talked so much."[22]

Two weeks later Stankevich informed his friend that the performance of *Kabale und Liebe* would take place on the next day, that he was hoping to see it, and that he was going to read Schiller in an hour or two with Marya Afanasevna.[23] From another passage in the same letter we learn which particular work of the German poet he was occupied with :

> Just now I am reading several scenes from *Don Carlos* to Marya Afanasevna. I have not read it for a long time, for this reason the excerpts have not interested me as much as the whole tragedy ! . . . But the scenes of Marquis Posa have touched me greatly—for I am used to identifying the thought of you with the idea of friendship; at any rate, if what I feel for you is not friendship then friendship should be relegated to the register of beautiful dreams : then it does not exist ![24]

As can be seen, Stankevich had a very personal reason for being "greatly touched" by the figure of Marquis Posa. Obviously he was still too young and inexperienced to recognize the tragic ambiguity inherent in Posa's character and in his dealings with Carlos and the King.[25] Toward the end of his letter Stankevich assured his friend he would describe to him the "wretched performance" of *Kabale und Liebe* as soon as he was able to, but for some unknown reason he did not keep his

[22] *Stankevich–Perepiska,* p. 216.
[23] M. A. Dokhturova, governess in the Beer family whose members were acquainted with Bakunin and Stankevich.
[24] *Stankevich–Perepiska,* p. 220.
[25] Cp. André von Gronicka, "Friedrich Schiller's Marquis Posa," *GR*, XXVI (October, 1951), 196–214.

promise. A later letter to Neverov (May 20, 1833) contains only a very brief reference to the performance of *Kabale und Liebe* indicating that he had finally seen the play "from the first row," and that Mochalov had acted in the role of Ferdinand. No explanation is given why, according to his earlier letter, the performance of the tragedy should have been "wretched."

This disappointment with the poor performance of *Kabale und Liebe* could not, of course, dampen Stankevich's interest in, and admiration for Schiller's intriguing and inspiring *dramatis personae*. We have seen how his fervent sentiment of friendship for Neverov had caused him to be personally touched by Schiller's dramatization of friendship in Marquis Posa's ambivalent relation to Don Carlos. Now, one month later, discoursing on the sentiment of love, he discovers his affinity to another figure of the drama :

I think about love like the *Prinzessin* Eboli but I do not squander this feeling. If I shall find my ideal, and if I shall not be rejected by her, if her love will be equal to mine, then "eine nur wird meine Liebe glücklich machen, doch diese einzige zur Göttin. . . ."[26]

That Stankevich should have chosen the treacherous and revengeful Princess Eboli as a model in matters of love seems a little strange, especially in view of the high ideals of moral self-education he had set up for himself and for his friends at that time. The Queen—pictured by Schiller as the embodiment of sublime spiritual nobility—would surely have been a better choice and more in keeping with Stankevich's philosophy of life.

For the summer vacation Stankevich went to Uderevka, the estate of his parents. Here he continued reading his beloved Schiller and diligently jotted down the thoughts and emotions roused in him by the German poet. Whatever he read, whatever he felt, he desired to share with his bosom friend Neverov. On

[26] *Stankevich–Perepiska,* p. 226.

July 24, 1833, after the reading of Schiller's poem "Resignation,"
he sent him the following commentary and interpretation :

It seems the poet expresses his desperate conviction : Two flowers
bloom for man—hope and enjoyment; he who plucks the one must
not demand the other; but the powerful imagination of the poet on
the wings of his ecstatic sentiment creates heroes who reach for
both—a conception not very appealing to an ordinary mortal dissatisfied with his eternal destiny. Eternity responds to the grumbling
of the poor son of the earth and annihilates him with its answer!
How much poesy is here! Of course, the poet does not say to himself : Let us elaborate such a conception! because in this case he
would elaborate it logically. No, he depicts a fact of life which has
appeared to his soul in a poetical light without realizing that this
fact expresses a great idea.[27]

Exception must be taken to Stankevich's expression "desperate
conviction." Also his phrase "poor son of the earth," which
implies compassion or sympathy with the plaintiff against
Eternity, calls for a critical consideration. Undoubtedly, the poem
may be regarded as a kind of aesthetic and religious confession
of faith of the young Schiller but there seems to be nothing
"desperate" about it. The poet simply asks for an aesthetic
uplifting of man above his limitations here on earth in return for
his renunciation of any claim to happiness in a hereafter. Nor
does Schiller in any way sympathize with the "poor son of the
earth" who is so terribly disappointed at discovering that there
is no reward prepared for him in the other world, despite his
renunciation of happiness on earth. This is what Schiller himself
has to say about the true meaning of his poem :

Der Inhalt desselben sind die Aufforderungen eines Menschen
an die andre Welt, weil er die Güter der Zeit für die Güter der
Ewigkeit hingegeben hat. Um des Lohnes willen, der ihm in der
Ewigkeit versprochen wurde, hat er auf Genuss in dieser Welt

[27] *Stankevich–Perepiska,* pp. 236–237.

resigniert. Zu seinem Schrecken findet er, dass er sich in seiner Rechnung betrogen hat und dass man ihm einen falschen Wechsel an die Ewigkeit gegeben.—So kann und soll es jeder Tugend und jeder Resignation ergehen, die bloss deswegen ausgeübt wird, weil sie in einem andern Leben gute Zahlung erwartet. . . . Das Gedicht ist also nicht gegen die wahre Tugend, sondern nur gegen die Religions–Tugend gerichtet, welche mit dem Weltschöpfer einen Akkord schliesst und gute Handlungen auf Interessen ausleihet, und diese interessierte Tugend verdient mit Recht jene strenge Abfertigung des Genius.[28]

On October 14, 1833, in an autumnal mood, Stankevich once again reverts to the theme of "Resignation" and cheerlessly informs his confidant that for him—as for Schiller—there are left now only "Zwei Blumen—Hoffnung und Genuss!"[29] The reason for his depressed state of mind is not hard to guess: Stankevich was not yet sure about his vocation and destiny in life. He believed that without hope he could not be happy. Consequently, he concludes with Schiller that he must not pluck the second flower, that is, *Genuss*. The fact that Stankevich had this poem "immer in Gedanken und auf den Lippen"[30] would seem to be indicative of the intensity of his moral and metaphysical struggles.

Stankevich's mood of listlessness and resignation continued into the following year. Even the gay and festive Easter holidays found him in a depressed frame of mind and he felt little inclined to join in the jubilation of the faithful in the Moscow cathedrals. A letter to Neverov reveals that he met Holy Easter "not very cheerfully" but, as it were, "in a human fashion: Until twelve o'clock Krasov and I did not go to bed; at first we read Schiller,

[28] *Schillers Sämtliche Werke*, Säkular–Ausgabe (Stuttgart & Berlin, n. d.), I, 337–338 (notes).

[29] *Stankevich–Perepiska*, p. 251.

[30] D. I. Cyzevskyj, "Schiller und die Brüder Karamasow," *Zeitschrift für Slawische Philologie*, VI (Leipzig, 1929), 11.

then we talked. I told him about my first love of whom I have often spoken to you."[31]

Stankevich did not bring his studies at the University of Moscow to a formal conclusion. Having given up the idea of completing his doctoral dissertation (due to "lack of time," as he said), he left for St. Petersburg to live exclusively for his private studies of philosophy and literature, for the theatre, and for his friends. Since he was the son of a wealthy noble family he could afford to live an independent life of meditation and leisure without the work and worry connected with an official position.

His enthusiasm for Schiller had not suffered by his transfer to the capital. A letter to his friend Vasily Ivanovich Krasov reveals that—for the second time in the course of one year—he had attended a performance of Schiller's *Kabale und Liebe* with the famous actor Karatygin playing the principal role. Stankevich lauded the "excellence" of his acting but at the same time, without being specific, he also spoke of "severe shortcomings."[32] Although Stankevich himself does not say so, one can assume that he went to see *Kabale und Liebe* for the second time, not only because of his enthusiasm for the play itself, but also because of his desire to compare the actors in St. Petersburg with the actors in Moscow.

Stankevich enjoyed the free and stimulating life in St. Petersburg, and loved especially its cosmopolitan atmosphere and Western orientation. But in the fall of 1834 we find him far away from the brilliant capital in the desolate village of Uderevka. It seems he departed from St. Petersburg not quite on his own accord, because in a letter to Neverov, dated September 19, 1834, he exclaims: "How furious I was that I would not be able to see

[31] *Stankevich–Perepiska*, p. 284. Letter of April 24, 1834.
[32] *Stankevich–Perepiska*, p. 398. Letter of July 8, 1834.

Schiller and Shakespeare!" Yet Stankevich could not stay inactive and angry for a long time.

To console himself to some extent for the "Paradise Lost" he continues his studies of Schiller: "I read several historical works of Schiller," he reports in the same letter to Neverov, "which are so picturesque and so animated that I would make an astonishing progress in history within a month if only Schiller would hit upon the idea to explain it all himself."[33] Also, Schiller's drama *Maria Stuart* must have occupied him during this fall of 1834 in Uderevka as can be deduced from another letter to Neverov: "I like *Maria Stuart,* but will God ever grant me to see it in Petersburg?—because in Moscow one has no desire to see it. . . ."[34] When writing these lines Stankevich undoubtedly was thinking of the "wretched" performance of *Kabale und Liebe* he had witnessed in Moscow in the spring of 1833.

In the summer of 1836 Stankevich stayed for some time in the famous resort town of Pyatigorsk north of the Caucasian mountains. Perhaps he hoped to improve his feeble health by availing himself of the excellent climate and the many warm sulphur springs in that area. Also in Pyatigorsk he occupied himself intensively with German literature. In a letter of June 14, 1836, he reports to Neverov: "I am reading Schiller, Faust, and Werther."[35]

After his return to Uderevka, Stankevich continued to pursue his philosophical and literary studies. Schiller remained his favorite and the German poet's views on life and society gave

---

[33] *Stankevich–Perepiska,* p. 290. Stankevich's high esteem of Schiller's historical writings has been borne out by modern criticism. Uncritical, but brilliant in form and style, they are unsurpassed models of historiography even today. Cp. Bernt von Heiseler: "Inbesondere ist es seine [Schiller's] Auffassung Wallensteins . . . die von der heutigen Forschung glänzend gerechtfertigt worden ist." *Schiller* (Gütersloh, 1959), p. 129.

[34] *Stankevich–Perepiska,* p. 301. Letter of November 20, 1834.

[35] *Stankevich–Perepiska,* p. 360.

him much food for reflection. In a letter to Neverov he praises
Schiller's profound understanding of nature and humanity, his
ability to discover with one single glance "all the best things in
God's creation." Paraphrasing the principal thoughts of one of
Schiller's poems he then writes: "A man is rough, cynical, cruel
—he needs the influence of a woman and family; only thus his
feeling of duty can become the comforting feeling of love."[36]
Stankevich does not mention the title of the poem, but there can
be little doubt that he was thinking of "Würde der Frauen"
whose second and third stanzas read as follows:

> Ewig aus der Wahrheit Schranken
> Schweift des Mannes wilde Kraft;
> Unstet treiben die Gedanken
> Auf dem Meer der Leidenschaft;
> Gierig greift er in die Ferne,
> Nimmer wird sein Herz gestillt,
> Rastlos durch entlegne Sterne
> Jagt er seines Traumes Bild.
>
> Aber mit zauberisch fesselndem Blicke
> Winken die Frauen den Flüchtling zurücke,
> Warnend zurück in der Gegenwart Spur.
> In der Mutter bescheidener Hütte
> Sind sie geblieben mit schamhafter Sitte,
> Treue Töchter der frommen Natur.

The year 1837 opened a new chapter in Stankevich's not very
eventful life. That year his dream of setting foot on the homeland
of Goethe and Schiller and of drinking at the very fountain of
German idealistic philosophy finally materialized. Although very
young he had gained much prestige among his countrymen by
the magnetism of his personality and his superior intellect. Leaving his native land, he deprived his friends of his intellectual

---

[36] *Stankevich–Perepiska*, p. 363. Letter of September 21, 1836.

leadership and himself of the possibility of influencing their minds by the spell of his personal presence. A serious decline in his philosophical and literary predominance was the inevitable result and, at the age of twenty-four, "his career of immediate influence was ended by his departure from Russia."[37]

Reasons of health made it seem advisable to Stankevich to spend some time in Karlsbad. Here his mind was occupied with Schiller and the dramatic figures the German poet had created. In a letter of October 8, 1837, Stankevich writes to Neverov : "I would like going to Eger to look at the room where Wallenstein was killed : I love this epoch and I do so, it seems, because of Schiller's tragedies."[38] One week later Stankevich gives a detailed account of his visit to Wallenstein's castle in Prague to his fiancée Lubov A. Bakunina with whom he had often read Schiller :

For a long time I could not master my imagination which sought in these walls not the traces of the historical Wallenstein but of the Wallenstein of Schiller's tragedy; against my own will I tried to persuade myself that Thekla was a dream, that she would not appear among the trees of the orchard, and that Max was perhaps a noble warrior but not Max. I strove to discover a particular lineament in Wallenstein's portrait—but I did not detect anything. The Countess—exactly as I imagined her in the tragedy : a good, feeble creature who perhaps was indispensable for such a tempestuous soul.[39]

The quoted passage is very characteristic of Stankevich who seemed, according to the expression of a compatriot, "created only for revery,"[40] and who interspersed his letters with citations from Schiller such as : "Nur der Irrtum ist das Leben"

---

[37] Bowman, *Vissarion Belinski*, p. 22.

[38] *Stankevich–Perepiska*, p. 386.

[39] *Stankevich–Perepiska*, p. 541.

[40] A. L. Volynsky, "V. G. Belinsky," *Russkie Kritiki* (St. Petersburg, 1896), p. 41.

("Kassandra"). Nothing could better illustrate the intensity of
Schiller's influence on Stankevich than his involuntary looking
for "the Wallenstein of Schiller's tragedy" and his fanciful
expectation that Max and Thekla would suddenly appear
"among the trees of the orchard." Schiller must have truly been
the master of Stankevich's imagination if his dramatic figures had
the power to displace the historic ones from Stankevich's own
mind—as the Russian himself admits—"for a long time." By
"Countess" Stankevich obviously means the Duchess of Friedland, Wallenstein's kindly but ineffectual wife. One may doubt,
however, if that "good, feeble creature" was really "indispensable" to an ambitious man such as Wallenstein. Looking at the
tragedy as a whole, one is rather inclined to come to a diametrically opposite conclusion.[41]

At long last, toward the end of October, 1837, Stankevich
arrived in Berlin, the Mecca of his philosophical dreams. He
immediately felt at home in the Prussian capital and was very
favorably impressed by the order and discipline prevailing in the
autocratically organized state. This sympathy for the existing
form of government in Germany—and Russia—becomes understandable in the light of his conviction that divine harmony
pervades the whole universe: "Es herrscht eine allweise Güte
über die Welt." Furthermore, Stankevich's philosophical allegi-
ance had shifted: "He started with Schelling and Schiller, went
through Kant and Fichte, and after that turned to Hegel."[42] But

---

[41] Cp. Karl Berger: "Der Willensmächtige [Wallenstein] will keinen
fremden Einschlag, am wenigsten eine Frauenhand in dem Gewebe seiner
Pläne dulden. Je weiter ihn sein Streben von der ruhigen Welt des Beste-
henden entfernt hat, desto mehr hat der sinnlich-gemütvolle Zauber zarter
Weiblichkeit die Gewalt über sein Wesen verloren; dies prägt sich in der
Stellung der schwachgemuten, zu leidender Ohnmacht verurteilten Herzogin
von Friedland aus. Für das stille Walten einer ängstlich auf Versöhnung der
Gegensätze bedachten Hausfrau ist kein Raum in einer so ganz auf den
Streit aller Kräfte gespannten Welt." *Schiller* (München, 1909), II, 418–419.
[42] D. I. Chizhevsky, *Gegel v Rossii* (Paris, 1939), p. 75. *N.B.*: "Chizhevsky"

it was to the *conservative* Hegel that he turned and to the reactionary metaphysics of the philosopher's later years.

The idea of freedom—as he had found it in *Kabale und Liebe* and *Don Carlos*—remained dear to Stankevich's humane and noble heart, but he conceived of it in a way that is characteristic of his helplessness in the face of social and political problems: "I esteem human freedom," he wrote to his father in 1838, "but I know well of what it consists, and I know that the first condition for freedom is legal authority."[43] No wonder then that he considered Germany as the model of a well-governed and well-organized state.

In Berlin Stankevich became a faithful disciple of Professor Karl Werder who agreed to read for him *collegia privatissima* on the German idealistic philosophers and on the aesthetics of Schiller. At frequent intervals Stankevich also visited the local theatre which, at times, gave him much pleasure and satisfaction. In a letter to his fiancée Lubov Bakunina, he gives, however, a rather critical account of a *Wallenstein* performance at the Berlin theatre:

During my stay they played *Wallenstein,* the last part. The matter went tolerably but Thekla—Mlle. von Hagen, an outstanding comic actress—offended me personally by her performance. She was the embodiment of insensibility combined with the most trivial grimaces, yet in comedy she was inimitable. Max was a youthful declaimer—as for the rest, tolerable. Wallenstein, played by Roth, I did not like at all although he drew terrible bursts of applause and is considered a good artist. His passionate declamation, his changing voice, did not fit the role of Wallenstein who is attractive by the strength of his soul, self-control, superiority over the others for which you forgive him all ambitious intentions. The stage decorations and costumes

is the English transliteration, "Cyzevskyj" the German transliteration of a Russian (or Ukrainian) original.

[43] *Stankevich–Perepiska,* p. 455.

were very striking. The march in the finale, together with Schiller's verses and the painted windows in the Gothic hall, makes a marvelous impression."

Stankevich's critical observations are revealing in several respects. First of all, they permit us—by way of deduction—to reconstruct the ideal image Stankevich had created in his mind of the two lovers Max and Thekla. Wallenstein's daughter, it appears, was to him the opposite of insensibility and triviality— in other words, the embodiment of tenderness and *uncommonness,* while Max appeared to him as the model of a genuine knight devoid of falsehood and empty declamation. Stankevich, himself a rapturous and sentimental type, did not see the light haze of sentimentality surrounding this pair of lovers which is obvious, however, to modern audiences. Apart from this he was entirely justified in having a high regard for these two noble characters and in resenting the assignment of their roles to actors who were unsuitable for this task.

Stankevich's characterization of Wallenstein as a man of strength, self-control, and superiority tallies with the Wallenstein of Schiller's drama, but it seems a little strange that he is ready to "forgive him all ambitious intentions"—strange in view of his lofty ideals of moral self-education, for he must have known that the expression "ambitious intentions" was just an apologetic euphemism for disloyalty and treason.

The year 1837 marks a turning point in Stankevich's attitude toward Schiller's aestheticism and philosophy of life. This is evident in Stankevich's changing views with respect to Schiller's concept of the "beautiful soul" *(schöne Seele).* In the definition of the German poet, a "beautiful soul" or "noble spirit" always acts, as if by intuition, in absolute agreement with his sense of duty. This concept, exalted for a long time by Stankevich and by

" *Stankevich–Perepiska,* pp. 544–545. Letter of November 11, 1837.

the members of his circle, became gradually to their minds an unsubstantial and completely visionary speculation, and a "beautiful soul," accordingly, a being existing in dream and Utopia only. A philosophical thinker like Stankevich could not fail to draw the manifest conclusions from this process of re-evaluation.[45] Belinsky went through a similarly painful reappraisal of Schiller's concept of the "noble spirit."

But whereas the disintegration of this idea constitutes a passing phase in the spiritual development of Belinsky, Stankevich himself never recovered from the collapse of his lofty ideal.[46] As a result of his changed views, he very often felt like a "superfluous man" living in a "shadow world of marginal existence." In a mood of melancholy resignation to his own impotence and ineptitude for coping with the problems of actuality he writes to his friend Bakunin :

Reality is the battleground of the truly strong man. The feeble soul dwells in the *Jenseits*, in a dreamy enthusiasm; . . . as soon as this dreamy something turns into *etwas* tangible, such a soul flings itself anew beyond the boundaries of reality. . . . That is my story and the manifest reason for my unhappiness.[47]

Stankevich's abandonment of Schiller's concept of the "nobility of the spirit" did not signify a diminution of his profound esteem

[45] Cp. Bowman: "With the rejection of that ideal existence in the 'Absolute' which the early Stankevich had striven to attain, the term 'noble spirit' is debased to mean the person of lofty aims who is unable to realize them in actual life, who is thereby condemned to inhabit a kind of purgatory between the actuality from which he has divorced himself and the life in the ideal which he has not attained. Living in this shadow world of marginal existence, the 'noble spirit' becomes the 'superfluous man,' separated from actuality by his 'noble' protest against its emptiness and vulgarity." *Vissarion Belinsky,* p. 43.

[46] Bakunin's turn to Hegel and Goethe was a major influence in this "re-evaluation" of Schiller by the members of the Stankevich circle. Cp. Bakunin, *Polnoye sobranie sochineniy,* ed. A. I. Bakunin (St. Petersburg [?] n. d.), II, 178.

[47] *Stankevich–Perepiska,* p. 650, Letter of January 9, 1838.

for the genius of the German poet. Stankevich's letters to his family and to Lubov Bakunina reveal, on the contrary, his continued enthusiastic interest in anything connected with the life and work of Schiller. Thus he informs his fiancée that Weimar was the first town in which he decided to stop for several days during a trip through Western Germany. He characterizes Weimar as "insignificant in itself as a town but hallowed by the memory of Schiller and Goethe."[48]

During his stay in Weimar, Stankevich did not fail to pay his respects to the widow of Goethe's son, Ottilie von Goethe, who received him with great cordiality. A letter to his brothers and sisters mentions also a visit to the graves of Schiller and Goethe early in the morning of May, 23, 1838. Stankevich does not elaborate on his feelings or reflections during that visit but limits himself to the laconic statement that the graves are "in the family tomb of the Dukes."[49] Nevertheless, the atmosphere of Weimar, charged with the spirit of Schiller and Goethe, was bound to exercise a powerful influence on his vivid imagination. Stimulated by this atmosphere he seriously thought of publishing, in collaboration with his friend Granovsky, an almanac or periodical similar to the *Xenien*.

Stankevich's feeling of affinity with Schiller must have been strong at that time, for communicating his idea of a common-enterprise journal to Granovsky he speaks of the parallels that exist between them and the authors of the *Xenien* and concludes with the terse affirmation : "We are Schiller and Goethe."[50] A bold affirmation, indeed, but one that will not be challenged once it is realized that it was used as a kind of metaphor to suggest the cordiality of his relationship with Granovsky, or as a turn of phrase to indicate his intention of satirizing literary mediocrity

[48] *Stankevich—Perepiska,* p. 568. Letter of June 24, 1838.
[49] *Stankevich—Perepiska,* pp. 176–177.
[50] *Stankevich—Perepiska,* p. 468.

in his native country. Another interpretation seems hardly conceivable, for Stankevich was too unassuming and intelligent, too perceptive to compare himself and his friend with Schiller and Goethe on a poetic level.

Even after his departure from Weimar Stankevich was occupied with the thought of the two German poets as can be seen from a letter to Granovsky written in Aachen. It is the intricate problem of the relationship between the dissimilar master spirits of German literature that puzzles him and causes him to attempt the finding of at least a personal and temporary solution, or a standard of comparison. After intense deliberation he comes to the following conclusions:

Schiller has a "rational reality" in his head; immediate human aspirations without any special respect of and attention to natural reality—a consequence of his intellectual-philosophical (not natural–philosophical) occupations; his task is clearer and more simple [than Goethe's], and he solves it with accuracy. In this fashion, I surrender to my uncertainties regarding these men. I clearly feel both their disparity and their genius but I must also know the reason why they are like that; later this will perhaps become clear to me and then I shall be able to find a more solid *Standpunkt.* . . . There is some truth in comparisons and deductions but the matter can undoubtedly be grasped only by an all-embracing and animated feeling.[51]

Stankevich's expression "rational reality" is suggestive of Hegel's often-quoted formula: "All that is rational is real and all that is real is rational." As a matter of fact, Stankevich had been under the influence of the conservative Hegel since 1835 or 1836. Probably due to the influence of this philosopher he characterizes Schiller as a "rational realist," a definition which is obviously tantamount to "subjective realist." As Schiller is set in opposition to Goethe it would then follow that Stankevich would

[51] *Stankevich–Perepiska,* p. 473. Letter of August 27, 1838.

have defined Goethe as an "objective realist." In the opinion of Stankevich the task of Schiller was "clearer and more simple" than Goethe's. This seems at the first glance a rather sweeping and peremptory statement which, however, is supported to a certain extent by Schiller himself who declares in a letter to Goethe : "Weil mein Gedankenkreis kleiner ist, so durchlaufe ich ihn eben darum schneller und öfter und kann eben darum meine kleine Barschaft besser nutzen und eine Mannigfaltigkeit, die dem Inhalte fehlt, durch die Form erzeugen."[52]

Schiller, however, was less sure about solving his task with "accuracy" than Stankevich suggests. It is only toward the end of his life that he appears relatively satisfied with his literary achievements. Thus, referring to his drama *Wilhelm Tell*, Schiller remarks in a letter to Körner : "Ich fühle, dass ich nach und nach des Theatralischen mächtig werde."[53] By saying : "I must also *know* the reason why they are like that" (that is, *why* Goethe and Schiller are so different), Stankevich falls into contradiction with his later statement, in which he said this matter "can undoubtedly be grasped only by an all-embracing and animated feeling."

If feeling is the only way of reaching an understanding of the differences between the two German geniuses, then his hope of gaining an insight into these differences by way of intellectual reasoning was certainly altogether illogical and unfounded. Stankevich must have been to some extent aware of these contradictions and inconsistencies in his thinking, since he consoles himself with the idea that "later this will perhaps become clear to me. . . ."

During these years Stankevich's weak health had steadily deteriorated. In the end he was compelled to leave Germany and

[52] *Friedrich Schiller–Briefe,* ed. Reinhard Buchwald (Leipzig, n. d.), pp. 355–356. Letter of August 31, 1794.
[53] *Ibid.,* p. 836. Letter of April 12, 1804.

seek refuge in the milder climate of Italy. Rome, Naples, and Florence were the principal stages of his sojourn in the European south. Schiller remained close to his heart, and when an occasion arose he recommended him to his friends. Thus, being a frequent guest in the house of a Russian family in Rome, he not only played piano with the daughter of his hostess, but also read Schiller's poetry with her.[54]

Stankevich's last reference to Schiller is dated February 1, 1840. It is contained in a letter to Granovsky, written from Florence a short time before his premature death. In this correspondence Stankevich passionately defends the German poet against the attacks of Belinsky and Bakuin who, at the time, were both passing through a phase of crass objectivism ("reconciliation with reality"):

The news regarding the literary efforts and concepts of our friends is not very comforting. What do they have against Schiller? Why this hatred? . . . Ridiculous people! They do not understand what reality is but I hope they will at least respect the word of Hegel. And if his authority carries great weight with them let them read what he says about Schiller in his Aesthetics, in several passages, and also about *Wallenstein* in his minor works. And about reality let them read in his Logic that reality, in the sense of spontaneity, external existence,—is something accidental; that reality, in its very essence, is reason, spirit. And if Schiller, according to their opinion, is not a poet of reality but of nebulousness then I suggest to them as a poet Svechin who describes how in a battle "the whip of many a fighter was broken to pieces."[55]

Stankevich felt personally offended by Belinsky's vitriolic assaults on Schiller[56] and the whole affair almost ruined their

[54] Maykov, "Zapiska I. S. Turgeneva," p. 14.

[55] *Stankevich–Perepiska,* p. 486.

[56] Belinsky had charged Schiller with rotten morality, abstract idealism, and dramatic impotence. Cp. Belinsky, *Pisma* (St. Petersburg, 1914), I, 346–350.

intimate friendship—a fact which, taken by itself alone, would suffice to reveal the scope and depth of Schiller's influence on Stankevich. In a letter to Botkin, written in February 1840, Belinsky expressed his surprise at the unexpected outburst of indignation on the part of his friend and indicated that he regretted the incident. From the apologetic tone of the letter one can deduce that Belinsky wanted a reconciliation with Stankevich, and that he felt ashamed of his sallies against the German poet.

The notice of Stankevich's death, several months later, came—especially under these circumstances—as a doubly heavy blow to Belinsky. In his article on Koltsov (1846) the great critic pays tribute to the memory of Stankevich who had given away the riches of his spirit to friends and to strangers, while remaining unknown to the world and to fame:

This was one of those remarkable men who are not always known to society but about whom mysterious and awe-inspiring rumors, emanating from the circle of people who were close to them, sometimes find their way also into society.[57]

At the age of seventeen, under the impression of Schiller's aesthetic world-view, Stankevich had written : "Art is becoming a God for me." Stankevich's student years at the University of Moscow were passed under this influence of the aesthetic principle and of Schiller. At this stage of his intellectual development he appreciated the writings of Schiller as a confirmation of Schelling's philosophy of nature and as a guide toward moral self-education. To these philosophical and didactic elements the optimistic humanism of the German poet must be added as a third factor which acted strongly upon the mind of the young Stankevich. Schiller's appeal to mankind : "Seid umschlungen

[57] V. G. Belinsky, *Sochinenia* (Kiev, 1911), II, 664.

Millionen !" was received with enthusiasm by the noble-minded Russian idealist.

The melancholy mood of disenchantment vibrating in the verses of Schiller's poem "Resignation" overwhelmed his sensitive soul and for many years remained his doleful companion. Equally powerful was the influence of Schiller's dramatic works. In contrast to Belinsky, he showed no sign of interest in the revolutionary drama *Die Räuber* but he was fascinated by *Kabale und Liebe, Don Carlos, Maria Stuart,* and *Wallenstein.* In *Don Carlos,* very significantly, he all but ignored the political aspect of the drama. But the emotional theme—love and friendship— aroused a sympathetic echo in his tender heart.[58]

The tragic figure of Wallenstein captivated his imagination to such a degree that he almost became the victim of dream-like hallucinations. In 1837 Stankevich turned away from Schiller's aestheticism and philosophy of life. But this rejection was not unconditional. There were moments when he, the "superfluous man," the "feeble soul," in despair over the cruel aspects of reality, flung himself anew "beyond the boundaries of reality." Moreover, Stankevich's abandonment of Schiller's aestheticism did not lessen his admiration for the poetic genius of the German poet. Witness his passionate defense of Schiller against the scathing criticism of his friend Belinsky. Toward the end of his life art was no longer a God for him.

Suffering, experience, and philosophical reflection had led him to the conviction that art was only "the first stage in the knowledge of God." Such a conviction was in accord with the basic tenets of Schiller's aestheticism and with the doctrines of romanticism in general. The contradictory nature of Stankevich's

---

[58] Another Russian, Alexander Herzen, thought of *Don Carlos* in terms of a tragedy of love and friendship and entirely ignored its political aspect. Cp. A. I. Gertsen, *Polnoye sobranie sochineniy i pisem,* ed. M. K. Lemke (St. Petersburg, 1919–25), II, 33.

personality here comes to light strikingly—for it was Stankevich the philosopher who rejected Schiller's aestheticism on logical grounds, while Stankevich the romanticist accepted it on the grounds of empathy.

II

Lermontov

"A RUSSIAN POET OF THE STATURE OF IVAN THE GREAT!" THIS
is how Belinsky summed up the profound impression Lermontov
had made upon him during their second meeting in the guard-
house in St. Petersburg.[1] Like Schiller, Mikhail Yuryevich
Lermontov (1814–41) is a poet of revolt and freedom, a poet of
youth, admired by young and ardent hearts. In 1830 he entered
the University of Moscow where he came into contact with the
romantic idealists of the Stankevich circle. He studied little but
as a reader of poetry he was insatiable. Pushkin, Byron, and
Schiller were his favorite authors at that time. In Russian literature Lermontov is generally regarded the greatest poet next to
Pushkin.

Although remarkable as a lyric poet, he is even more excellent
as a prose writer. His famous novel *A Hero of Our Times* (1840)
may be considered his surest claim to immortality. There is a particular atmosphere of irony and tragedy about this novel which
makes it hard to speak of it in terms of simple prose fiction. "This
atmosphere," observes a Russian critic, "together with the perfec-
tion of the verbal and narrative form, is what has induced people
by no means extravagant or paradoxical to call *A Hero of Our
Times* the greatest Russian novel, thus placing it above *War and
Peace*."[2]

[1] V. G. Belinsky, *Polnoye sobranie sochineniy* (Moskva, 1956), XI, 509.
Letter to Botkin dated April 16, 1840.
[2] D. S. Mirsky, *A History of Russian Literature* (New York, 1949), p. 157.

In Lermontov's development, translations play a significant role because they are closely connected with his own poetic production. But his work as a translator—his methods of translation and their gradual elaboration—also throw much light on his relation to the literature of the West. In 1829, at fourteen, Lermontov began translating and Schiller was the first whom he tried his hand at successfully. The following poems of the German poet were translated by Lermontov : "An Emma," "Die Begegnung," "Der Handschuh," "Das Kind in der Wiege," "Teile mir mit," and also part of Schiller's version of the witches' scene from *Macbeth* (1, 4).[3]

In addition, he gave a free rendering of two of Schiller's ballads ("Der Taucher," and "Der Handschuh") uniting them into one single poem entitled "Ballad." The choice of these poems reveals the types of Schiller's poetry in which the young translator was interested at that particular time. Thus, the poems "An Emma" and "Die Begegnung" belong to the amorous-lyrical and the elegiac genre respectively. "Teile mir mit" is an epigram, "Das Kind in der Wiege" a philosophical distich, "Der Handschuh" a ballad, and the fragment from *Macbeth* a dramatic dialogue with broadly narrative elements.

Lermontov's own lyric production was at that time dominated by elegiac meditations and lyrical monologues. Only occasionally did he dwell on epic themes, but he did not elaborate them in the form of short poems. Very significantly, his translation of "Der Handschuh" is the first genre poem he dared to write outside of the category of poetry proper. There is no uniformity in his treatment of the original as is apparent from the way in which he reproduces the poems of the German poet.

The poem "An Emma" is translated rather exactly in three

---

[3] M. Yu. Lermontov, *Polnoye sobranie sochineniy* (Moskva–Leningrad, 1948), I, 363 (notes).

stanzas, each stanza containing six lines. But of "Die Begegnung" he translates only the first two stanzas, and although the metre and the stanzaic structure of the original are preserved, many deviations and errors may be found in his text. Like the preceding translation, this was probably little more than a poetic exercise. Lermontov's treatment of the elegiac distich is particularly interesting. In one case ("Das Kind in der Wiege"), he renders the distich by an analogous form, limiting himself to a shortening of the second verse and changing somewhat the distribution of the accents.

In another case ("Teile mir mit"), he renders the distich by a completely different form, namely by a rhymed four-foot iambic quatrain. The "Ballad" consists of fifteen stanzas, each stanza containing two verses which rhyme in couplets, while the fragment from *Macbeth* is characterized by a combination of four-foot and three-foot iambs. The translation of "Der Handschuh" is noteworthy as "Lermontov's first experiment, and one of the first experiments in Russian poetry, in the field of purely tonic verse."[4] In fact, the poem is rendered in an unusual and characteristic form, the distinguishing marks of which are strophic differentiation and extraordinary metrical freedom. In its loose sequence of verses of entirely different syllabic and phonetic structure Lermontov comes very close to the rhythm of the original, which Zhukovsky does not. "For the year 1829," a critic remarks, "this was an exceedingly audacious and original system of rhythms which overthrew all rules of traditional Russian poetics."[5]

In the same year, 1829, the Moscow theatre gave a performance of Schiller's drama *Die Räuber* and Lermontov, then a student in the exclusive Boarding School for Children of Noble

[4] Lermontov, *Poln. sobr. soch.* (M.–L., 1948), I, 365 (notes).
[5] *Literaturnoye Nasledstvo* (Moskva, 1941), XLIII/XLIV, 134.

Parents, obtained permission to attend the show. The famous Mochalov played the part of Karl Moor. His splendid interpretation made a tremendous impression on the precocious boy. After the performance Lermontov wrote triumphantly to his aunt M. A. Shan-Girey:

Do you remember, you asserted at that time that our [Moscow] actors are inferior to the actors in Petersburg. What a pity you have not seen here *The Gambler* and *Die Räuber,* you would now hold another opinion![6]

It seems that Lermontov saw Mochalov not only in *Die Räuber* but also in *Kabale und Liebe* and in other dramas of the German poet.[7] Under the impression of these performances he began to try his hand at the dramatic kind of poetry. The result was a Schillerean "Storm and Stress" tragedy entitled *The Spaniards* (1830). At first glance one might think that *The Spaniards* is a historical drama presenting the times of the Spanish Inquisition. But this is not the case. Behind the national and historical costume—as in *Don Carlos*—hides the poet's philosophy of life.[8]

In fact, an analysis of the two dramas reveals striking parallels. Fernando, the hero of *The Spaniards,* can be easily compared to Marquis Posa, the actual hero of *Don Carlos.* Following the example of Posa, who champions the cause of the persecuted Protestants of the Netherlands, Fernando champions the cause of the persecuted Jews of Spain and even risks his life to save an old Jew from the hands of the Inquisition. Like the Marquis, he is opposed to religious fanaticism. Alvarez, boasting of the

---

[6] Lermontov, *Poln. sobr. soch.* (M.–L., 1947), IV, 400. Hereafter abridged to "PSS."

[7] Cp. *Lit. Nasl.,* XLIII/XLIV, 22.

[8] Cp. Eichenbaum: *"The Spaniards* is, of course, not a historical but a socio-political drama. Spain is, so to say, only a cipher, or a historical symbol suggested to Lermontov by Schiller's *Don Carlos."* *Klassiki Russkoy Dramy* (Leningrad–Moskva, 1940), p. 111.

merits of one of his ancestors who had tortured and burned at the stake "more than three thousand infidels" receives the sarcastic reply : "Oh, he was certainly a holy man; undoubtedly he was canonised for that ?"[9] With bitter words Fernando denounces the iniquity and inhumanity of the Inquisition tribunals to which often a slanderous denunciation is enough to put an innocent upon the rack.

Although a faithful Catholic, he rejects indignantly this kind of Christianity, calling it an abominable superstition. In this connection a passage from Schiller's letter to Reinwald in which he speaks of his plans regarding *Don Carlos* deserves to be mentioned :

Ausserdem will ich es mir in diesem Schauspiel zur Pflicht machen, in Darstellung der Inquisition die prostituierte Menschheit zu rächen und ihre Schandflecken fürchterlich an den Pranger zu stellen. Ich will—und sollte mein Karlos dadurch auch für das Theater verloren gehen—einer Menschenart, welche der Dolch der Tragödie bis jetzt nur gestreift hat, auf die Seele stossen.[10]

Little has been realized of this grandiose intention. On the other hand, Lermontov seems to have carried it out in *The Spaniards,* although, in youthful exuberance, he distorts Schiller's majestic-pathetic tendency into a grotesque-pathetic one. Wicked Father Sorrini, who does not shrink from using crime to attain his aims, is the embodiment of the Inquisition. With regard to baseness he surpasses his model Domingo in *Don Carlos,* and there can be little doubt that the Russian more than shares Schiller's antipathy against priestcraft and the Inquisition. Incidentally, there is a character also named Domingo in *The Spaniards.*

[9] Lermontov, *PSS,* III, 163.
[10] *Friedrich Schiller–Briefe,* ed. Reinhard Buchwald (Leipzig, n. d.), pp. 40–41. Letter of April 14, 1783.

The figure of Franz Moor represents another parallel to Sorrini. Both villains covet a girl who has given her heart to someone else; both attempt to lure her into a private chamber; both
receive a slap in the face for their insolence; both threaten to
use force—Sorrini points a dagger, Franz draws his sword—in
order to have their way. An influence of Schiller's hero may also
be seen in Sorrini's materialism and atheism. Like Franz Moor,
Sorrini consoles himself with the idea that there is no hell and
no heaven, no avenger and no judgment; like Franz Moor, he
sees in religion only a fairy-tale invented by clever priests to
keep the ignorant mob in fear and subjection. Finally, both
heroes cause the ruin of their rivals by means of lie and slander.[11]

In the drama of the German, wicked Franz is contrasted with
noble-minded and heroic Karl. Similarly in *The Spaniards,*
wicked Sorrini is contrasted with noble-minded and heroic Fernando, who was characterized by a critic as "a copy of the
famous, magnanimous exiles of romanticism."[12] Among the
"famous exiles of romanticism" Karl Moor appears to be a very
close parallel to Fernando. In bitter loneliness the two "sublime
villains" face a cold, strange, hostile world. "I have no more a
father, I have no more a love!" cries Karl Moor full of furious
grief.[13] Like an echo resounds Fernando's lament: "Fatherland!
Home!—an empty jingling of words; for their value is unknown to me. Fatherland is the country where one has relatives,
house and friends; but I have neither relatives nor house nor
friends under this sky!"[14]

Against the hostility of the world Karl Moor reacts with hate

[11] Lermontov, *PSS, III,* 228–230; Schiller, *Sämtliche Werke,* Säkular-
Ausgabe (Stuttgart & Berlin, n. d.), III, 137–143. Hereafter abridged to
"SW."
[12] I. I. Zamotin, *M. Yu. Lermontov* (Varshava, 1914), p. 57.
[13] Schiller, *SW, III,* 32.
[14] Lermontov, *PSS,* III, 199.

and scorn and revenge. The idea of revenge dominates his life: "My handicraft is retaliation—revenge is my trade."[15] Fernando reacts in a similar way: "I have no hope in heaven, I have no hope on earth—to revenge I dedicate now my soul."[16] Like Karl Moor, who wants to poison the ocean and sound the bugle of rebellion throughout nature, he dreams of world-shaking deeds of revenge which will make mankind shiver.[17] Also in the motivation of the idea of revenge Lermontov imitates the German poet. Karl Moor becomes a criminal because he has appealed in vain to humanity, sympathy, and forbearance. Fernando becomes a criminal because he has appealed in vain to the humanity and sympathy of Father Sorrini. Innocent blood stains Fernando's hands when he murders Emilia—but he is a noble-minded, heroic, pathetic criminal like the robber Moor.

In lonely grandeur the two majestic malefactors challenge God and the existing order of society. True, Karl is the chief of a gang of robbers, but he has nothing in common with them. They are only "roguish thieves, miserable instruments of his greater intentions."[18] Fernando's loneliness may be paralleled with the sublime loneliness of Karl Moor. Fernando exclaims: "I am alone . . . and against me the whole world! The whole universe against me: how great I am!"[19] After the example of Schiller, who also stigmatizes the corruption of justice and public life in Germany, Lermontov denounces the moral, political, and religious conditions and the depraved courts in Russia: "Where is still a court of justice in Spain? It is nothing but a gang of robbers!"[20]

After moments of titanic defiance, Karl Moor's burning soul becomes immersed in the sombre waters of melancholy and senti-

[15] Schiller, *SW*, III, 79.
[16] Lermontov, *PSS*, III, 241.
[17] Schiller, *SW*, III, 30; Lermontov, *PSS*, III, 224.
[18] Schiller, *SW*, III, 80.
[19] Lermontov, *PSS*, III, 260.
[20] Schiller, *SW*, III, 63–64, 77; Lermontov, *PSS*, III, 204, 260.

mental yearnings.[21] Heroic Fernando succumbs to similar moods:
"Look at the moon," he says to Emilia, "how beautiful it is!
And the little clouds around it!—The moon, the moon!—How
much sentiment vibrates in this word!"[22]

The finale in the two dramas is almost the same. After Karl
Moor has stabbed Amalia he throws his weapon scornfully to the
ground and leaves to surrender to the courts. It has finally
dawned on him that he is not appointed to anticipate Divine
Providence.[23] Parallel to this, Fernando, seeing that Emilia cannot
be saved from the clutches of the priest, stabs her with his dagger.
Then he attempts to kill Sorrini. In his failure he perceives a
hint from Heaven. He flings his dagger contemptuously away
and surrenders to earthly justice.[24]

Another influence of Schiller may be seen in the figure of
Emilia who resembles both Amalia and Luise Millerin. Like
Luise, who dreams of the time when noble titles will be cheap
and hearts will rise in price, she defends the principle of the
nobility of the spirit.[25] When her stepmother forbids her to see
Fernando because he is not of noble birth she answers: "Believe
me, not in patents of nobility is nobility, but in the heart!"[26]
Both in *The Spaniards* and in *Kabale und Liebe* the catastrophe
of the lovers derives from the insuperable gulf between aristocracy and bourgeoisie. The consciousness of the gulf dividing
her from her lover is rooted so deeply in Emilia's heart, that she
considers her situation as irremediable from the very beginning.
As in the case of Luise Millerin and Amalia, the thought of
breaking the barriers of her environment and founding a new
existence in another land does not occur to her. Following the

---

[21] Schiller, *SW*, III, 87–89, 98.
[22] Lermontov, *PSS*, III, 178–179.
[23] Schiller, *SW*, III, 154–156.
[24] Lermontov, *PSS*, III, 259, 264–265.
[25] Schiller, *SW*, III, 307.
[26] Lermontov, *PSS*, III, 158.

model of Amalia, the only way out she can think of is to seek refuge behind the walls of a cloister.[27]

Don Alvarez in *The Spaniards* may be compared to President Walter in *Kabale und Liebe*. Both figures represent the high aristocracy, both are proud of their ancestry and their blue blood, both cherish ambitious plans for the future of their children. Alvarez is beside himself with astonishment and rage when he learns that Fernando, a foundling, wants to marry his daughter Emilia. The mere idea of such a marriage appears to him a mortal insult.[28] This parallels the fury of President Walter who cannot imagine that his son should have "serious intentions" regarding the "bourgeoise canaille" Luise. In both dramas the ambition and class-prejudice of the fathers drive the lovers into the arms of death.

Lermontov's drama is characterized by an exaggerated number of monologues and speeches "aside," and the action is continuously interrupted by the interspersed poems, ballads, and songs. In spite of this and its immature style which sounds like a bad imitation of the "Storm and Stress" style of the German poet, *The Spaniards* is an interesting phenomenon in the field of tragedy. Lermontov appears here, in emulation of Schiller, as a champion of freedom and as a critic of society. The flame of rebellion glows in the drama.

It is the same revolutionary spirit which also smolders in the audacious political poems of the thirties. Lermontov himself testifies to it when he says that in this play it was his intention to present "the untamable ardor of the soul—and the rebellious fire of wild passion."[29] On the strength of its themes of freedom and revolt *The Spaniards* may be placed in line with the revolu-

---

[27] Lermontov, *PSS*, III, 213; Schiller, *SW*, III, 85.
[28] Lermontov, *PSS*, III, 161.
[29] Lermontov, *PSS*, III, 157.

tionary tragedies of the Decembrist poets.[30] An American critic, nevertheless, maintains that "Lermontov never became a lover of civic liberty," that he was "unmoved by the republican and revolutionary moods of Schiller, the while he followed him in his furious denunciations of social life and customs."[31]

Lermontov's second drama, *Menschen und Leidenschaften,* was written and completed in the same year as *The Spaniards,* that is in 1830. It is certainly a very revealing title for the work of a Russian dramatist. "With this title," says Eichenbaum, "the literary dependence of the play on the dramas of the "Storm and Stress" period—especially on Schiller *(Die Räuber, Kabale und Liebe)*—is emphasized."[32] Schiller's influence is evident both in the subject matter (family conflict) and in the bombastic, forcedly tense and vigorous style. "In prose," Eichenbaum continues, "these characteristics of Lermontov's youthful style look particularly crude and unmotivated—like an awkward imitation of the pathetic style of Schiller."[33]

Yury Volin, the hero of *Menschen und Leidenschaften,* suffers not only because of the quarrels and intrigues disrupting his own family, but also because of the badness and injustice of mankind. He experiences the family conflict as a tragedy of society, as a conflict between Good and Evil. This is characteristic of the so-called "family dramas" of the German poet. Like Karl Moor, Yury had once been an enthusiast and a champion of freedom. "Whenever freedom was mentioned," he says to his friend Zarutskoy, "my heart started trembling and my cheeks grew red-hot as fire."[34] But like Karl Moor, he has lost faith in the goodness

[30] Cp. *Klassiki Russkoy Dramy,* p. 112.
[31] Clarence A. Manning, "The Dramas of Schiller and Lermontov," *PQ,* VIII (1929), 13.
[32] *Klassiki Russkoy Dramy,* p. 112.
[33] *Ibid.* See also Henri Troyat, *L'étrange destin de Lermontov* (Paris, 1952), p. 25.
[34] Lermontov, *PSS,* III, 280; Schiller, *SW,* III, 18.

of the human heart and he discards his dreams of world-brother-hood and freedom: "The dream is dead for I have become acquainted only too well with man."[35] And in melancholy despair, he sheds bitter tears about his loneliness and ejection from the ranks of mankind.[36]

It can be assumed that the collision of Lermontov's youthful dreams of freedom with the realities of Russian life contributed to the genesis of this drama in more than one respect. The yearning for freedom out of which the work grew is comparable to the mood and atmosphere dominating the life of the German poet when the latter was a student in the Karlsschule. The very name of the hero is symbolical: Volin is derived from either "vola" (freedom) or "volny" (free). He appears enthusiastic, idealistic and romantic—but not romantic in the conventional sense of the word. He is, as a critic says, "not a romanticist of enchantment but a romanticist of disenchantment."[37] Yury's sociopolitical utopianism ("The unrealisable dream of a universal world-brotherhood") reminds us of Karl Moor's fanciful dreams of a free German republic, of Posa's impracticable plans of reform, of Ferdinand's democratic-revolutionary question of whether his patent of nobility was older than the handwriting of heaven in Luise's eyes. The scenes unmasking the outrages of feudalism (for instance, the mistreatment of the kitchen boy by the lady of the manor, II, 1) prove, however, that Lermontov's enthusiasm for freedom applied not only to an abstract and nebulous mankind.

Here he shows real sympathy with the serfs suffering under the arbitrary rule of their feudal lords. This may be an echo of the poet's own boyhood experiences in Tarkhany, the estate of his grandmother Yelizaveta Alekseyevna, but it may also be

---

[35] Lermontov, PSS, III, 281; Schiller, SW, III, 30.
[36] Lermontov, PSS, III, 282; Schiller, SW, III, 80, 89.
[37] Zamotin, op. cit., p. 58.

parallel to some scenes in Schiller's *Die Räuber*. A hidden protest against feudal arbitrariness resounds in part of the monologue of Franz (malicious destruction of the peasants' fields by
the feudal lords, I, 1). Another passage that may have influenced
Lermontov is to be found in the narration of the robber Raz-
mann, where Karl Moor is described as protector of the weak
and poor and as an avenger of the oppressed serfs.[38]

The catastrophe in *Menschen und Leidenschaften* can be compared to the finale in *Kabale und Liebe*. Disillusioned, embit-
tered, despairing, Yury ends his life—on the model of Ferdinand
—by means of a poisoned drink. Also the motivation of the
suicide is identical in the two dramas; both heroes depart from
life because of the alleged unfaithfulness of their loved ones. Too
late they realize that this "unfaithfulness" was nothing but a
product of their imagination and jealousy. The perception of
the truth hits them hard, but in the face of death they forgive
the culprit who has brought about their misfortune. The hero's
father in both dramas is the villain and the originator of the
catastrophe.[39]

In contrast to Lermontov's first drama, *Menschen und Leidenschaften* contains the complicated motives of slander, error, and
misunderstanding. It is, for instance, due to the intrigues and lies
of the maid Darya that innocent Yury incurs his father's curse
and repudiation. This may be compared to the intrigues and lies
of Franz, because of which Karl Moor was cursed and repudiated by his father. Error and misunderstanding dominate the
garden scene where Yury sees his friend Zarutskoy kneeling
before Lubov. Through his naive credulousness Yury destroys—
like Karl Moor—his happiness and his life. And like Schiller's
hero he flies into desperate rages against his foolishness and

[38] Schiller, *SW*, III, 15, 63.
[39] Lermontov, *PSS*, III, 335; Schiller, *SW*, III, 420.

self-deception. But it is too late and he dies calling himself a villain and a suicide.[40]

Yury Volin represents in the drama the world of faith, enthusiasm, love, and ideals. He perishes as an innocent victim in a struggle of interests and passions. There is no guilt on his part and consequently no atonement. But evil—as in the drama of the German poet—does not triumph and there is no victorious villain ruining an innocent and noble-minded hero. The improvement in the dramatic technique is evident : from the simple motivation of the tragic catastrophe in *The Spaniards* Lermontov has progressed to the complicated motivation of *Menschen und Leidenschaften*. As in *Die Räuber* and in *Kabale und Liebe* the final catastrophe strikes principally the culprits. Marfa Gromova, the wicked grandmother, has an apoplectic fit and goes out of her mind. Her intriguing maid Darya faces the grim prospect of deportation to Siberia. Nobody rejoices on account of Yury's death and nobody derives profit from it.[41]

Another case of Schiller's influence may perhaps be seen in the family quarrel about Yury's education abroad. The scene apparently implies a knowledge of the philosophical systems of the time. Actually, however, Lermontov had only a superficial knowledge of philosophy and his enthusiasm for German philosophy and for Kant must thus be derived from his acquaintance with the aesthetic and philosophical works of Schiller.[42] "Philosophy," declares Nikolay Mikhalich, "does by no means lead to atheism but it is, on the contrary, its most efficient antidote and best medicine against blind fanaticism."[43] Like Schiller, the Russian believes in the high educational values of philosophy; like Schiller, he sets his hopes for the future of mankind on the

---

[40] Lermontov, *PSS*, III, 333; Schiller, *SW*, III, 112.
[41] Cp. *Klassiki Russkoy Dramy*, p. 113.
[42] Zamotin, *op. cit.*, pp. 59–60.
[43] Lermontov, *PSS*, III, 293.

idealism of Kant which, he trusts, will liberate the human race from the chains of ignorance and spiritual servitude.

In the year 1831 Lermontov again took up the subject matter of the drama *Menschen und Leidenschaften* and elaborated it in such a way that a completely new play was produced. This new play, *A Strange Man*, is largely autobiographical, like the two preceding plays. It differs, however, from *The Spaniards* and from *Menschen und Leidenschaften* owing to the philosophical deepening of the personal background of experience. The personal sufferings of the hero dissolve in the great ocean of human suffering and the family conflict assumes the importance and symbolism of historical events. Out of his brooding, disconsolate eyes stares, sphinxlike, the old unfathomable problem of Good and Evil which also had ruined the noble-minded enthusiasts Karl Moor, Fiesco, Ferdinand, and Posa.[44]

In contrast to *Die Räuber*, this is not a tragedy of struggle but a tragedy of suffering and decline, the softness of which may be paralleled with the lyrical passivity of *Kabale und Liebe:* for Lermontov's drama represents, as it were, the sum total of his early lyric poetry. In *A Strange Man* he tries to tie his many intellectual poems into a single dramatic unit and to transform the image of his lyric hero into a tragic hero.[45]

This tragic hero is Vladimir Arbenin. He may be characterized as a man who has suffered from childhood under the "heavy burden of self-knowledge," who despises mankind, like Karl Moor, and revolts against the existing order of the world. The spirit of the great robber awakes in his breast when he indignantly exclaims: "How ridiculous man is ! . . . I see now, one must be cruel to live with them."[46] Like Karl Moor, he denounces the indolence, triviality, and injustice of his century: "I am not

[44] Cp. *Lit. Nasl.,* XLIII/XLIV, 22.
[45] Cp. Lermontov, *PSS,* III, 475 (notes).
[46] Lermontov, *PSS,* III, 340, 401.

made for the people of the present century . . . Suffer! suffer!—
how long has mankind already listened to this humbug? . . ."[47]
The existence of evil is an eternal sting in his heart, and as he
sees no way out he quarrels with destiny and God, a "terrible
plaintiff against Divine Providence" like the robber Moor. Also
in this the two figures resemble each other that they never lose
faith completely in a supreme Ruler of heaven and earth.[48]

Lermontov's protest against the outrages of feudalism resounds
again and with much greater vehemence than in *Menschen und
Leidenschaften*. After the example of Ferdinand, Fiesco, Posa,
and Tell who champion the rights of the oppressed people, and
particularly on the model of the noble-minded robber Moor who
protects the peasants against the cruelty of the barons, Arbenin
acts as defender of the tormented serfs.[49] The shocking story of
the old peasant—he tells of the tortures inflicted upon his native
village by the lady of the manor—puts Arbenin into a paroxysm
of horror and indignation.[50] Eichenbaum calls this scene "a
flaming protest against the system of serfdom, one of the strongest
pictures on this topic in Russian literature in the first third of
the nineteenth century."[51]

Another influence of Schiller may be seen in the motives of
curse and revenge. Vladimir Arbenin, repudiated and cursed by
his father, pronounces words which sound like an echo of Karl
Moor's outbursts against the dragon brood of mankind:

I see! I see! Nature arms against me; in my soul I carry the seed
of evil; I was made to destroy the order of nature. . . . Woe! woe
to him who has caused this heart to wither! He shall have to pay for
it: through him I have become an outcast; from this minute: be off
sympathy!—Day and night I will sing my father a ghastly song

---

[47] Lermontov, *PSS*, III, 341, 348–349; Schiller, *SW*, III, 16–18.
[48] Lermontov, *PSS*, III, 367, 397; Schiller, *SW*, III, 71, 88, 121, 127, 131.
[49] Schiller, *SW*, III, 63, 205, 252, 317, 326, 330, 333, 390; IV, 150–166.
[50] Lermontov, *PSS*, III, 365–366.
[51] Lermontov, *PSS*, III, 485 (notes).

until his hair stands on end and repentance begins to devastate his soul![52]

Like Karl Moor, he has hoped for pity and forgiveness. When he realizes that he has hoped in vain he flies into a terrible rage: "But I will avenge myself, I will cruelly avenge myself! . . . I will squeeze tears out of his eyes—and when he cries I shall laugh!"[53]

Besides the motives of revenge and rebellion, a note of elegy and melancholy vibrates in Arbenin's soul: "Once I too was happy and innocent . . . how it hurts that I am not as good, that my soul is not as pure as I should like!"[54] This is perhaps parallel to Karl Moor's lament for the lost paradise of his childhood days: "My innocence! My innocence! . . . everybody is happy . . . I alone am repudiated, I alone am excluded from the ranks of the pure . . . ."[55] In both heroes this mood of loss and contrition is associated with a conviction of the absolute vanity of human striving. "Brother," says Karl Moor, "I have seen mankind, their little worries and their giant projects—their divine plans and their dirty affairs . . . this lottery of life . . . blanks are the result—perhaps there was no prize in it."[56]

Vladimir expresses similar thoughts: "How this moon, how these stars seek to convince me that life has no meaning at all! —Where are now my giant projects? What was the purpose of this megalomania? All is finished!"[57] Evil misgivings oppress his soul—the inevitable end, madness and death, hovers like a black cloud over his existence.[58] This may be compared to a passage in *Die Räuber* where Karl Moor says: "I understand—Ruler in

[52] Lermontov, *PSS*, III, 378; Schiller, *SW*, III, 30–32.
[53] Lermontov, *PSS*, III, 379.
[54] Lermontov, *PSS*, III, 341, 344.
[55] Schiller, *SW*, III, 88–89.
[56] Schiller, *SW*, III, 87.
[57] Lermontov, *PSS*, III, 386.
[58] Lermontov, *PSS*, III, 342–343.

Heaven—I understand—the twigs are falling down—and my autumn has come. . . . Soon—soon all will be finished. . . ."[59] For a last time hope flames up in Arbenin's heart that his disconsolateness and despair may be healed by the love of Natasha, that it may be possible for him to enjoy happiness and peace at her side in spite of the hostility of fate. His hope proves fallacious— as fallacious as that of Karl Moor who for one moment had hoped that in spite of everything he could be happy in the arms of forgiving Amalia.[60]

Along with *Die Räuber, Kabale und Liebe* seems to have exercised considerable influence upon the drama of the Russian. Both in *A Strange Man* and in *Kabale und Liebe* we see an increasing estrangement between father and son which is quickly brought to a climax by a cruel, coolly calculating order of the father. Ferdinand's reaction is furious indignation and the desperate threat: "While you lead her away to the pillory I will tell the capital a story about how one becomes president."[61] Vladimir utters a similar threat: "I already begged you not to destroy in me the last spark of filial humility so that I shall not be forced to repeat this accusation in front of the whole world."[62] Like Ferdinand, he defends himself against the reproach of ingratitude: "Ungrateful?—You have given me life: take it back, take it back if you can. . . ."[63] Like Ferdinand, he curses the moment of his birth and the wicked one who is his father; like Ferdinand, he declares that he cannot be the son of a villain any longer:

Yes, I am your son and therefore I must become the enemy of everything that is holy, your enemy . . . out of gratitude!—Oh,

[59] Schiller, *SW*, III, 121.
[60] Schiller, *SW*, III, 152–154; Lermontov, *PSS*, III, 386.
[61] Schiller, *SW*, III, 347.
[62] Lermontov, *PSS*, III, 372.
[63] Lermontov, *PSS*, III, 374.

if I could concentrate my feelings, my heart, my soul, my breath
into one word, into one sound, then this sound would be a curse to
the first moment of my life, a thunder-clap which would shake your
entrails, father . . . and it would dissuade you from calling me your
son any longer!⁶⁴

Finally, a possible influence of *Don Carlos* may be seen in the
delineation of the character of Princess Sofya who shares more
than one trait with Princess Eboli. Both ladies are in love with
a man whose heart already belongs to someone else, and both
begin to frame evil intrigues as a result of their disappointment.
Jealousy and desire of revenge burn in Eboli's wounded heart:

> Das durfte sie? Das sollte ungerochen
> Der Gauklerin gelungen sein? gelungen,
> Weil sich kein Rächer meldet?—Nein, bei Gott!
> Ich betete sie an—Das fordert Rache!⁶⁵

A similar jealousy and desire of revenge causes Sofya to make
the resolve: "No! They [Natasha and Arbenin] shall not be
happy . . .I swear by this sky, I swear by my soul: all poisonous
means of womanly cunning will I use to annihilate their happiness. . . ."⁶⁶ The two princesses resemble each other even in the
striking plot-detail that their hatred extends not only to the more
lucky rival but also to the lover and that, in the end, bitter repentance overwhelms both.⁶⁷

After the completion of the drama *A Strange Man* Lermontov
concentrates more and more on the problem of Good and Evil.
Vladimir's words: "In my own heart I carry the seed of evil;
I am made to destroy the order of nature" surely allude to the

---

⁶⁴ Lermontov, *PSS*, III, 374; Schiller, *SW*, III, 316–319, 343.
⁶⁵ Schiller, *SW*, IV, 98.
⁶⁶ Lermontov, *PSS*, III, 348.
⁶⁷ Lermontov, *PSS*, III, 390–391; Schiller, *SW*, IV, 219.
  Cp. "Schiller's Influence on the Early Dramas of Lermontov," *PQ*,
XXXII (October, 1953), 396–410.

figure of Yevgeny Arbenin in the tragedy *A Masquerade* (1835)
with which the poet inaugurates the period of his maturity as a
dramatist. On the model of the German dramatist, he endeavors
to construct a completely new kind of tragedy, realizing in the
figure of the hero an aesthetic principle stated in Schiller's essay
"Über die tragische Kunst":

Zu einem weit höhern Grad steigt das Mitleid, wenn sowohl
derjenige, welcher leidet, als derjenige, welcher Leiden verursacht,
Gegenstände desselben werden. Dies kann nur dann geschehen, wenn
der letztere weder unsern Hass noch unsere Verachtung erregt,
sondern wider seine Neigung dahin gebracht wird, Urheber des
Unglücks zu werden.[68]

With these words Schiller proclaims the principle of double
compassion : with the victim and with the originator of the misfortune. Initially, this principle appears connected with the idea
of a moral purpose which collides with the purposelessness of
nature. The catastrophe is consequently the work of blind chance
and the psychology of the hero can be rightfully neglected because he is bound to become the cause of the misfortune "against
his inclination." Later Schiller abandons the idea of moral purposefulness (at least with regard to aesthetics) and places the
principle of strength in the foreground. This exempts the playwright from the necessity of taking his heroes exclusively from
the category of "good characters":

Wieviel mehr wir in ästhetischen Urteilen auf die Kraft als auf
die Richtung der Kraft, wieviel mehr auf die Freiheit als auf
Gesetzmässigkeit sehen, wird schon daraus hinlänglich offenbar,
dass wir Kraft und Freiheit lieber auf Kosten der Gesetzmässigkeit
geäussert, als die Gesetzmässigkeit auf Kosten der Kraft und Freiheit
beobachtet sehen. . . . Ein Lasterhafter fängt an, uns zu interes-
sieren, sobald er Glück und Leben wagen muss, um seinen schlimmen

[68] Schiller, *SW*, XI, 164.

Willen durchzusetzen; ein Tugendhafter hingegen verliert in demselben Verhältnis unsre Aufmerksamkeit, also seine Glückseligkeit selbst
ihn zum Wohlverhalten nötigt. Rache, zum Beispiel, ist unstreitig
ein unedler und selbst niedriger Affekt. Nichtsdestoweniger wird sie
ästhetisch, sobald sie dem, der sie ausübt, ein schmerzhaftes Opfer
kostet.[69]

Schiller's thesis of the superiority of strength and freedom over
the direction of strength and over moral regularity brings us very
close to the problems of Good and Evil raised in the drama
A Masquerade. We now understand why Lermontov takes his
hero from the wicked class of characters and why Arbenin's vile
and ignoble act of vengeance produces an aesthetic effect of
astonishing force. Like the German poet, Lermontov is interested
solely in the *expression* of strength—for the *direction* of strength
he does not care at all. By risking his life and happiness to carry
out his evil designs, Arbenin arouses our interest and even that
higher sort of compassion which Schiller refers to in his treatise
"Über die tragische Kunst."

It is a long road leading from Lermontov's passionate, enthusiastic, noble-minded heroes Fernando *(The Spaniards)*,
Yury *(Menschen und Leidenschaften)*, Vladimir *(A Strange
Man)*—who despite their opposition against the existing form of
society perish almost without resistance—to the fanatical, cold-
blooded, wicked hero of *A Masquerade*. Yevgeny Arbenin is not
the kind of man to think of impotent submission to fate, of irreso-
lute resignation or feeble forgiveness. From the very beginning
he appears as an active, forceful character who has lost his belief
in the power of so-called Good. Like Karl Moor, before his conversion, he takes the "sword of vengeance" into his own hands,
resolved to deal the corrupt society one avenging blow after the
other. The figure of Arbenin proves that Lermontov himself has
lost faith in the power of Good.

[69] Schiller, *SW*, XI, 273.

At its representatives he now looks down with pity and contempt : he sees in them only weak and passive characters who
are unable to resist the power of Evil. Equipped with this knowledge, he creates in Yevgeny Arbenin a hero who *deliberately*
passes from Good to Evil. Arbenin's fight against society and
the order of the universe results not from the fact that a "spark
of heavenly fire" still glows in him but from the fact that he has
preserved in his soul the primitive force of fighting and reveng-
ing. In other words : the faculty of volition. Here again Lermontov proves himself a disciple of Schiller who, in the essay "Über
das Erhabene," unconditionally defends the freedom of human
volition :

"Kein Mensch muss müssen" sagt der Jude Nathan zum
Derwisch, und dieses Wort ist in einem weiteren Umfange wahr,
als man demselben vielleicht einräumen möchte. Der Wille ist der
Geschlechtscharakter des Menschen, und die Vernunft selbst ist
nur die ewige Regel desselben. Vernünftig handelt die ganze Natur :
sein Prärogativ ist bloss, dass er mit Bewusstsein und Willen vernünftig handelt. Alle andere Dinge müssen : der Mensch ist das Wesen,
welches will.[70]

From this thesis it is only a step to the conclusion drawn by
Schiller, that in tragedy there is no room for a philosophy of
moral purposefulness, a higher order of things, a kind of universal will which regulates and directs the world and "dissolves the
single discordant sound in the great harmony." Having discovered the grandiose charm of chaos in nature, Schiller vigor-
ously turns against the champions of the harmony philosophy
to which he himself had paid homage not so long ago :

Also hinweg mit der falsch verstandenen Schonung und dem
schlaffen verzärtelten Geschmack, der über das ernste Angesicht
der Notwendigkeit einen Schleier wirft und, um sich bei den Sinnen

[70] Schiller, *SW*, XII, 264.

in Gunst zu setzen, eine Harmonie zwischen dem Wohlsein und Wohlverhalten *lügt,* wovon sich in der wirklichen Welt keine Spuren zeigen. Stirne gegen Stirn zeige sich uns das böse Verhängnis. Nicht in der Unwissenheit der uns umlagernden Gefahren—denn diese muss doch endlich aufhören—nur in der Bekanntschaft mit denselben ist Heil für uns. Zu dieser Bekanntschaft nun verhilft uns das furchtbar herrliche Schauspiel der alles zerstörenden und wieder erschaffenden und wieder zerstörenden Veränderung—des bald langsam untergrabenden, bald schnell überfallenden Verderbens, verhelfen uns die pathetischen Gemälde der mit dem Schicksal ringenden Menschheit, der unaufhaltsamen Flucht des Glücks, der betrogenen Sicherheit, der triumphierenden Ungerechtigkeit und der unterliegenden Unschuld, welche die Geschichte in reichem Mass aufstellt und die tragische Kunst nachahmend vor unsre Augen bringt.[71]

With these words Schiller deals a deadly blow to the idea of moral purposefulness and lays down the aesthetic principle of strength. On the basis of this principle he proceeds to divide the "Lebenswege" of men into two great categories: a realistic one and an idealistic one. Since man is the being who wills, it is possible for him to assert his will in two ways: "Entweder *realistisch,* wenn der Mensch der Gewalt Gewalt entgegensetzt, wenn er als Natur die Natur beherrschet; oder *idealistisch,* wenn er aus der Natur heraustritt und so, in Rücksicht auf sich, den Begriff der Gewalt vernichtet."[72] It is evident that the material for a tragedy, as Schiller understands it, ought to be taken from the first category (although, in practice, Schiller himself did not always act according to this principle: cp., for instance, Max Piccolomini!).

In this respect Lermontov follows his model both dramatically and philosophically. Arbenin's life represents a "pathetical drama of man struggling with destiny, of happiness fleeing irresistibly,

---

[71] Schiller, *SW,* XII, 279–280. [Italics Schiller's.]
[72] Schiller, *SW,* XII, 265. [Italics Schiller's.]

of security betrayed, evil triumphant," as Schiller had pictured
it for a true tragic playwright in his essay "Über das Erhabene."
Arbenin appears as the incarnate principle of strength and
double compassion, for even after his murdering of the innocent
Nina we feel sympathy and pity for him because with Nina he
"destroys his own happiness, his hope for salvation, and his belief in Good."[73]

Beside the principles of strength and double compassion *A
Masquerade* contains also the principle of justification of Evil.
Arbenin's "Lebensweg" represents itself as the "Lebensweg" of a
man whom Schiller would have defined as "realistic" : free and
proud, Arbenin asserts his will by opposing force to force. By
introducing the principle of justification of Evil, Lermontov does
take, unquestionably, a step away from Schiller, and yet the
principle of justification of Evil can be traced back to the
aesthetic treatises of the latter :

In ästhetischen Urteilen sind wir also nicht für die Sittlichkeit an
sich selbst, sondern bloss für die Freiheit interessiert, und jene kann
nur insofern unsrer Einbildungskraft gefallen, als sie die letztere
sichtbar macht. Es ist daher offenbare Verwirrung der Grenzen,
wenn man moralische Zweckmässigkeit in ästhetischen Dingen
fordert und, um das Reich der Vernunft zu erweitern, die
Einbildungskraft aus ihrem rechtmässigen Gebiete verdrängen will.
Entweder wird man sie ganz unterjochen müssen, und dann ist es
um alle ästhetische Wirkung geschehen; oder sie wird mit der
Vernunft ihre Herrschaft teilen, und dann wird für Moralität wohl
nicht viel gewonnen sein. Indem man zwei verschiedene Zwecke
verfolgt, wird man Gefahr laufen, beide zu verfehlen. Man wird die
Freiheit der Phantasie durch moralische Gesetzmässigkeit fesseln
und die Notwendigkeit der Vernunft durch die Willkür der Einbildungskraft zerstören.[74]

---

[73] Cp. Lermontov, *PSS*, III, 477 (notes).
[74] Schiller, *SW*, XI, 274, "Über das Pathetische."

Schiller, as can be seen, limits the justification of Evil to "aesthetic things." Lermontov, however, consciously passes these limits, throwing himself into the whirl of real life and actual passion. He unmasks the inner rottenness of the so-called "great world"; he sharply condemns "misconceived forbearance and indolent, effeminate taste." He proceeds to disturb the complacent cheerfulness of society by hurling an "iron verse" into their eyes—a verse "soaked in wrath and bile." And in the end he unchains a storm of rebellion which is equivalent to a revolt against the whole order of human society; against God and morals.[75] *A Masquerade* is a complicated play, but above all its obscurities and contradictions rises the pathetic figure of Arbenin, the great sufferer, whose monologues exceed by far the limited frame of a sentimental melodrama. By unveiling the social and philosophical basis of the drama, the monologues raise it to the dignity of a sublime lyrical tragedy, comparable to the philosophical tragedies of Schiller, the melodramatic deviations of which may be interpreted as the result of "Lermontov's search for new solutions in the field of style and motivation."[76]

Lermontov's transition from the philosophical to the psychological drama had already been prepared by his *A Masquerade.* Early in 1836 the poet started working on a new play in which this change to realism and psychological analysis was actually accomplished. In *A Masquerade* a picture of society in grand style is presented, but the new play, *The Two Brothers,* leads us back into the narrowness of domestic life. Lermontov, "as it were, repeats thus the dramatic road Schiller had taken from *Die Räuber,* via the *Wallenstein Trilogie,* to *Die Braut von Messina.*"[77] The difference between the two poets consists chiefly in

[75] Cp. *Lit. Nasl.,* XLIII/XLIV, 28.

[76] *Klassiki Russkoy Dramy,* pp. 119–120. Cp. "The Influence of Schiller's Aesthetics on the Dramas of Lermontov," *PQ,* XXX (October, 1951), 393–402.

[77] *Klassiki Russkoy Dramy,* p. 124.

the fact that Schiller arrives at the art form of classical Greek tragedy whereas Lermontov's line of development progresses from the paradoxical–philosophical and declamatory–pathetic manner to psychological–realistic motivation.

In spite of this important difference, many elements in the drama of the Russian remind us of Schiller. The plot parallels the plots of *Die Räuber, Die Braut von Messina,* and *Don Carlos.* In each case blood relations fight for the possession of the beloved woman. In each case the struggle ends with the ruin of the better, more humane, more noble-minded hero. Also the motives of exasperated struggle, envy and jealousy, are nearly identical. The brothers Yury–Alexander in Lermontov's drama can easily be compared to the brothers Karl–Franz in *Die Räuber.*

Noble-minded Yury corresponds to Karl, wicked Alexander corresponds to Franz. Hatred toward father and brother, and a scorching passion for his brother's sweetheart loom large as the moving forces of Alexander's evil actions. Like Franz Moor, he hates his brother, both for being their father's coddled favorite and for being his more lucky rival in love. He hates his father because of the partiality with which the old man has concentrated all his affection and tenderness on Yury alone. A true "Storm and Stress" character, Alexander persists in his implacable grudge even at his father's bier : "I don't care a damn for my father, I don't care a damn for the whole world! . . ."[78] Sometimes, notwithstanding his wickedness, he yields to moods of melancholy and repentance which recall the figure of the contrite robber in the scene on the Danube : "Alone, always alone, rejected like Cain—God knows for whose misdeeds. . . ."[79] In his attitude towards God and religion Alexander can be compared

[78] Lermontov, *PSS,* III, 152.
[79] Lermontov, *PSS,* III, 141; Schiller, *SW,* III, 88–89. Cp. also Byron.

to Franz. Alexander's desperate cry: "If only I could pray . . . .!"
vibrates with the same note of deep uncertainty and agony as
Franz Moor's convulsive attempt to pray when everything is at
stake and "the water reaches his soul."[80]

Another parallel to Schiller may be seen in Alexander's passion
for his brother's sweetheart Vera. On the model of Franz Moor
pestering Amalia with his declarations of love, Alexander haunts
and torments Vera. Both villains talk of "boundless sacrifices"[81]
on behalf of their beloved, both allegedly burn with the desire
"to become a slave"[82] of the desired lady. Both, finally, seeing
that their protestations are met with disdain and scorn, throw
off their mask of love to get by brutish force what they had been
unable to obtain by artifice and flattery.[83]

Alexander's noble-minded brother Yury shares several characteristics with Karl Moor. There is, first of all, his youthful
frivolity and passion for gambling. "Has he [Yury] perhaps
ruined himself in a game of chance?"[84] Dmitry Petrovich wonders, while Alexander does his best to slander and defame his
brother who is absent. Karl Moor, it will be recalled, is guilty
of the same lightheadedness and of the same sin of gambling.[85]
Also the principal motive of *Die Räuber,* the motive of revenge,
had a strong impact on the figure of Yury Radin.

When Yury discovers that it was his own brother who had
disturbed his nightly rendezvous with Vera he exclaims furiously:
"Brother! . . . from this moment on—torn to pieces are the
bonds of blood and friendship—great evil you have done to me—
evil that cannot be undone—this calls for revenge!"[86] This is

[80] Lermontov, *PSS,* III, 129; Schiller, *SW,* III, 144.
[81] Lermontov, *PSS,* III, 123; Schiller, *SW,* III, 33.
[82] Lermontov, *PSS,* III, 129; Schiller, *SW,* III, 83.
[83] Lermontov, *PSS,* III, 132, 143; Schiller, *SW,* III, 38, 84.
[84] Lermontov, *PSS,* III, 133.
[85] Schiller, *SW,* III, 7, 25.
[86] Lermontov, *PSS,* III, 147.

parallel to Karl Moor's fit of rage at the frontier inn after he has received the faked letter : "I have no longer a father, I have no longer a love, and blood and death shall make me forget that something was ever dear to my heart!"[87]

The figure of old and sick Dmitry Petrovich (father of Yury and Alexander) bears much resemblance to old and sick Maximilian Moor. Dmitry Petrovich is as foolishly infatuated with his darling Yury as Maximilian Moor is infatuated with his darling Karl; and Alexander, after all, has some reason to be furious at the unequal distribution of fatherly affection. "With me you have never been so cheerful as now with my brother!"[88] Alexander bitterly remarks to his father, seeing his delirious joy on account of the home-coming of his darling Yury. The whole scene recalls Franz Moor hurling his complaint of partiality against his father and reminding him of how "dull mediocre Franz" was neglected from infancy and placed behind "talented Karl."[89] Dmitry Petrovich is weak-minded enough to serve Alexander as an instrument for his plans of revenge, just as decrepit Maximilian Moor unsuspectingly serves the vengeful purposes of villainous Franz.[90] In the face of death Dmitry Petrovich imparts his fatherly benediction upon Yury. This is parallel to Maximilian Moor giving his blessing to Karl a short time before dying.[91]

The influence of *Don Carlos*, noticed already by Zamotin,[92] is less conspicuous. Nevertheless, the figure of Vera may be compared to the figure of the queen in several respects. Both have made unusually brilliant matches : Vera has married a prince, Elizabeth a king. Both are unhappy, for their hearts are beating

[87] Schiller, *SW*, III, 32.
[88] Lermontov, *PSS*, III, 118.
[89] Schiller, *SW*, III, 8–9.
[90] Lermontov, *PSS*, III, 133; Schiller, *SW*, III, 5–13.
[91] Lermontov, *PSS*, III, 151; Schiller, *SW*, III, 148.
[92] Zamotin, *op. cit.*, p. 21.

for someone else. Elizabeth Valois is the victim of intrigues and circumstances, and she explains her marriage by saying that she had been forced to bow to fate. She meets her royal husband with respect and awe, not with love or passion.[93] Vera, too, is a victim—the victim of her illusions and emotions. She does not love her husband and finally realizes that her marriage has been a fatal miscalculation: "It was a madness, a mistake! . . . "[94]

An additional parallel between the two dramas is the fact that the princesses' hearts are ruled by young lovers, although both are married to old men. From Elizabeth's conversation with Don Carlos we learn how much she suffers on account of her forced matrimony. Neither her matrimonial vow nor her heart forbid her to fall into her lover's arms, but only the sense and consciousness of her duty.[95] Vera, it is true, goes even a step farther than the queen, admitting frankly that she is still in love with Yury.[96] But like Elizabeth ("no further word—for the sake of my peace!"), she begs her lover for mercy and consideration: "Happy I cannot be any more, peace is all I still desire—will you grudge me even this?"[97] On the model of Schiller's heroine, Vera makes her appeal in the name of duty.[98]

The dramatic novelty of *The Two Brothers* lies in the fact that the play contains not one but two heroes who both assert their rights and claims to the heroine and the leading role. An analogous situation prevails in Schiller's *Die Braut von Messina* where two brothers, Don Manuel and Don Cesar, fight for the same maiden and alternately stand in the centre of interest. The objection might be raised that the two dramas are constructed on different dramaturgical principles and, consequently, are not

[93] Schiller, *SW*, IV, 38.
[94] Lermontov, *PSS*, III, 124.
[95] Schiller, *SW*, IV, 38.
[96] Lermontov, *PSS*, III, 142.
[97] Schiller, *SW*, IV, 36; Lermontov, *PSS*, III, 142.
[98] Lermontov, *PSS*, III, 142, 146.

comparable. However, one should remember that *Die Braut von Messina*, although a fate drama, does not conceive of fate in the classical Aeschylean sense, but in the almost modern Euripidean sense which allows free play to the character and psychology of man.

As in the German drama, inherited character is also of great importance in *The Two Brothers*. Yury and Alexander are drawn as contrasting characters like Don Cesar and Don Manuel; and Alexander's gloomy thoughts, feelings, and actions are explained by the circumstances and conditions of his unhappy childhood. In the second act Alexander sets forth the reasons of his wickedness in a long speech.[99] Here we have the essence of that psychological material which exists to a great extent also in *Die Braut von Messina*.

But a significant difference between the two dramas must not be passed over in silence. Whereas in *Die Braut von Messina* the wicked brother commits suicide to atone for his crime, in *The Two Brothers* the romantic idea of justification of evil still holds its ground—in an attenuated form because it is subordinated to the psychological motivation.[100] But as in the drama *A Masquerade* the villain triumphs over the weakness and passivity of the noble-minded hero. Incidentally, a reference to Schiller may perhaps be seen in the title of the Russian play. *The Two Brothers* reminds us of *Die feindlichen Brüder* which was the original title of *Die Braut von Messina*.[101]

Summarizing, we may say with Manning "that the dramas of Schiller, especially *Die Räuber* and *Kabale und Liebe*, exercised a great influence upon the dramas of Lermontov."[102] To this

[99] Lermontov, *PSS*, III, 130.
[100] Cp. *Klassiki Russkoy Dramy*, p. 124.
[101] Cp. "Schiller's Influence on Lermontov's Drama *The Two Brothers*," *PQ*, XXXV (April 1956), 186–190.
[102] Manning, "The Dramas of Schiller and Lermontov," p. 19.

dramaturgical influence must be added the philosophical influence of Schiller's aesthetic writings. Even in his first play, *The Spaniards,* Lermontov endeavors to raise the family conflict to a higher socio-philosophical level by introducing into it Schiller's ideals of tolerance, humanity, and freedom, and by employing Schiller's principle of aesthetic strength. His second play, *Menschen und Leidenschaften,* represents a considerable progress in the direction of the philosophical drama of the German poet. The family conflict here assumes the character of universal social and moral collisions. The hero, Yury Volin, does not perish as a victim of accidental circumstances or due to the bad will of a wicked individual as in *The Spaniards,* but he is ruined by the very organization of human life and by the very order of the universe.

Obviously, Lermontov imitates here the Schillerean tragic catastrophe which manages without the guilt of the hero and without a triumphant villain. In his third drama, *A Strange Man,* the former lyric hero is transformed into a tragic giant and the whole drama rises to the level of a "social and ethical humanism which unveils the defects of the contemporary society." [103] As in the preceding play, there are no real villains in the drama. We see only ordinary people carried away by the torrent of their petty passions, people who scarcely realize how inhumanly, abominably, treacherously, jealously they behave. With this mean and insignificant society Lermontov contrasts Vladimir Arbenin who carries the "heavy burden of self-knowledge" on his shoulders—a noble, enthusiastic, high-minded youth like his model Karl Moor.

After the completion of the drama *A Strange Man* Lermontov's dramatic endeavors concentrate on the problem of Good and Evil already raised here with great poignancy, Vladimir's

[103] Lermontov, *PSS,* III, 475 (notes).

cry : "I carry in me the seed of Evil; I am created to destroy the order of nature!" prepares the way for the figure of Yevgeny Arbenin in the drama *A Masquerade* which marks the peak of Lermontov's achievements as a dramatist.

This drama leaves but little doubt that Lermontov's Evil is an Evil generated by the guilt of Good. It is an Evil which exists as an eternal reproach to Good because it continuously unveils Good's appalling weakness. The poet does not represent Evil as an expression of strength in general, however (regardless of its direction); rather he depicts it as a conscious revolt against the helplessness and indolence of Good—as a phenomenon, not of nature but of history. From this standpoint Lermontov consequently passes to his apology for Evil. From this standpoint he manages to construct the drama in such a way that the originator of the catastrophe, the personification of Evil and Vice, rouses in us not only fear and horror but also sympathy and compassion. In other words : in *A Masquerade* Lermontov realizes in dramatic form Schiller's principle of double compassion, compassion with the victim *and* with the orginator of the misfortune. On this contradictory demand of double compassion rests also the hidden philosophical and dialectical depth, the power, vitality, and poignancy of this remarkable drama.

In his last drama, *The Two Brothers,* Lermontov continues to elaborate the problem of Good and Evil raised in *A Masquerade.* Noteworthy is his passing from philosophical drama to psychological and realistic analysis and from lyrical verse to ordinary prose. What is really new in *The Two Brothers* is only the introduction of *two* tragic heroes. Plot and motivation remind us of *Die Räuber,* but the drama can also be paralleled with *Don Carlos* and *Die Braut von Messina.* In the development of the poet *The Two Brothers* represents a stage of transition—a first step towards prose, an unconscious preparation for the novel *A Hero of Our Time*.

The figure of Alexander Radin occupies an important intermediate position between Arbenin *(A Masquerade)* and Pechorin *(A Hero of Our Time)*. The drama as a whole may be viewed as an attempt to solve the most vital moral problem of the romantic drama; the attempt to develop a correlative psychological elaboration of both the good and the wicked hero. Yury and Alexander are "two final links of an invisible chain drawing near each other by withdrawing from each other."[104] In this sense we can call *The Two Brothers* an experiment, after the completion of which Lermontov was ready to move to the novel. In *A Hero of Our Time*, written in the years 1838–40, the poet shows that he has extinguished all traces of Schillerean pathos. From the standpoint of his newly-won philosophical and historical perspectives he boldly places the problem of Good and Evil in the light of a realistic psychological analysis.

Schiller's influence on Lermontov is therewith ended. Russian history and the grandiose world of the Caucasus became the two principal sources of Lermontov's inspiration during the last years of his life.

---

[104] Lermontov, *PSS*, III, 478 (notes).

III

Belinsky

Lermontov was not the only young Russian who was carried away by the brilliant performances of *Die Räuber* and *Kabale und Liebe* during the Moscow theatrical seasons of 1829–30. Mochalov's inspired acting, in the parts of Karl Moor and Ferdinand, stirred the imagination of another remarkable young man, Vissarion Grigoryevich Belinsky (1811–48), wakening in him the ambition to write a similar play—a play designed to denounce serfdom and oppression, prejudice and privilege. Thus, under the "fresh influence of Schiller's *Die Räuber* and *Kabale und Liebe*,"[1] Belinsky's dramatic tale *Dmitry Kalinin* (1831) came into being. That the drama was conceived under the aegis of the German poet is confirmed by the testimony of Belinsky's university friend Prozorov. According to his explanation, *Dmitry Kalinin* was the fruit of Belinsky's enthusiasm for the theatre and the "still novel magnetism of Schiller's *Die Räuber* and *Kabale und Liebe* which, at that time, were often performed on the stage."[2] Belinsky's dramatic attempt consists of five acts and is written in a highly exuberant prose. The following is a synopsis of this little known play :

Dmitry Kalinin, a released bondsman, has set his affections on

[1] A. N. Pypin, *Belinsky* (St. Petersburg, 1908), p. 44.
[2] *Polnoye sobranie sochineniy Belinskogo*, ed. S. A. Vengerov (St. Petersburg, 1900), I, 137. See also O. P. Peterson, *Schiller in Russland* (New York, 1934), pp. 156–157, and L. Silberstein, "Belinskij und Cernysevskij," *Jahrbücher für Kultur und Geschichte der Slaven*, N. F. VII, Heft II (Breslau, 1931), 165.

Sofya, the daughter of his former master and benefactor, Lesinsky. A letter from Andrey, Lesinsky's eldest son, revoking the release and ordering him to return to the estate cruelly destroys his dreams of an eventual union with Sofya. Sursky, Dmitry's friend, suggests a secret marriage. At a party in the house of Lesinsky he explains his plan to Sofya. The girl agrees to a secret marriage. At this moment Dmitry appears. He embraces Sofya before the dumbfounded guests. Then he kills Andrey, the author of his misfortune. After a struggle, Dmitry is seized and thrown into prison. He escapes and appears again in the house of Lesinsky. The two lovers experience an instant of bliss and forgetfulness.

Soon, however, they awaken to the tragic hopelessness of their situation. Prince Kizyayev has proposed to her, and Sofya will have to marry him in accordance with the wishes of the whole family. In a fit of despair she begs her lover to stab her and then to kill himself. Dmitry refuses at first, but finally he gives in. Sofya dies in his arms. Yet before he has time to pierce his own heart the door opens and Ivan, the old servant of the house, appears with a letter in his hand. Dmitry reads the letter with growing fury and despair. He learns that Lesinsky was his own father and Sofya—his sister. Overcome by horror, shame, and repentance, he stabs himself with his dagger.

The play caused a scandal at the university and the authorities decided to expel the writer of this "immoral piece." This banishment from the university is the only exciting incident in Belinsky's otherwise quiet and uneventful life.[3]

Dmitry Kalinin is a youthful production with all the typical faults and with few merits. However, it must be conceded that its author had noble intentions and that it is of interest to students of literature who desire to fathom the theories, idiosyncrasies, and violent impulses of the future remarkable critic at the earliest

---

[3] N. N. Yengalychev, "V. G. Belinsky," *Russkaya Starina*, XV (St. Petersburg, Jan. 1876), 81.

stage of his literary activity. Throughout the play the influence
of *Die Räuber* is unmistakable. *"Dmitry Kalinin,"* observes a
Russian scholar, "represents a youthful and passionate tragedy
imbued with hatred towards slavery, overflowing with sanguinary
effects, with clear and distinct traces of Schiller's *Die Räuber."*[4]
At the very beginning of the drama a motif of revenge is sounded
which is reminiscent of the German play : "And if I decide to
live," Dmitry Kalinin declaims, "then only for the sake of
revenge !"[5] This seems to be an echo of the words of Karl Moor :
"My handicraft is retaliation—revenge is my trade."[6] In Act
IV Sofya sings a melancholy and pathetic song, accompanying
herself on the guitar—a parallel to Amalia in *Die Räuber* who
sings a song in a similar pining mood. But the most striking
approximations to *Die Räuber* are to be found in Dmitry
Kalinin's bombastic monologues :

The most terrible thing in the drama are Kalinin's monologues
which overflow with romanticism and Schiller's *Die Räuber*. Thousands of venomous vipers, diabolical curses, infernal ecstasies, thirst
of blood, murders and devastations, thousands of daggers piercing
the heart in one instant, the fiery tartarus of the soul, million times
more horrible, a host of furies shaking their torches, etc., etc.,—this
whole dictionary of romanticism is exhausted by Belinsky with that
lack of moderation which is characteristic of all his raptures.[7]

Dmitry's denunciation of serfdom and social prejudice and his
defence of freedom and the equality of all men introduce a
humanitarian, almost revolutionary element into the drama. In
the opinion of a Russian critic, this humanitarian coloring of

[4] Aleksey Veselovsky, *Zapadnoye vlianie v novoy Russkoy Literature*
(Moskva, 1906), pp. 217–218.
[5] V. G. Belinsky, *Dmitry Kalinin, Sbornik obshchestva lubiteley rossiyskoy
slovesnosti na 1891 god* (Moskva), p. 487.
[6] Schiller, *SW*, III, 79.
[7] *Poln. sobr. soch. Belinskogo*, ed. Vengerov, pp. 131–132.

Dmitry Kalinin's monologues is only an echo of such tragedies as
Die Räuber and *Kabale und Liebe*.[8]

Belinsky's dependence upon the violent and bombastic style of
Die Räuber can be traced throughout the five acts of his play.
Here are a few examples that will illustrate this dependence.
After his escape from prison Dmitry appears again in the house
of Lesinsky and relates his shocking experiences to Sofya :

At first I was put in chains and thrown in with a mob of desperate
criminals. The members of this wild and ferocious gang described
their crimes to each other with a ghastly roar of laughter. One of
them narrated how he had torn a suckling baby into two pieces all
the while bursting with guffaws; another,—how he had smashed the
skull of a ninety-year-old man with his naked fist; a third,—how he
had butchered a whole family, and how he had amused himself
watching the death convulsions of his victims . . .[9]

This passage bears a strong resemblance to the boastful speeches
of the Schillerean robbers describing their misdeeds during the
sacking of the city, in particular to the scene of Schufterle brag-
ging about the slaughter of bedridden old men, sleeping women,
climaxing with the violent death of an innocent child :

Wie ich von ungefähr so an einer Baracke vorbeigehe, hör ich
drinnen ein Gezeter, ich guck hinein, und wie ich's beim Licht
besehe, was war's? Ein Kind war's, noch frisch und gesund, das
lag auf dem Boden unterm Tisch und der Tisch wollte eben angehen.
Arms Tierchen! sagt' ich,—du verfrierst ja hier, und warf's in die
Flamme.[10]

Like Schiller's hero, Dmitry quarrels with Divine Providence
that permits his life and happiness to be wrecked by such human
monsters as Lesinsky and his family, "Serpents, crocodiles, tigers

[8] Yury Veselovsky, "Schiller kak vdokhnovitel Russkikh Pisateley," *Russ-kaya Mysl*, II (Moskva, 1906), 8.
[9] Belinsky, *Dmitry Kalinin*, p. 522.
[10] Schiller, *SW*, III, 71.

feeding on the bones and the flesh of their neighbors and drinking their blood and tears like water."[11] His despair after the receipt of the fateful letter shows a striking similarity to the parallel scene in *Die Räuber.*[12] In this connection the use of the "tiger" metaphor can be singled out as especially striking. Cursing his father and renouncing every bond of relationship between himself and his parent Dmitry exclaims: "Oh, now bite my heart, grim tiger-despair, tear it into millions of shreds as long as it keeps beating! Qualms of conscience, serpents of repentance, suck the juices out my veins, dry out the marrow in my bones!"[13]

Another "Storm and Stress" tragedy of Schiller, *Kabale und Liebe,* has also exercised influence on Belinsky's youthful production. In both dramas the catastrophe of the lovers springs from the insurmountable gulf between the nobility and the common people. The only difference is that the social status of the principal characters has been reversed: Dmitry represents the common people, whereas Sofya represents the aristocracy. To *Die Räuber* and *Kabale und Liebe* one may add *Die Braut von Messina* as a probable source of inspiration to the Russian playwright. The motif of the brother who unknowingly loves his own sister, used by Belinsky in this drama, appears to lend some support to this thesis.

Belinsky's attitude toward the German poet in a more mature period of his literary career is both interesting and significant. Interesting, because Schiller played an especially outstanding role in Belinsky's artistic and spiritual development. Significant, because from the middle of the thirties onward Belinsky becomes the recognized leader of literary taste in Russia. "In no other particular fact," observes a Russian scholar, "can one so clearly

[11] Belinsky, *Dmitry Kalinin,* p. 528.
[12] Schiller, *SW,* III, 30–32.
[13] Belinsky, *Dmitry Kalinin,* pp. 529–530.

see those fruitful changes which occurred in the *Weltanschauung* of the great critic as in his relations to Schiller."[14]

Starting with the *Literary Reveries* (1834) where he places Schiller next to Byron, Belinsky was "one of Schiller's most faithful and enthusiastic admirers on Russian soil."[15] The author of *Die Räuber* and *Don Carlos* seemed to him a new Prometheus bringing celestial light to the darkened minds of men. In this his first article he ecstatically exclaims: "Schiller has given us the mysteries of heaven, has unveiled to us the wondrous beauty of life . . . !"[16] Referring to the principal characters in *Die Räuber* and in *Don Carlos* he affirms: "I love Karl Moor as a man, I worship Posa as a hero."[17] It is in the *Literary Reveries*, too, that he summons the shadow of the "divine dreamer Posa,"[18] whose political utopia continues to cast a spell on his restless and heaven-storming imagination. In the same article, speaking of the poetry of Derzhavin, he warns his countrymen not to seek in Derzhavin's songs the sweet yearning for heaven nor the sublime dreams of the great and sacred things in life characteristic of Schiller's inspiring poetry.

There are indications that Belinsky occupied himself, not only with Schiller's dramatic works and with his poetry, but also with his aesthetic and philosophical writings. An acquaintance with Schiller's theoretical treatises is revealed by his article on the novels of Gogol where the Russian critic, discoursing on poetry in general, distinguishes between "ideal" and "real" poetry. This distinction may be an echo of Schiller's treatise *Über naive und sentimentalische Dichtung*. In his article Belinsky considers a

---

[14] *Schiller*, ed. S. A. Vengerov (St. Petersburg, 1900), I, i–ii.
[15] Yury Veselovsky, "Schiller kak vdokhnovitel . . . ," p. 8.
[16] V. G. Belinsky, *Sochinenia* (Kiev, 1911), I, 14. Hereafter references to this edition will be abridged to "Soch."
[17] Belinsky, *Soch.*, I, 15.
[18] Belinsky, *Soch.*, I, 65. Cf. Bernhard Schultze, *W. G. Belinskij* (München, 1958), p. 54.

phase in the development of literature in which *ideal* and *real* poetry meet and achieve an organic fusion. As examples of such lofty achievement he cites the works of Byron, Pushkin, Mickiewicz, and Schiller. In addition to Schiller's philosophical writings, Belinsky undoubtedly was also familiar with the historical works of the poet.

As a student he had frequented the lectures of Professor Pogodin which "opened before him new perspectives in the study of history, and in which he heard the names of Lomonosov, Karamzin, Schelling, Schiller, Herder, Niebuhr, Guizot and other representatives of Russian and foreign science."[19]

Belinsky remained for a long time under the spell of Schiller's powerful first dramatic creation. Years after the enthusiastic acceptance of *Die Räuber* in the Moscow student circle and in a period of estrangement from Schiller's idealistic philosophy of life, he still remembered, not without pleasure though in a mocking vein, the tremendous impression the play had produced in his imaginative mind. "Having read *Die Räuber*," he admits in a letter to Bakunin, dated September 10, 1838, "I was ready to stick a wooden dagger under my waistcoat."[20]

Whereas some of his friends took exception to the rhetorical tone of *Die Räuber* Belinsky himself saw nothing detrimental in it : for to him Schiller was "a phrasemonger without being a phrasemonger,"[21] and he, therefore, felt little inclined to put up with this attack on excessive and unnatural oratory—particularly aimed at Karl Moor's great monologues. Referring to the scene in which Karl tells the robbers about his father, the critics of Schiller maintained, for instance, that a man in a similar situation would be able to utter perhaps two or three words at the most. In defense of the German poet Belinsky responded to these

---

[19] *Literaturnoye Nasledstvo* (Moskva, 1950), LVI, 338.
[20] Belinsky, *Pisma* (St. Petersburg, 1914), I, 253.
[21] Belinsky, *Pisma*, I, 231.

censors that in his opinion, such a man would not utter a single word, but speechlessly point at his father with his hand. Despite the length of the monologue Belinsky did not see a trace of oratory in Karl's words:

> The point is that not a *character* is speaking here but the *author himself;* that in this whole work there is no truth of life but there *is* truth of feeling; there is no reality, no drama, but there *is* a wealth of poesy; unreal conditions, unnatural situations, but certainly feeling and depth of thought; in short : the point is that one must not take Schiller's *Die Räuber* as a drama, as a representation of life, but as a lyrical poem in the form of a drama—a fiery and seething poem. Karl Moor's monologue must not be understood as the natural, ordinary expression of feelings of a character who is in the known situation but as an ode, the meaning or theme of which is the expression of indignation at monstrous children trampling on the sacredness of filial duty.[22]

In this sense Belinsky places all dramas of Schiller (except *Maria Stuart* and *Wilhelm Tell*) in the category of *Die Räuber,* "that wild, flaming dithyramb erupting like lava from the depths of a young, dynamic soul . . ."[23] Schiller is to him not so much a great dramatist as a great poet endowed with divine inspiration which, however, sometimes works as a block preventing him from penetrating deeper into life and from reproducing it in all its substance and essence. In the opinion of Belinsky, Schiller's drama *Die Räuber* suffers from such an excess of inspiration. Everything in it—plot, characters, situations—seems to have been devised for the expression of the author's ebullient ideas and sentiments. But in the definition of the mature Russian critic, who

[22] Belinsky, *Soch.,* I, 103. Cf. A. Lavretsky, *Estetika Belinskogo* (Moskva, 1959), pp. 320–321.

[23] *Ibid.* Belinsky's view of Schiller exercised a profound influence on the Schiller image of Dostoyevsky and Vyacheslav Ivanov. Cp. Dostoyevsky's letter to his brother Mikhail of January 1, 1840, and Ivanov's essay "On Schiller" (1905).

had left his own excessively emotional first dramatic attempt far behind, a drama must mirror reality quietly and dispassionately and the personality of the author must disappear because of the very nature of the dramatic genre which is objectivity in the highest degree. Schiller, according to Belinsky, nearly always expresses only himself, even in his *Wallenstein,* and it is only in *Wilhelm Tell* that he is a true and real dramatist. This criticism is not meant to diminish the stature of the German poet. Belinsky warns his countrymen :

Notwithstanding, do not accuse him of onesidedness or lack of genius; there are minds, there are characters so original and wonderful, so unlike the ordinary people that they seem strangers to them; and, dissatisfied with the world, they create a world of their own and live exclusively in it. Schiller was such a character. Submitting to the spirit of the time, he wanted to be realistic in his productions, but idealism remained the dominant characteristic of his poetry owing to the power of his genius.[24]

Belinsky finds it hard to decide to which of the two kinds of poetry, *idealistic* or *realistic,* he should give preference. After some hesitation and deliberation, however, he comes to the conclusion that the realistic poetry, "born of the spirit of our positivistic times," better satisfies the needs of the contemporary generation. Moreover, he thinks it can be grasped more easily by the great masses of the people than the idealistic poetry. It is precisely on account of their realistic elements that he expects Schiller's *Die Braut von Messina* and *Jungfrau von Orleans* to find sympathetic reception among his countrymen—certainly a strange definition of "realistic" on the part of the Russian critic! Belinsky's turn toward realism is significant because it is the first step in the direction of his later "reconciliation with reality" and wholesale condemnation of Schiller's idealism.

[24] Belinsky, *Soch.,* I, 104.

When *Die Braut von Messina*—in the abridged stage translation by Rotchev—had reached the boards of the Moscow theatre,
Belinsky took the occasion to express his opinion regarding the
merits of the play. He classified it as a "lyrical tragedy" and as
an attempt of Schiller to revive the ancient Greek drama. In
the expression "lyrical tragedy" the Russian critic places the
accent on the word "lyrical" for to him Schiller was essentially a
lyric poet despite his achievements in all three genres of literary
production. As elements typical of the classical Greek tragedy
Belinsky cites predestination, inescapable fate hovering above the
heroes, and the introduction of the ancient Greek chorus into the
plot. Belinsky dislikes the idea of predestination; it exercised on
his soul an unpleasant and anti-poetical impression—like the
squeaking of a rusty spring. But he was overwhelmed by the
lyrical power of the play :

Schiller's tragedy is a sublime work of its kind : a glowing,
passionate, impetuous flame of inspiration. Schillerean pathos, soul-
tearing, tragic situations, magnificent verse, waves of lyricism flow-
ing in a majestic stream—these are the distinguishing characteristics
of *Die Braut von Messina*. We did not think for a moment that a
lyrical tragedy could be performed on stage and exercise from it any
effect at all; but now we have fully convinced ourselves that if the
play as a whole were capably staged, even with a merely intelligent
and faithful, if not inspired and impassioned performance of the
principal characters, it would exert a stronger and more awe-
inspiring impression on the spectators than all the other tragedies
of Schiller.[25]

Belinsky's enthusiasm for the German poet cooled but once,
namely during the brief period of his "reconciliation with reality"
(1838–40).

Toward the end of 1837 the Russian critic began to show

[25] Belinsky, *Soch.*, II, 673.

signs of weariness and growing disgust with the whole system of abstract idealism. He was longing for a change and for closer contact with reality. The abstract and philosophical aspect of Schiller's poetry prompted him to take an increasingly critical attitude toward the works of the German poet. With indulgent irony he refers to Schiller as "that strange half-artist and half-philosopher,"[26] and he reproaches him because in his soul "the philosophical element continuously was struggling with the artistic element, defeating it often. . . ."[27] In contrast to Schiller, the "half-poet," he places Goethe and Pushkin, the "purely poetic characters," the *true, real* and *authentic* poetic geniuses who created unconsciously. In Schiller he did not find "that tranquillity which was an indispensable condition of free creation, that objective, dispassionate eye which can be discerned in the works of Goethe, the Olympian. . . ."[28]

Belinsky's turn toward realism was encouraged by the teachings of his friends Katkov and Bakunin who led him away from Schiller and Schelling to the moral idealism of Fichte, and thence to Hegel. "From him [Bakunin] Belinsky learned the meaning of Hegelean reality, and he assimilated so completely the ideas he heard from him that they became his innermost conviction. But he paid for it with mental agony and struggle."[29] When, in October 1839, Belinsky arrived in St. Petersburg he was brimful of Hegel and the Hegelean reality. As a result, his first articles in Krayevsky's review, *Otechestvennye Zapiski,* "caused considerable consternation among his readers by their unexpectedly enthusiastic conservatism and 'official nationalism.'"[30] From Bakunin, too, he learned the principles of a new aesthetics,

[26] P. V. Annenkov, *Literaturnye vospominania* (Leningrad, 1928), p. 226.
[27] *Lit. Nasl.,* LVI, 114.
[28] I. I. Panayev, *Literaturnye vospominania* (Leningrad, 1950), p. 185.
[29] Pypin, *Belinsky,* p. 193.
[30] D. S. Mirsky, *A History of Russian Literature* (London, 1927), p. 212.

according to which truth resided only in objectivity. From this conception came the inescapable conclusion, consistently drawn both by Bakunin and Belinsky, that subjectivity in poetry amounted to negation of truth and poetry. Belinsky did not hesitate to apply these new concepts to the poetry of Schiller with the result that his attitude toward him—in view of the German poet's "abstractness" and "subjectivity"—became more and more critical and, in the end, downright hostile.

At first, it is true, Schiller was to him still a remarkable man and a poet but no longer a *great* poet who could be ranked with Homer, Pushkin, and Goethe. "Reality" and "Objectivity" became sacred watchwords by which he lived, dreamed, and swore. "Reality!" he would exclaim upon arising and on retiring. All through the day and night, "Reality" surrounded him : he felt it everywhere and in everything, even in himself, in that new and strange transformation of his personality and of his beliefs which became more perceptible every day.

This change in Belinsky's views and attitude, however, was brought about not solely by the teachings of his friends, but also by his stringent personal circumstances. His former enthusiasm for the abstract Schillerean ideals of the Good and the Beautiful, for a nebulous mankind and humanity, had detached him from practical life to such an extent that in the end, he found himself facing a general bankruptcy in almost every phase of his private affairs. To avoid a catastrophe there was only one thing for him to do : to descend from the lofty heights of abstract idealism and bow to the necessity of "recognizing reality and giving room to its demands on his personal life."[31]

The concept of realism embraced by Belinsky was of the most conciliatory and conservative type. To the artist Belinsky assigned from now on the task of contemplating "glorious reality" and of

[31] Pypin, *Belinsky*, pp. 191, 194.

not meddling in political and governmental affairs. Art he defined as "recreation of reality." Consequently, its task was not to correct or beautify life but to show how it was in "glorious reality." Quite obviously, these reactionary ideas—absolute reconciliation with reality, unconditional submission to the established order of society—were derived from the teachings of the old conservative Hegel who legitimizes the Prussian autocratic state with his slogan : "Was wirklich ist, ist wahr." The Russian public "were not aware of the hidden logic of the critic's philosophical evolution, and that he now was living up to Hegel's famous proposition : 'All that is, is rational.'"[32] Their shock at Belinsky's sudden turn-about was, therefore, well justified. On the other hand, as a critic has pointed out, one should not put all blame on Belinsky for his conclusion that the existing social and political regime was rational :

If Belinsky interpreted Hegel's thesis "whatever is real is rational, whatever is rational is real" too narrowly, it must be admitted that there was ample precedent for this in the conservative spirit of Hegel's later years and in the work of his right wing followers.[33]

A Russian critic (Plekhanov) emphasizes that "what is usually considered Belinsky's mistake (in interpreting the doctrine of "reasonable reality") in fact corresponded to the interpretation of Hegel which was prevalent in Germany at the time."[34] Furthermore, Belinsky's reliance on his friends for his knowledge of Hegel makes it doubtful that his comprehension of Hegel's philosophy could have been exact and complete. Nor is it likely that he was interested in becoming an authority on Hegel and the intricacies of the Hegelean system :

[32] Mirsky, *A History of Russian Literature*, p. 212.
[33] B. Malnick, "V. G. Belinsky," *SEER* (London, May 1949), p. 369.
[34] V. V. Zenkovsky, *A History of Russian Philosophy* (New York, 1953), I, 264.

He [Belinsky] sought in Hegel a philosophically adequate solution of his own ideological problem, the fulfillment of an intimately personal intellectual and spiritual need. If he can be considered a faithful follower of Hegel, it is because in spite of useless repetition of Hegelean terms and Hegelean formulas, he continued to work toward a conviction that reality is justified and that art is justified only by its fidelity to reality. . . . Yet in Belinsky's defense it can be said that he grasped the meaning of the principle that nothing is real except idea, and that his vacillation between a reality of idea and a reality of appearance is inherent in Hegel's original doctrine. To say that nothing is real except idea does not limit the area of idea, which in the Hegelean system tends to be all-embracing. If Belinsky in his excess of political conservatism seems to have misinterpreted the Hegelean formula. "What is rational is real and what is real is rational," perhaps the original formula can be accused of containing the seeds of its own misinterpretation.[35]

Hand in hand with Belinsky's mounting veneration of Hegel went a new interest in Shakespeare with all its consequences in the fields of literature and criticism. Belinsky's article on *Hamlet* (1838) "signifies his passage to the ideas of Hegel and to the so-called reconciliation with reality which culminated in his essays on 'The Anniversary of Borodino,' on 'Menzel, the Critic of Goethe' and on Griboyedov's *Woe from Wit.*"[36]

During Belinsky's period of "reconciliation with reality" Schiller became a real touchstone for the views of the Russian critic. For years he had lived under the spell of the German poet whose noble idealism transported him into realms of "abstract heroism" and into a position of "guardianship over humanity." Having convinced himself of the reasonableness of reality, he rejected Schiller and Schiller's noble idealism and almost began hating

[35] H. E. Bowman, *Vissarion Belinski* (Cambridge, Mass., 1954), p. 101.
[36] Ettore Lo Gatto, *Storia della Letteratura Russa* (Firenze, 1944), p. 244.

him—for the very same qualities by which he had been previously carried away :

From his [Belinsky's] present aesthetical point of view, true poetry excludes all subjectivity and tendentiousness which he had perceived in Schiller. Belinsky, of course, expressed his current opinion in the most peremptory fashion so that in the end his friends simply accused him of misunderstanding Schiller.[37]

Belinsky defended himself by pointing out the possibility of divergent opinions about the same subject and continued to label Schiller's poetry as rhetorical, unbalanced, dogmatic, prejudiced, and downright naïve. In a letter to Bakunin, dated October 12, 1838, he curtly declares : "I believe in your esteem for Schiller : do believe, for your part, in my lack of esteem for him. Each of us has his reasons and we are both right."[38] Belinsky then goes on to criticize severely Schiller's inability to draw a convincing picture of a female character. As an example he cites the figure of Thekla, "that tenth, last, improved, corrected, and revised edition of one and the same woman of Schiller's." Belinsky's opinion on this subject had been entirely different in the days of the *Literary Reveries* where he spoke of "those two flowers of paradise—Max and Thekla—with their heavenly love."[39]

But *Literary Reveries* was written in 1834, and Belinsky had returned from heaven and paradise to the earth and to a soberly realistic point of view both in practical life and in literature. As a result of his "reconciliation with reality" his style also becomes drastic and earthy, especially when he refers to Schiller. In his attack on Thekla, the Russian critic had been satisfied to use a mild form of sarcasm as a weapon. In his attack on another female character of Schiller he is far more virulent and caustic :

[37] Pypin, *Belinsky,* 198.
[38] Belinsky, *Pisma,* I, 265.
[39] Belinsky, *Soch.,* I, 65.

And *Die Jungfrau von Orleans*—can I help it?! As far as I am concerned, *Die Jungfrau von Orleans,* excepting a few lyrical passages which have a particular significance of their own, is—a sheep's bladder, no more! I repeat, perhaps I am wrong and, while understanding Shakespeare and Pushkin, have not yet risen to an understanding of Schiller; but I am no less touchy and proud than you, and no less than you satisfied . . . with my natural feeling for the perception of artistic impressions.[40]

This is turgid and blunt language but it tallies with the vehement temperament of our "furious Vissarion." In the same letter to Bakunin, however, he replaced bluntness with irony and a sneer when referring to "that trivial fair-souledness chanted by the great poet Schiller in *Die Räuber, Kabale und Liebe, Fiesco,* and in many other works."[41]

Belinsky expressed himself still more sharply in the following year (1839). Now he views *Die Räuber* and *Kabale und Liebe* as poetic miscarriages and monstrosities and, in general, as totally insignificant phenomena in the field of art. From the standpoint of absolute truth and higher ethics he condemns them as decidedly immoral. Referring specifically to *Kabale und Liebe* he observes :

This play is one of the most fair-souled works of Schiller; there is much more childishness in it than in *Die Räuber.* No trace at all of artistic value and creative power; poetic fire, however, one cannot deny. Nevertheless, as this fire has not come from creative inspiration by the objective perception of life but from his struggle against reality, therefore it is like so many fireworks : much noise and crackling—and little significance.[42]

Also the plot of the drama is now judged by Belinsky very severely. In his opinion, the plot is based on an empty misunder-

[40] Belinsky, *Pisma,* I, 265–266.
[41] Belinsky, *Pisma,* I, 281.
[42] Belinsky, *Soch.,* I, 710–711.

standing. As for the characters, he calls Louise "an ideal cook and sentimental phrase-monger." Ferdinand seems to him "a little Othello with sword and epaulettes." Only Louise's parents and Wurm appear to him as "something like people showing signs of reality." Yet despite his mordant polemics, Belinsky cannot completely free himself of his fascination by his former model and idol. "Schiller's life," he admits in a letter to Bakunin written in October 1838, "is better than fiction and it is impossible not to find pleasure in his biography."[43]

In the years of his "reconciliation with reality" and accompanying Shakespeare worship, Belinsky was apt to judge very severely, even fanatically, any literary endeavors which, by their nature, were bound to "tamper" with the sacred writings of the idolized English bard. It is therefore, not surprising to see him indignantly point an accusing finger at two literary villains convicted of having committed such an offence :

About Goethe I have found out a nice thing—as a young man he perpetrated a sacrilegious and godless act : he disfigured *Romeo and Juliet,* that is to say he tampered with it in his own way. But he repented and never put it in print, in contrast to Schiller who, having disfigured *Macbeth,* had the insolence to bring this distortion before the world.[44]

One month later, on November 8, 1838, Belinsky writes in a letter to his friend Stankevich :

I have broken completely with Schiller. God be with him—he had his fun with me . . . I am not very sorry for his women, either. And in general—as a poet—he has lost all significance for me. Perhaps the wildness of my nature reveals itself here—so be it ! Alone and by myself I will be.[45]

[43] Belinsky, *Pisma,* I, 306.
[44] Belinsky, *Pisma,* I, 307.
[45] Belinsky, *Pisma,* I, 310.

Belinsky then lauds the "healthy and normal poetry of Goethe" expressing satisfaction that Aksakov has abandoned the illusory world of Hoffmann and Schiller and finally found his way back to reality and to Goethe. In a letter to Panayev dated August 19, 1839, Belinsky reaffirms his sympathy for the author of *Faust* and his aversion for Schiller: "Incidentally, after the articles about the second part of *Faust* and Dante I have become still more stubborn, and now they had better not even speak to me of Schiller's dramas. I have found out already a long time ago that they are pretty rickety."[46] They had not seemed so "rickety" to Belinsky when he wrote the *Literary Reveries*. At that time he praised enthusiastically the dramas of Schiller as "a whole gorgeous and infinite world" created by a "prolific imagination."[47] At that time, comparing the dramatic achievements of the German poet to the tragedies of Ozerov he had exclaimed:

Bring a man to a Shakespeare or Schiller performance who possesses no learning, no education, but with an inborn intelligence and receptivity to the beautiful; not being versed in history, he will nevertheless grasp at once what is going on. Not understanding historical personages, he will perfectly understand the human ones; but if he looks at a tragedy by Ozerov he will understand nothing at all.[48]

Homer, Shakespeare, and Pushkin were the "three gods of art" in whose glorification and defence Belinsky almost daily "raved and fumed." Contrasting Shakespeare as a poet of infinitely higher caliber, with the author of *Die Jungfrau von Orleans,* he did not tire of censuring the German's one-sidedness and subjectivity. From Belinsky's newly-won point of view Schiller had become the very opposite of Shakespeare, for Schiller had ex-

---

[46] Belinsky, *Pisma,* I, 335.
[47] Belinsky, *Soch.,* I, 65.
[48] Belinsky, *Soch.,* I, 45.

pressed in his works only one aspect of human life—the "beautiful," and only one side of man's nature—his "sacred hopes and dreams."[49]

In defence of Pushkin, the Russian critic staged a violent attack on Granovsky who had just been appointed to a professorship of history at the Moscow University. In one of his lectures Granovsky had asserted that Schiller was superior to Pushkin. In the eyes of Belinsky such an allegation was tantamount to literary blasphemy. Boiling with anger he spitted the unfortunate scholar on his sharp and merciless pen : "And how he [Granovsky] understands Pushkin—long live idiocy! Pushkin sadly lagging behind Schiller! And in our opinion Schiller behind Pushkin—a sparrow is no match for an eagle!"[50] At that stage Belinsky's esteem for Schiller had gone into such decline that he ranked the mediocre work of an obscure poet (Kudryavtsev's *The Flute*) higher than all the philosophical dramas of the German. In a letter to Stankevich, dated October 2, 1839, referring to his above-mentioned devastating judgment on Schiller's dramas, he seeks to explain and justify his views :

In my attacks on Schiller you may see, if not bitterness, then a somewhat savage joy in being able to blast him legitimately. It was a collision between our personalities : Schiller was my personal enemy at that time. I had to make an effort to control my hate for him and remain within the limits of my own brand of decency. Why this hate?—For his subjective-ethical point of view, for his terrible concept of duty, for his abstract heroism, for his aesthetic war on realism, for all I suffered in his name! You will say that it is not Schiller's fault if I understood his great genius falsely and, of course, also one-sidedly, and if I grasped only his bad side without grasping his good one : yes, but it is not my fault, either, that I could not understand him better.[51]

[49] *Belinsky—Stati i materialy* (Leningrad, 1949), p. 149.
[50] Belinsky, *Pisma*, I, 341.
[51] Belinsky, *Pisma*, I, 346–347.

Belinsky thereupon recalls how the reading of Schiller's "Storm and Stress" dramas (especially *Die Räuber, Kabale und Liebe* and *Fiesco*) had imbued him with a fierce animosity for the established order of society in the name of an abstract social utopia constructed in thin air. How *Don Carlos*, "that anemic phantasmagoria of faceless images and rhetorical personifications, that apotheosis of philosophical love for mankind without content," had propelled him into an abstract heroism which caused him to despise and hate mankind, wildly and morbidly, all the while clearly realizing, despite the delirium of unnatural ecstasy, that he was a thing of naught. How *Die Jungfrau von Orleans*, "this drama with two elements as sharply separated from one another as water is from oil when poured into the same vessel," with its hateful catholicism and its insipid theatricalism, had driven him into a similar abstract heroism, into a similar empty, impersonal, conventional emotionalism.

Although he admits that there is powerful romantic poetry in the mystical figure of Joan of Arc he hastens to stress that he has now grown cold toward mysticism. The other characters, however, he considers utterly dull and trivial because of Schiller's total inability to rise to an objective delineation of human beings or of dramatic action. Then, with caustic sarcasm, he turns on another of Schiller's heroines—Thekla. There had been a time, he confesses, when Thekla had represented to him the ideal of womanhood outside of which there was no woman. Under the spell of this "heavenly woman" he and his friends had arrived at the conclusion that it was base and dishonest to enter into a love-affair with a girl. But then he discovered that this "heavenly woman" was an idea, a grey and pithless abstraction born in the brain of the idealistic Schiller—and *not* a living being.

Disillusioned and in despair, he turned to the alternative of

seeking consolation in a brothel since, as he says, it is impossible
for a man to live without a woman. "Do you see now," he asks
his friend Stankevich, "where the idealistic Schiller has led us!"[52]

And Belinsky goes on to remind his friend that Schiller, too—
a victim of his own contradictions—used to drop in at "such
places." Moreover, it was that idealist Schiller who, having
married, soon grew cold toward the woman of his choice and
began to treat her badly, and who, as an act of self-justification
and final flight from all reality, wrote his poem "Die Ideale" in
which he took leave of all the "ghosts" of life : poetry, knowledge, glory, and love—isolating himself with but two ideals :
friendship and work. In the poem "Resignation" he proceeded
to sacrifice all private and personal affairs on the altar of
humanity—and stepped out into emptiness with empty hands.

Belinsky points to Schiller's "universality" as being the cause
of this world-flight—a veritable Moloch devouring its own children and not as Schiller mistakenly thought, the eternal Love
revealing itself wherever there is life. Finally, in his poem "Der
Kampf" Schiller takes leave of virtue which oppresses him, sends
it to hell and, in a savage frenzy, exclaims : "I want to sin!"
And now Belinsky asks :

What kind of life is this where reflection poisons every minute of
blissfulness that comes of the high tide of life, where universality tells
you to regard every human enjoyment as a sin, where religion
reveals itself as medieval Catholicism, Cato's stoicism—as redemp-
tion! Now I understand the saying of Heine that the Christian
religion gives all to the spirit, and that it must be abolished so that
the body may enter into its rights : I remember, these words of
Heine enraged you but the crank was right from his point of view
because Christianity manifested itself to him in the abstract form
of the Middle Ages. This is the reason why I have come to hate

[52] Belinsky, *Pisma,* I, 347–348.

Schiller : the cup overflowed, my spirit craved for liberation from stifling dogmatism.[53]

Belinsky's frenzy for "objectivity," as we have already mentioned, had been brought about by the teachings of Bakunin. In the beginning the master was well satisfied with the success of his efforts and the great zeal of his disciple. But when all of a sudden "frantic curses poured down on the noble advocate of mankind and humanity—Schiller," the teacher became alarmed. Seeing the fury and intoxication of his pupil, he tried to stop him, but it was too late : Vissarion "had already broken loose from the chain and ran amuck screaming at the top of his voice."[54]

And he found plenty in the German poet to scream about. There was, for instance, Schiller's advice to Goethe to let Duke Alba listen in the corner of the room during his son's conversation with Egmont so that the villain would be either moved and repent, or suffer the torments of his own fury :

The height of fair-souledness, the model of dramatic impotence! Mishel [Bakunin] wanted to hide this fact from me and, as usual, he himself let the cat out of the bag : I howled with joy. This is the moment when the persecution of fair-souledness began in the name of reality.[55]

Belinsky does not explain why such a suggestion (to let Duke Alba listen in the corner of the room) would appear to him as "the height of fair-souledness" and brand Schiller as dramatically impotent. Belinsky evidently considers it totally unrealistic and the height of sentimentality to have that man of action— Alba—listen to his son's conversation with Egmont "to be converted!" This amounted to a flagrant and outrageous violation

[53] Belinsky, *Pisma,* I, 347–348.
[54] Belinsky, *Pisma,* I, 349.
[55] *Ibid.* Cf. D. Chizhevsky, "Schiller v Rossii," *Novy Zhurnal,* XLV (New York, 1956), 119–120.

of the principle of artistic objectivity, and the effect of such a scene, in the eyes of Belinsky, would have been neither dramatic suspense nor genuine heart-felt emotion, but rather disgust and ridicule.

Very opportunely, the names of Goethe and Heine began to emerge at that time (Autumn, 1839) in the talks and discussions of the Belinsky circle. Poems by Goethe were recited either in the original or in a translation. To Belinsky, the apostate from fair-souledness and idealism, these poems sounded like the revelation of a new gospel. He plunged into them with a feeling of delight and heavenly rapture. The gate of a new life, of a whole new world seemed to have been flung open in front of him :

Down with the yoke of duty! To hell with the rotten morality and the idealistic philosophy! Man can live—all belongs to him, every instant of life is great, true, and sacred! Then, well-timed for me, came the translations of the beloved Heine, and soon we read *Romeo and Juliet* to find out what a woman is like. . . . Poor Schiller![56]

Describing Aksakov's trip to Germany and his zealous quest of Schillerean traces and relics, Belinsky cannot refrain from shooting another barbed arrow at the author of *Wallenstein:* "In Germany he [Aksakov] looked for the vestiges of Schiller and raved in beatitude that he drank coffee from the same cup from which *the creator of Thekla* had once drunk."[57]

Stankevich felt deeply hurt by his friend's attacks on Schiller and their relations deteriorated. In a letter to Botkin, written in February 1840, Vissarion complains bitterly about this fact :

An odd fellow, Stankevich—he got angry at me on account of Schiller. I don't understand how one can be angry because of con-

[56] Belinsky, *Pisma,* I, 350.
[57] Belinsky, *Pisma,* I, 357. [Italics Belinsky's.]

victions. I love Shakespeare, it's true, no less than he loves Schiller,—
why then be angry? One can quarrel—even violently, but be angry
. . . certainly *this is Berlinotheticism?*[58]

The truth is that Belinsky felt ashamed of the letter in which
he had so ferociously assailed the German poet and his dramatic
works. As he himself puts it: "It's terribly stuffy and there is no
end of childishness in it." Moreover, he really had no desire to
quarrel with Stankevich about Schiller and even less to get angry
and break off relations. Therefore the conciliatory tone in his
letter to Botkin and the attempt to represent all as a sorry misunderstanding:

The matter is clear: one of us does not understand the issue;
understanding it, however, depends on one's spiritual resources and
on the time; consequently it is ridiculous to become furious. I esteem
Schiller for his spirit, but his dramas, from an artistic point of view,
are for me such as if they did not exist at all.[59]

The argument, advanced in defense of Schiller, that he had paid
tribute to the spirit of his time with his philosophizing poetry
was completely idle and irrelevant in the eyes of Belinsky. He
answered it with an ironical reference to Voltaire who, with his
rationalism and venomous blasphemies, not only paid tribute to
the spirit of the times but also gave it the fullest possible expression. But from this, according to Belinsky, it does not yet follow
that Voltaire is equal to or more sublime than Homer, Shakespeare, and Pushkin: "Once more—we are lucky that Pushkin's
nature did not succumb to reflection: that's why he is a great
poet."[60]

The year 1840 marks a new turning point in Belinsky's attitude toward Schiller. The critic's reconciliation with reality
comes to a close and, as if awakening from a dream and regain-

[58] Belinsky, *Pisma,* II, 56. [Italics Belinsky's.]
[59] *Ibid.*
[60] Belinsky, *Pisma,* II, 68.

ing consciousness, he begins to shake off the vestiges of a philosophy which tallied badly with his true nature and temperament. "It was the impact of St. Petersburg, 'Chinese empire of material animal life,' that transformed Belinsky's view of Russian society and shattered his 'reconciliation to reality'."[61] The abandonment of his hitherto implacable and ferocious opposition to Schiller, characterized as a "turning point of tremendous importance in Belinsky's *Weltanschauung*" by a Russian critic,[62] is signalized in a letter to Bakunin written on February 26, 1840:

> I no longer wage war against fair-souledness. Petersburg and your brother Nikolay have forced me to reconcile myself with him [Schiller] and even to like him. I have seen clearly that I am below fair-souledness and that I have no right to attack something to which I have never been able to rise. Fair-souledness is a great and sacred state of the spirit and a thousand times more sublime than my . . . reality. I understand now that in assailing Schiller for his fair-souledness I confused Schiller with myself, with you, and with Aksakov with whom the great German spirit did not have and does not have anything in common.[63]

Belinsky is now once more willing to recognize that Schiller is a great poet even when placed alongside Pushkin. He considers Schiller a more popular poet in the sense that he is accessible both to abstract minds and to the great mass of the people whereas Pushkin, in his opinion, can be grasped only by those who possess a profound feeling for concrete reality. For this reason, according to the critic, the officers and officials in St. Petersburg can fathom the greatness of Schiller, but Shakespeare they call great only for propriety's sake, being afraid to be branded as ignorant. In Pushkin, however, they absolutely do not see anything great at all.

[61] Malnick, "V. G. Belinsky," p. 370.
[62] *Schiller,* ed. Vengerov, I, ii.
[63] Belinsky, *Pisma,* II, 78.

In March, 1840, Belinsky gets more closely acquainted with the writings of E. Th. A. Hoffmann. The quaint mixture of realism and fantasy in Hoffmann's works appeals to him—he is at once deeply fascinated and especially by the tale entitled *Meister Martin der Küfner*. Without hesitation he proclaims its author a great poet worthy to have a place beside the greatest ones : "Schiller, Goethe, and Hoffmann : these three are one—the profound, soulful, many-sided German spirit !"[64] As we can see, his reconciliation with Schiller has progressed considerably. He even expresses the wish that Bakunin undertake the translation of Schiller's correspondence with Goethe. Yet it is E. Th. A. Hoffmann now with whom he has fallen in love so passionately that he would not give him up for anything in the world—certainly not for Schiller. Though he no longer condemns Schiller out of hand, his newly-won esteem of the German poet is conditional. "Belinsky now clearly sees in him the romanticist, and this romantic element prompts him to take a critical attitude."[65] He recognizes Schiller's genius, he appreciates his personality, he has a high esteem for some of his works—but as to his tragedies : ". . . it's even nauseating to think of them !"[66] He cannot help comparing Schiller with the great English playwright, and the result of each such comparison is devastating to the German :

A short time ago I read again aloud *Richard II*. Ooh ! . . . No, brother, say what you will, but concerning Schiller one of us grossly misunderstands the other. All you [Botkin] write about him is true, and yet, his tragedies, in all conscience, one does not have the strength to read.[67]

[64] Belinsky, *Pisma,* II, 95.
[65] F. F. Nelidov, *Ocherki po istorii noveyshey Russkoy Literatury* (Moskva, 1907), p. 82.
[66] Belinsky, *Pisma,* II, 107.
[67] Belinsky, *Pisma,* II, 133.

Belinsky's critical and often sarcastic attitude toward Schiller comes to a sudden end in October 1840. As if transformed by a flash of intuition, with the destructive zeal of an iconoclast, he turns violently against Hegel, the apologist of Prussian autocracy, and the golden calf of Reality. Again, as in his youth, "in dazzling brilliance shines Schiller, the singer of emancipation."[68] In a mood of contrition and self-denunciation he writes to Botkin :

I curse my infamous proclivity to reconciliation with foul reality ! Long live the great Schiller, the noble advocate of humanity, the bright star of salvation, the emancipator of society from the bloody prejudices of tradition ! Long live reason, death to obscurantism— as the great Pushkin exclaims ! Human personality is now more sublime to me than history, more sublime than society, more sublime than mankind. This is the idea and concept of the century ! My God, it's terrible to think what had happened to me—a delirium, a derangement of the mind—I feel like a convalescent.[69]

Hand in hand with his reawakened passion for Schiller goes an increasing antipathy for the realistic kind of poetry and for Goethe whom he now blames for the absence of historical and social elements in his works and for his pompous satisfaction with reality as it is. These shortcomings of Goethe he considers the principal reason why the humane poetry of Schiller, although less artistic than Goethe's, has found among mankind a greater response.[70]

Belinsky's reconciliation with Schiller reaches its climax when he comes to recognize his affinity with Schiller. Completely under his spell again, he concedes that he cannot even think of him "without losing his breath." With great zeal and enthusiasm

---

[68] A. Veselovsky, *Zapadnoye vlianie,* p. 224.

[69] Belinsky, *Pisma,* II, 163. Belinsky's Schiller image was not quite the real Schiller. Cf. M. Malia, "Schiller and the Early Russian Left," *Harvard Slavic Studies* (Cambridge, Mass., 1957), IV, 186.

[70] Belinsky, *Soch.* II, 11 ff. "On the Poetry of Lermontov."

he studies books, periodicals, and letters containing facts on or critical appraisals of the German poet. Anything Botkin, the Schiller-enthusiast, says about Schiller he now accepts unquestioningly thanking him warmly for his "wonderful enlightenment." In a letter of December 30, 1840, Belinsky carries his self-identification with and idolization of the German dramatist *ad absurdum:*

Yes, I have finally realized my kinship with Schiller : I am bone from his bones, flesh from his flesh,—and if anything in life and history must and can interest me then it is he, created to be my god, my idol,—for he is my highest and noblest ideal of man.[71]

As for his former idol Hegel, he had good reason to be angry with him. "Since it was under the banner of Hegel that he had defended all reality as rational, it was in Hegel that Belinsky was bound to see the symbol of all that he now repudiated."[72] He had been a faithful and enthusiastic disciple of the German philosopher, and under the influence of his teachings he had resigned himself to the dreary Russian reality, praising Zagoskin (author of nationalistic historical novels) and similar "infamous characters" and despising Schiller. Now, after the rediscovery of his kinship with Schiller, he solemnly swears that it is "better to die" than to be reconciled to the absolutism of Hegel's philosophy, and the fate of an individual appears to him as infinitely more important than the most momentous Hegelean "generalities," whether it be "the health of the Chinese Emperor or the destinies of the whole world."[73]

As can be seen, Belinsky is not very consistent in his thinking. Not so long ago he had condemned Schiller on the very grounds of his "vague generalities" of which he now accuses Hegel and absolves Schiller !

[71] Belinsky, *Pisma,* II, 196.
[72] Bowman, *Vissarion Belinski,* p. 138.
[73] Belinsky, *Pisma,* II, 213.

Belinsky's new enthusiasm for Schiller reflects itself in a striking way in his attitude toward Goethe. On March 1, 1841, in a letter to Botkin, Belinsky comments on Goethe's drama *Egmont*. His criticism is favorable, in fact, he calls the drama a "wonderful and precious work." But he hastens to make clear to his friend the real reason for his enthusiasm : he likes it so much because "there is something Schillerean in its construction."[74] As in the days of the *Literary Reveries,* Schiller is once again a source of continual inspiration and delight to Belinsky. Reading a biography of the German poet, he cannot help bursting into "tears of rapture and tender emotion," and his heart "wants to jump out of his breast." Belinsky then urges his friend Botkin to write a detailed *Life of Schiller* in the Russian language : "It would be a great work and you could carry it off excellently. And what a boon that would be for our society!"[75]

One month later, on April 6, 1841, Belinsky confirms his literary and philosophical "conversion" in a letter to Bakunin :

Yes, now neither Hegel nor the philosophical hoods are my heroes any longer; even Goethe is great only as an artist but loathsome as a personality; now again there have risen before me the colossal images of Fichte and Schiller in all the brilliance of resplendent greatness : the prophets of humanity, the heralds of the Kingdom of God on earth, the priests of eternal love and truth not only in a scholastic sense and in Brahmin contemplation but in living and intelligent *Tat*.[76]

In the wake of his reconciliation with Schiller the Russian critic develops a new and lively interest for social and political

[74] Belinsky, *Pisma,* II, 221.
[75] Belinsky, *Pisma,* II, 221. The same letter contains a vehement condemnation of Hegel. According to M. Karpovich, the letter had a great influence on Dostoyevsky (epitomized in Ivan Karamazov's rebellion against God). Cp. "Dostoyevsky, Belinsky, Schiller," *Novy Zhurnal,* XLV (New York, 1956), 282–283.
[76] Belinsky, *Pisma,* II, 232.

problems. Mankind and human rights—civil liberty, freedom of
thought—had once again become important issues and high
ideals for Belinsky. As a result of his reconversion he begins
viewing the world and its struggles through the prism of Schiller's
exalted soul, and everything appears to him in another light. As
if by magic his eyes are turned to personalities that bear a kinship or resemblance to the German poet. Thence his passionate
enthusiasm for Béranger, the champion of civil liberty and freedom of thought, "the French Schiller."[77] Hearing a recital of
Schiller songs in St. Petersburg, Belinsky is moved to rapture :
it has been a thrilling and memorable evening to him. In a
letter to Botkin of February 6, 1843, he ecstatically looks back
upon the concert, recalling the singular emotional experience it
had been and the refreshment it had bestowed on his soul "with
the beneficial dew of tears."[78]

While his love for Schiller grows and becomes more fervent
every day, Belinsky develops almost simultaneously an increasing
aversion for Goethe. In the words of a Soviet critic :

No less characteristic of Belinsky during these years is his contrasting the "philistine spirit" and "egoism" of Goethe with the sublime
civic spirit of Schiller, this "poet of humanity." Schiller is "a lofty
soul tempered in the fire of the civic spirit of classical antiquity,"
the 'Tiberius Gracchus of our century" (Pisma, II, 350, 246–47). It
is in this sense that he is called in an anonymous article a "descend-
ant of Arminius" (that is, of Arminius, the liberator of the ancient
Germans.)[79]

At first Belinsky feels a dislike only for Goethe's temperament
and "loathsome personality." Later, he extends this dislike to
some of his works and characters. In a letter of March 8, 1843,
addressed to the sisters of his friend Bakunin, the critic bitterly

[77] Belinsky, *Pisma,* II, 250.
[78] Belinsky, *Pisma,* II, 335.
[79] *Lit. Nasl.* LV, 349.

attacks Egmont who, according to his opinion, plays with the feelings of Klärchen in an utterly irresponsible way. Indignantly he exclaims :

The sacred nature and great soul of Schiller tempered in the embers of ancient civility could never have given birth to such a rotten ideal of a self-mocking personality that trifles with the sacred and lofty things of life.[80]

Belinsky's last reference to Schiller is contained in a letter to Botkin written from Dresden on July 7, 1847. Commenting on Botkin's friendship with Krayevsky, the critic exclaims with apparent cordiality : "I congratulate you on your new friend ! To find a friend on earth is a great thing, as Schiller often used to say so well, especially a friend with a feeling heart, such a one, in one word, as A. A. Krayevsky."[81] The following lines of the letter, however, leave no doubt that the whole passage must be understood in the light of irony and sarcasm. Belinsky makes no secret of his true feelings regarding Krayevsky : angrily he brands him a "scoundrel" and "blood-sucker" who has caused the destruction of his health.

In view of the many twists and turns in Belinsky's spiritual development it seems fitting to retrace the principal stages of his attitude toward Schiller. Summarizing, one can say that, except for the brief period of his "reconciliation with reality" (1838-40), Belinsky's sentiment toward the German poet was one of lively sympathy interspersed with frequent bursts of ecstatic enthusiasm and idolatrous adoration. In the days when he wrote *Dmitry Kalinin* and the *Literary Reveries* his Schiller worship was founded on imponderables—its principal characteristics were intolerance of even the slightest criticism directed at Schiller and elemental emotionalism.

[80] Belinsky, *Pisma,* II, 350.
[81] Belinsky, *Pisma,* III, 246.

Subsequently his utterances and judgments became more balanced and more critical. He qualified his irrational and impulsive Schiller cult with a number of corrections and reservations, taking, for instance, vehement exception to the dramatic works of the poet. Nevertheless, in spite of great efforts to find a judicious and more objective approach to Schiller, he did not lose completely his previous instinctive enthusiasm for him. Deep down in his heart he kept a flame burning for the noble man from Germany. At times this flame threatened to be extinguished, but after his abrupt break with Hegel it soon shone again with its former brilliance. In the forties, Schiller once more becomes to him the "advocate of mankind," the "poet of humanity," the "passionate priest of the sublime and the beautiful." In his articles *On Pushkin* (1844) the great critic puts Schiller at the head of the whole artistic literature of the nineteenth century as the principal task of which he regarded the energetic and unanimous propagation of active humanity, freedom, and brotherhood. "From this moment on the unshakable glory and the tremendous influence of Schiller in Russia were established forever and nobody attempted any longer to question his importance."[82]

It would be an exaggeration to call Belinsky a spiritual brother of the German poet; however, there are several characteristics he has in common with him. Both men inscribed their names in the annals of literature as merciless critics of the shortcomings and vices of human society, yet it is in the sphere of temperament and pathos that Belinsky's kinship with Schiller stands out most strikingly. A truly Schillerean hatred of despotism, a noble passion for dignity and freedom, for the welfare and happiness of all people pervades his life and his works.[83] His fervent love

[82] *Schiller,* ed. Vengerov, I, iii.
[83] "We must be careful, however, to avoid the mistake of confusing Belinskii's socialism with the socialism of to-day, with Marxist socialism." Thomas G. Masaryk, *The Spirit of Russia* (New York, 1955), I, 363. In fact, according

of the good and the beautiful, of an abstract humanity, borders on fanaticism and exceeds by far the harmonious inspiration characteristic of Schiller's visionary dreams of brotherhood. In his obsession with making mankind happy the Russian sometimes goes to tyrannical extremes: "People are so stupid," he laments in a letter to Botkin, dated September 8, 1841, "that it is necessary to lead them toward happiness by force. . . *fiat justitia— pereat mundus!*"[84]

Belinsky was not very proficient in the German language. In a letter to Bakunin of November 15, 1837, he confesses:

My German language goes badly. I started working on Schiller's *Die Räuber* but, apart from the fact that this drama does not have for me the thrill of novelty, it is written in such a sententious and elaborate style that even those who know the German language are unable to understand many passages, and I, if I do not understand one passage, lose the desire to continue.[85]

This lack of proficiency in the German language should be kept in mind when Belinsky's critical utterances on the German poet are considered. On the other hand, although deeply deploring his "shameful inactivity" in this respect and although denouncing himself as a member of a "pitiful generation,"[86] he nevertheless felt that he was more entitled to judge the supreme figures in German literature than some of the authorities on that subject. Thus, four years after his first confession of deficiency in the German language, Belinsky boldly proclaims both his com-

to Belinsky, the individual must not be sacrificed to the whole. In this respect Belinsky's socialism appears to be close to the socialism of Lassalle. About the tendency to sovietize Belinsky, cp. Gleb Struve, "A Belinsky Centenary Bibliography," *SEER* (London, May 1949), p. 546. See also René Wellek, "Social and Aesthetic Values in Russian Nineteenth-Century Literary Criticism," *Continuity and Change in Russian and Soviet Thought,* ed. E. J. Simmons (Cambridge, Mass., 1955), p. 388.

[84] Belinsky, *Pisma,* II, 269.
[85] Belinsky, *Pisma,* I, 156.
[86] Belinsky, *Pisma,* II, 129–130.

petence in German letters and his ignorance of the German
language. There is even a note of self-satisfaction when he
asserts: "I understand Goethe and Schiller better than those who
know them by heart—and I do not know German."[87]

Reviewing the critic's observations and verdicts on Schiller one
may concede that, in general, his self-satisfaction is not unjustified. Not many writers in Russia in the first half of the nineteenth
century can vie with Belinsky in point of comprehension and
interpretation as far as Schiller's general spirit is concerned. In
his student days he had already instinctively recognized that Schiller was a great poet—great because endowed with genius, with
invisible wings which carried him up into regions of eternal
beauty. As a mature man and critic he re-examined his former
idol with cooler and more discerning eyes and found again that
the German's stature as a poet was truly that of a colossus.[88]

From then on he valued Schiller as the proclaimer of sublime
truths, a voice calling his human brethren from earth to heaven,
an organ of inexhaustible love. Thus, in his essays on Pushkin,
he does honor to Schiller by naming him the "poet of humanity,"
the "priest of the freedom of the spirit," but he also pays tribute
to Schiller's poetry—the poetry of a man who sacrificed his life-
blood on the altar of universal love:

In Schiller's poetry his heart eternally bleeds to death with the
most impassioned, fiery, and noble blood of love for man and mankind, of hate for religious and national fanaticism, for prejudices,
stakes, and whips which divide people and force them to forget that
they are brothers to each other.[89]

[87] Belinsky, *Pisma,* I, 244.
[88] As with Schiller so with Pushkin, Gogol, Dostoyevsky: Belinsky did
sense with amazing quickness and certainty—on a narrow basis of factual
content—the "greatness," the "genius" of a writer. That is, doubtless, a
strong point in this critic.
[89] Belinsky *Soch.,* III, 347. See also F. P. Schiller *Fridrikh Schiller*
(Moskva, 1955), pp. 10–11.

It was in 1843 that these lines were written. Belinsky died in 1848 but his admiration for Schiller's "great soul" and his fervent sympathy for his works did not fade in his heart to the very end.

IV

Bakunin

MIKHAIL ALEKSANDROVICH BAKUNIN (1814-76), A RUSSIAN aristocrat of royal ancestry who is principally known as the father of modern anarchism, can justly be considered one of the most colorful figures in the literary and sociopolitical history of the world. His political and revolutionary activity was marked by a series of fantastic adventures which carried him from the barricades of Prague (1848) and Dresden (1849), where he fought together with Richard Wagner, to the dungeons of Schlüsselburg and, finally, to exile in Siberia. His incredible flight from Siberia (1861) to Japan, America, and England, his collaboration and break with Herzen (1861–64), his epic struggle for the control of the First International (1862–72), his revolutionary activity in the Paris Commune (1871)—all this constitutes an exciting and important chapter in the chronicles of mankind.

In his youth Bakunin frequented the circle of Stankevich where he became the friend of Belinsky and Herzen. It was Bakunin who introduced Belinsky to the philosophy of Fichte and Hegel. Having left the army in 1835, he turned to literary and philosophical studies and quite seriously thought of entering upon an academic career. At that time Bakunin had no interest in social and political problems and no one, not even he himself, could suspect that he was destined to become the bugbear of European governments and the rival of Karl Marx in the international revolutionary movement.

116

Bakunin's first contact with the works of Schiller occurred several years before he entered the Stankevich circle. In a letter to his sisters of March 2, 1830, he makes a brief reference to the German poet : "Rotchev has translated two tragedies of Schiller (*Wilhelm Tell* and the *Macbeth* fragment) into the Russian language and one must admit that both of these tragedies are not lacking in beauty."[1]

Bakunin was also familiar with Schiller's *Die Räuber,* and it seems that this drama made an extraordinary impression upon him for he hastened to share his enthusiasm with his younger brothers, supplying them with a copy of *Die Räuber* and urging them, on the model of Karl Moor, to revolt against authority, discipline, and scholastic humdrum. Schiller's inflammatory drama and the instigations of the older brother did not fail to catch the imagination of the youngsters who promptly decided to follow the footsteps of the admirable robber. A whole episode ensued, which, fortunately, did not have serious consequences :

Ses quatre frères plus jeunes que lui font leurs études au collège de Tver. Ils reçoivent la visite de Michel (Bakounine), qui s'empresse de leur ouvrir les portes du paradis philosophique où lui-même vient de pénétrer. Grisés par les paroles de leur aîné, excités par les lectures romantiques qu'il leur fournit, et notamment par les ouvrages de Herder et les "Brigands" de Schiller, les jeunes gens ne peuvent plus supporter la vie monotone du collège de province. Ils décident de fuir, préparent tout un plan d'évasion, montent dans la charrette d'un paysan qu'ils ont soudoyé, mais qui, s'étant méfié au dernier moment les restitue à leur famille ![2]

After his resignation from the army Bakunin came to Moscow and actively participated in the philosophical and literary pursuits of the Stankevich circle. From 1835 to 1840 he played a

[1] M. A. Bakunin, *Sobranie sochineniy i pisem* (Moskva, 1934–35), I, 42. Hereafter abridged to "SSP."

[2] Hélène Iswolsky, *La vie de Bakounine* (Paris, 1930), p. 38.

considerable role in the circle, and on many occasions he energetically asserted his outstanding qualities of leadership, especially in the field of philosophy, over his equally talented but less forceful or less eloquent companions. The meetings of the circle were characterized by heated arguments about the new European literature, "and the works of Goethe, Schiller, Jean Paul Richter . . . were read and discussed with the ardor and pathos symptomatic of the young romanticists of that time."[3] In the study of German philosophy and literature Bakunin was able to advance more rapidly than most of his friends (for instance, Belinsky) because he was far better equipped linguistically:

One advantage that Bakunin had over some of his future colleagues in the intellectual world of the thirties and forties was his extremely good comprehension of the German language. He read with ease the original German texts, and his few translations from German into Russian were valuable at that time.[4]

In addition to the testimony of others, we have also the testimony of Bakunin himself that Schiller, among other German authors, was studied by him during his stay in Moscow. In a letter of March 11, 1836, he writes to his sister Varvara: "You want to know how I spend my time. I live with Stankevich. We study together history and philosophy. We read together the German writers: Goethe, Schiller, Jean Paul Richter, Hoffmann, and others."[5] With these young Russians, philosophy and literature were inextricably interlaced—an attitude very much in tune with the romantic mood of their life. This is especially true in the case of Bakunin. Fichte was the German philosopher who fascinated him most in those days, in fact, Fichte's *Anweisung zum seligen Leben* became his constant and inseparable companion.

---

[3] A. A. Kornilov, *Molodye gody Mikhaila Bakunina* (Moskva, 1915), p. 93.
[4] E. T. Weiant, *Sources of Modern Mass Atheism in Russia,* Dissertation (Basel, 1950), p. 69.
[5] Bakunin, *SSP,* I, 235.

But Fichte's romantic subjectivism combined in Bakunin's soul immediately with the poetic idealism of Schiller and other German writers. In the words of a literary historian : "Fichte is fused in Bakunin with German poetry (Schiller, Jean Paul Richter, Hoffmann, Bettina von Arnim) into some kind of revolutionary–romantic entity. He covets truth as it is and not truth as it is adapted to certain conditions."[6]

When Bakunin's sister Varvara conceived the idea of publishing an anthology for children, Mikhail encouraged her wholeheartedly and suggested that she take her material from a few well-chosen German authors. This is what Bakunin suggests to her in a letter of January 4, 1837 : "Your idea of compiling a collection of tales for children is very excellent . . . translate a number of passages from Schiller and Jean Paul Richter, particularly passages that can be understood by children."[7]

In contrast to Belinsky, Bakunin's literary output is relatively small. During the period from 1838 to 1840, the year of his departure from Russia, several articles by him appeared in Moscow periodicals the most important of which, for our purposes, is his widely-famed introduction to the "Gymnasiale Reden" of Hegel. This foreword appeared in the periodical *Moskovsky Nabludatel,* a magazine edited by Belinsky, in March 1838, and consists chiefly of an exposition of Bakunin's philosophical views and a devastating attack on Fichte's subjective idealism. Bakunin anticipates here Belinsky's reactionary interpretation of the Hegelean thesis, "All that is real is rational" :

Building on a Hegelean foundation, he [Bakunin] arrives at a position opposed to that of Kant, his former leader in philosophy, and opposed above all to that of Fichte, speaking of extreme subjectivism as egoistic self-contemplation and "the annihilation of any possible love." He condemns Schiller, the Kantian revolté; he

[6] D. I. Chizhevsky, *Gegel v Rossii* (Paris, 1939), p. 89.
[7] Bakunin *SSP,* I, 414–415.

condemns Voltaire and the French philosophers of the eighteenth century; and he condemns Saint-Simon. All are repudiated owing to their hostility to Christianity. Like Granovskii, Bakunin expressly defends the doctrine of immortality.[8]

In German idealistic philosophy Bakunin sees a bulwark against the evil influence of the materialistic French rationalism of the eighteenth century. He admits that Kant and Fichte were useful as a defense against the yoke of French materialism, but both committed the error of putting too much stress on the subject which was bound to lead to a flight from reality and to egotistic self-contemplation and finally, to a destruction of all objectivity. Although Schiller had also begun as a subjectivist, he did manage in the course of time to liberate himself from the peril of excessive abstraction :

Schiller, as a pupil of Kant and Fichte, also started out on subjectivity which is clearly expressed in his two fair-souled dramas, in his *Die Räuber* and in *Kabale und Liebe,* where he rebels against the order of society. But Schiller's rich nature carried him out of abstractness, out of this world of empty phantoms, and each new year of his life was a step towards reconciliation with reality. In his essay on aesthetical education he laid the first foundation of a rational philosophy which aimed at the concrete union of subject and object. Schelling derived this union from an absolute origin and, finally the system of Hegel completed this long striving of reason towards reality : What is real is rational, and what is rational is real.[9]

It now seems obvious that Hegel's proposition can be construed both as an apology for existing conditions and as a vindication of revolutionary resistance to them. At that moment, however, Bakunin apparently was not yet aware of the dialectic ambiguity

[8] Thomas G. Masaryk, *The Spirit of Russia* (New York, 1955), I, 436.
[9] Bakunin, *SSP,* II, 171.

inherent in Hegel's exciting proposition. In addition, there was a wave of pessimism then sweeping through the ranks of the Russian intellectuals, and Hegel's justification of Prussian absolutism ("What is real is rational") was "a sop to those who, though dissatisfied with the regime of Nicholas I, felt quite powerless to challenge it."[10] To be sure, to Bakunin this doctrine became more than "a sop." For about two years he embraced it enthusiastically in the sense of an unconditional yielding to the prevailing political and social conditions. "The reconciliation with reality," he declares in his above-mentioned introduction, "in every relationship and in every sphere of life is the great task of our time, and Hegel and Goethe are the leaders of this reconciliation of return from death to life." Turning then to Russian reality in particular, he concludes : "Let us hope that the new generation shall come to feel its kinship to our glorious Russian Reality and that having renounced all false pretensions to intellectual brilliance, this generation shall at last grasp the legitimate obligation to be Russian men in reality."[11]

As can be seen, Bakunin understands Hegel in the most limited and conservative sense. Any opposition to the existing order of society is roundly condemned. Only "finite reason" prevents man from seeing "that in life all is good and wonderful and that suffering is indispensable as a purification of the spirit, as a transition from darkness to clarity and enlightenment." Schiller is accused of "fair-souledness" (samo-osklablenie: "grinning at one's own self," explains Bakunin), a very serious accusation for "fair-souledness in the eyes of an orthodox Hegelianist was considered a mortal sin."[12] From this point of view Bakunin's rejection of Die Räuber and of Kabale und Liebe becomes not only

[10] Max Nomad, Apostles of Revolution (Boston, 1939), p. 148.
[11] Bakunin, Polnoye sobranie sochineniy, ed. A. I. Bakunin (St. Petersburg [?] n. d.), II, 178.
[12] Yu. Steklov, M. A. Bakunin (Moskva, 1926–27), I, 57.

understandable but even logical and necessary. The former artillery officer, turned passionate worshiper of the conservative Hegel, was bound to feel repelled by the excess of subjectivity and introspection swirling through the pages of Schiller's "Storm and Stress" productions. Schiller's revolt against the established order must have then seemed ridiculous to him—a foolish desire to change his "rational fatherland" according to his infantile chimeras. As a contemporary recalls :

For his youthful protests, for his thirst of justice, truth, and humanity, Schiller was declared by this idealism of Bakunin a puerile genius who never was able to rise from his ardent, beautiful feelings to the quiet contemplation of the ideas and universal laws governing mankind and to an objective understanding of things.[13]

It should be noted that Bakunin's condemnation of Schiller was never as sweeping and unconditional as was Belinsky's. Even in Bakunin's most critical utterances on the German poet there is always a note of indulgence—the kind of forbearance a wise man displays toward the pranks of a talented youngster. Bakunin's Russian biographer, Kornilov, remarks in this connection :

As far as Schiller is concerned, it is noteworthy that Bakunin's opinion of him is not characterized—even in this article written in March 1838 [Bakunin's introduction to the "Gymnasiale Reden" of Hegel]—by that onesidedness with which Belinsky looked at Schiller at this time.[14]

Bakunin's relatively mild criticism of Schiller, conditioned by his newly-won feeling of philosophical superiority and the innate didacticism of his temperament, may also be attributed to his conviction, clearly expressed in his introduction to the "Gymnasiale Reden," that Schiller had to a large degree overcome his abstract subjectivism and that "each new year of his

[13] P. V. Annenkov, *Literaturnye vospominania* (Leningrad, 1928), p. 214.
[14] Kornilov, *Molodye gody Mikhaila Bakunina,* p. 449.

life was a step towards reconciliation with reality." That Schiller outgrew the extreme subjectivism of his youthful dramas is indubitably true : there is no "egotistic self-contemplation" in such figures of the mature Schiller as Max Piccolomini, Johanna, or Wilhelm Tell.

Much less obvious and clear, however, appears Bakunin's statement about Schiller's progressive reconciliation with reality for which, incidentally, he fails to give any tangible proof. Perhaps he thought—as Belinsky did—of the philosophical poem "Die Ideale" where Schiller takes leave of the phantoms of life, and love, and glory, reconciling himself to the reality of indefatigable illusionless work. To be sure, Bakunin refers to Schiller's letters *Über die ästhetische Erziehung des Menschen,* but one is at a loss to see any connection between Bakunin's "reconciliation with reality in all circumstances and in all ways of life" and Schiller's evolutionary "construction of a true political freedom" through the aesthetic education of the individual. If the figure of Wilhelm Tell can be regarded as the mouthpiece and interpreter of the mature poet's point of view, then we may say that Schiller was indeed far from any reconciliation with reality as Bakunin understood it.

Consistency apparently was not one of Bakunin's virtues. Hardly had he managed to condemn Schiller in March, 1838, when, only one month later, he already advises his brother Nikolay to turn to the study of Schiller for the development of his character and the education of his aesthetic sensibility :

In one letter it is impossible to explain everything; when we shall see each other we shall speak about many things. At this moment, however, I will say only one thing : the content of real life, of real religion, and of real philosophy, that science of sciences, is love, and your fiery soul surely will believe and understand this. And here is a first piece of advice : Read the poetic works of Goethe,

Schiller, Hoffmann; read Pushkin, Gogol, develop in yourself an aesthetic sensibility.[15]

All this, especially the reference to "love," sounds like an echo from the *Anleitung zum seligen Leben* and the question arises whether Bakunin had ever been serious in his disparagement of Fichte. Interesting, too, that Mikhail does not advise his brother, as one would expect, to "reconcile himself with reality" but—a strange advice for a foe of fair-souledness!—to "develop an aesthetic sensibility," which reads like a sentence taken from Schiller's letters *Über die ästhetische Erziehung des Menschen.* Perhaps an American critic is right in his assumption that "the young ex-officer [Bakunin], turned seeker after truth, had at first become a conservative, at least with his head. With his temperament, however, he was more inclined to oppose that "reality" which his mind had told him to accept."[16] Such an assumption seems to be borne out by Bakunin's reaction to the hate-Schiller campaign unleashed by his friend and pupil Belinsky in the autumn of 1838.

By that time, under the direct influence of Mikhail's enthusiasm for the conservative Hegel, Belinsky's views on reality, the reprehensibility of struggling against it, nay, the absolute futility of any such attempts, had definitely crystallized.[17] Bakunin, very surprisingly, instead of rejoicing at the docility of his pupil, suddenly disavowed him and refused to recognize the validity and correctness of his ideas. In his answer to Belinsky's letter of September 10, 1838, "he specifically rises against both his friend's 'reality' with its 'iron claws and iron jaws' and also against his view of Schiller as an abstract and empty phrasemonger"[18] although in his foreword to Hegel's "Gymnasiale Reden" he him-

[15] Bakunin, *SSP,* II, 179. Letter of April 15, 1838.
[16] Nomad, *Apostles of Revolution,* p. 148.
[17] See preceding chapter, esp. pp. 91–94.
[18] Steklov, *M. A. Bakunin,* I, 64.

self had given a very similar appraisal of the German poet.

Bakunin's short-lived rejection of Schiller is reversed towards the end of September 1838. Writing to Belinsky and alluding to the latter's misunderstanding of Schiller, he refers, in general terms, to "a tragedy of Schiller which, surrounded by the magic aura of art, remains forever beautiful, regardless of all possible attacks by one who does not understand its profundity."[19] In a letter, dated September 25, 1838, to his sister Varvara, Bakunin again has high praise for Schiller just as he had in the days preceding his reconciliation with reality: "I have just finished reading *Maria Stuart* by Schiller. What a wonderful work! Do you know, Belinsky who was a desperate Schiller-enthusiast in olden times now abuses Schiller in a reckless way so that it is disgusting to listen to him."[20]

After his discharge from the army Bakunin became an avid and indefatigable reader. He decided that he must make up for his previous laziness and negligence and began to pore over the most diverse disciplines: universal history, Greek grammar, the Koran, mathematics, philosophy, and literature. After his "reconciliation with Schiller" in the spring of 1839, Bakunin went through one of his most intensive periods of intellectual effort and wide reading:

His [Bakunin's] mixed reading is reflected during this period in a strong element of eclecticism in his philosophy. He returned to Schiller, whom, in the days of their extreme Hegelianism, Belinsky and he had rejected as abstract and sentimental. He read a biography of Fichte and hailed his old master once more as "a true hero of our age. . . ."[21]

Bakunin, the teacher, had returned to Fichte and Schiller but Belinsky, his disciple, continued his virulent attacks on the Ger-

[19] Bakunin, *SSP*, II, 203–204.
[20] Bakunin, *SSP*, II, 207.
[21] E. H. Carr, *Michael Bakunin* (London, 1937), p. 74.

man poet. As a result, their intimate relations cooled considerably and a complete break became unavoidable in the end. In a
letter to Stankevich of May 13, 1839, written after Belinsky's
break with Bakunin and Botkin, Bakunin alludes to the reason
for Belinsky's hostile attitude toward Schiller: "He [Belinsky]
abuses (or, at least, abused—now I don't know which) Schiller
as a fool claiming that he allegedly brought great harm to him
by his idealistic philosophy."[22] The "great harm" done to him
by Schiller consisted in the eyes of Belinsky of the fact that the
German, by his idealism, had propelled him into the role of
"guardianship over humanity" and into an attitude of "abstract
heroism." The ironical tone of the letter makes it abundantly
clear that Bakunin has cast aside his animosity for Schiller and
that he now holds a view of the German poet diametrically
opposed to that of his overzealous pupil Belinsky.

The didacticism of Bakunin's nature reveals itself very
strikingly in his mentor-like relations with his brothers and sisters.
"By virtue of his sex he [Bakunin] dominated the elder group,
in which he was the only male. By virtue of seniority he towered
over the younger group, consisting of his five brothers."[23] Moreover, Bakunin's personality fitted him eminently for the precep-
torial role in the family circle which he obviously enjoyed. He
watched over the education of his brothers and sisters and told
them what to read and study. Bakunin's letters to his sisters are
full of deliberations on the lofty calling of womanhood and the
essence of love. "Love is a mystery," he writes in 1839 to his
sister Tatyana, developing his theory of love "on the model of
Schiller and Hegel."[24] By the middle of September 1839,
Bakunin dispatched a long letter to his sisters enlarging upon the
female psychology and depicting the image of an ideal woman:

[22] Bakunin, *SSP*, II, 241.
[23] Carr, *Michael Bakunin*, p. 5.
[24] *Mikhail Bakunin*, Sbornik (Moskva, 1926), p. 157.

I do not know, my dear girls, if I shall succeed in expressing to you what I have desired to tell you for a long time regarding the false perspective of your life, that false perspective to the development of which I contributed much, very much. Read Schiller's poem "Würde der Frauen" and you will find in it a complete definition of a woman. A woman has a complete revelation of truth in her soul, a revelation consisting of original moral sentiment (sittliches Gefühl) which one can call her spiritual instinct and which must be her guide in her further development. This original revelation takes the place of the abstract way or logical thinking which is the exclusive prerogative of the man and which is impossible for a woman. The essence of man's consciousness is abstractness : in order to attain full development, full knowledge, he must at first lose everything in abstract thought; he cannot be guided by an inner feeling the harmonious reign of which must be destroyed under the leveling of abstractness—of which he must not be afraid because, in fact, in it is enclosed the seed of restoration, the return of everything, lost through logical thinking. But a woman, despising the voice of her inner sentiment deprives herself of the only gauge, the only means of recognizing truth; if she gives up her moral sentiment a woman loses much more than a man—she loses everything because the moral sentiment of a woman is much fuller and richer than the sentiment of a man. The moral sentiment of a woman is love embodied in her pure and beautiful personality, and by giving it up she loses an infinite and innate source of truth and love. A woman, exactly in the same way as a man, is capable of infinite development, with that difference only that the guide of a man's development is abstract thought, logic, precision founded solely on itself and finding its justification in itself, but the guide of a woman can only be her innate wealth of innermost moral sentiment which accepts thought only when it corresponds to its intrinsic content, when it is no more than the outspoken consciousness of its secret, innermost life. In short, the difference between a man and a woman consists in this that the former must reject a measure of his inner sentiment for the sake of his full development; a woman, however, while enriching herself with thought, with knowledge, with experience of life, must never detach herself from her moral sentiment which must serve her as the guiding star in life.[25]

As can be seen, Bakunin follows very closely Schiller's trend of thought in his exposition of the moral status of the sexes in the world. Though Bakunin mentions in his letter only the poem "Würde der Frauen" it is not improbable that he also knew Schiller's other poems on the same subject, viz., "Macht des Weibes," "Tugend des Weibes," "Das weibliche Ideal." Bakunin's reference to "the abstract way of logical thinking which is the exclusive prerogative of the man" may also be an echo of Schiller's distich "Weibliches Urteil:"

Männer richten nach Gründen, des Weibes Urteil ist seine
Liebe; wo es nicht liebt, hat schon gerichtet das Weib.

Bakunin's expression "love embodied in her pure and beautiful personality" may have been inspired by the concluding lines of Schiller's stanza "Tugend des Weibes:"

Eine Tugend genüget dem Weib, sie ist da, sie erscheinet,
Lieblich dem Herzen, dem Aug lieblich erscheine sie stets.

And, finally, what Bakunin says of a man's abstract thought as opposed to a woman's wealth of "innermost moral sentiment"— by dint of which she exists as an autonomous and harmonious entity—seems to bear resemblance to certain lines in Schiller's poem "Das weibliche Ideal:"

Dünke der Mann sich frei! Du bist es, denn ewig notwendig
Weisst du von keiner Wahl, keiner Notwendigkeit mehr.
Was du auch gibst, stets gibst du dich ganz, du bist ewig nur eines,
Auch dein zärtester Laut ist dein harmonisches Selbst.

[25] Bakunin, *SSP,* II, 264, 265.

It should be noted, however, that Schiller, in all probability, was not the only one who contributed to the molding of Bakunin's ideas on the high calling of womanhood. According to the Soviet critic N. Brodsky, Bakunin's views in this matter reflect, besides the influence of Schiller, also the influence of "some kind of Hegelianist."[26] Another, more tangible evidence that the German poet had really reconquered Bakunin's heart at that time (1839–40) may be seen in the fact that he had placed a picture of Schiller on his desk. Thanking his friend Natalya Beer for a piece of embroidery she had done for him, Bakunin says in his letter of mid-February, 1840 : "I put it [the embroidery] on the table under the portrait of Goethe and Schiller drawn by Aleksandra [one of Bakunin's younger sisters]."[27] Bakunin's new interest in Schiller is also confirmed by a letter of Granovsky to Stankevich, dated February 12-24, 1840 : "We read Schiller together with Mishel [Bakunin]. He is of our opinion [that is, does not agree with Belinsky in his negative attitude toward Schiller]."[28]

The year 1840 opens a completely new chapter in Bakunin's life. After many efforts and frustrations, he finally succeeded in realizing his long-cherished dream of going abroad. His goal was Berlin, the home of philosophy, the Mecca of the members of the Stankevich circle. He arrived in Berlin on July 25, 1840, and without delay began a life of earnest studies. His teacher in philosophy was Professor Karl Werder, a faithful follower of Hegel, who also lectured on the plays of Shakespeare and Schiller. Bakunin became acquainted with the left-Hegelian Arnold Ruge, with the utopian communist Weitling, and with the poet Georg Herwegh. As a result of these new friendships, Bakunin soon lost interest in the orthodox interpretation of Hegel offered

[26] *Mikhail Bakunin,* Sbornik, p. 159.
[27] Bakunin, *SSP,* II, 298.
[28] Bakunin, *SSP,* II, 467.

by Professor Werder. This was the beginning of Bakunin's political and revolutionary activity.

We have already mentioned that the year 1840 was a turning point in Bakunin's life. It should be added that it was a turning point not only in his external biography but, above all, a radical change in his world outlook and in his whole philosophy of life, involving his passing from orthodox-reactionary conservatism to atheistic-revolutionary internationalism. In his youth, particularly during the period of his "reconciliation with reality," his model of a poet was the Olympian Goethe who, from the tranquil heights of his greatness, did not notice the sufferings of the un-enlightened rabble, while Schiller was ridiculed for his tendency to revolt against the established order.

Later, after his departure from Russia, "the rebels, on the contrary, are in every way glorified by him [Bakunin] and revolt is declared the principle trait of human nature."[29] Thus, as leader of the Anarchist wing in the International and as apostle of world-wide destruction, Bakunin, in a strange cycle, returns to the author of *Die Räuber* and the "fair-souledness" of his youth.

Bakunin's return to Schiller, or more exactly, to the ideals of the brigand Karl Moor, has found alarming expression in a pamphlet entitled *The Catechism of a Revolutionist* published in Geneva in the spring of 1869:

Together—the original manuscript is supposed to have been in Bakunin's handwriting—they [Bakunin and his disciple Nechayev] concocted a hair-raising document called *The Catechism of a Revolutionist*, which, though it managed, as Marx and Engels said, to fuse into a single ideal the romantic attitudes of Rodolphe, Karl

---

[29] Steklov, *M. A. Bakunin*, I, 59. For details about Bakunin's revolutionary activities abroad see Josef Pfitzner, "Michael Bakunin und Preussen im Jahre 1848," *Jahrbücher für Kultur und Geschichte der Slaven*, N. F., VII, Heft III (Breslau, 1931), 231–284.

Moor, Monte Cristo and Macaire, must be noted for its importance as the first complete statement of a revolutionary point of view that was to continue to figure in Russian history.[30]

The image of the ideal revolutionist, as depicted by the *Catechism,* emulates the hero of Schiller's *Die Räuber* in several respects. Like Karl Moor (before Karl Moor's ultimate conversion), Bakunin's revolutionist aspires "to improve the world through horrors, and to uphold the laws by lawlessness." Like Karl Moor, he is a doomed man, possessed by one idea : ruthless revenge upon society for all its injustices and oppressions; and like the great robber, he has broken with all the conventions and moral codes of established society.

Following his Schillerean model, the revolutionist has no personal interests or feelings : he is calculating, cool, and ready to give his life for his idea. His sole business—like that of Karl Moor—is "destruction, terrible, complete, universal and ruthless." For this purpose (another analogy to *Die Räuber!*), the true revolutionist must be ready to ally himself with all kinds of outlaws and scoundrels. For Bakunin believed that the only true revolutionists in Russia were "the brigands and rebel Cossacks like Stenka Razin and Pugatchev, who had incited the masses and led them against the Tsars."[31]

Even in his chief works, written between 1871 and 1874, which are eminently political in character, Bakunin takes the occasion to comment upon Schiller and German literature. Thus, in *State and Anarchy,* describing the social and political situation of Germany in the second half of the eighteenth century : the misery of the population, the servility of the intellectuals, the despotism of the rulers, Bakunin suddenly turns to literature and observes :

[30] Edmund Wilson, *To the Finland Station* (New York, 1940) p. 275.
[31] Helen Iswolsky, *Soul of Russia* (New York, 1943), p. 99.

This was the situation of Germany even in the second half of the eighteenth century when, by some kind of miracle, all of a sudden, out of this bottomless abyss of vulgarity and degradation surged a magnificent literature created by Lessing and completed by Goethe, Schiller, Kant, Fichte, and Hegel.[32]

In Bakunin's opinion, this literature constitutes the greatest and well-nigh only merit of modern Germany. With its bold and sweeping scope it has increased human understanding and opened up new horizons of thought. Its chief dignity, according to Bakunin, consists in the fact that it is national and yet, at the same time, humane and universal in the highest degree.

In the same work, reflecting on the shortcomings of the German educated classes during the classical period of German thought ("from Lessing to Goethe"), Bakunin sharply criticizes the representatives of German culture for their "hovering between heaven and earth." He deems them unfit for life or, even worse, condemned to perpetrate in reality the exact opposite of what they had idolized in their poetic or metaphysical flights. Thereupon, turning to the Germany of his own experience, he caustically remarks:

Thus is explained the amazing and rather common phenomenon which strikes us in Germany still today: that the fervent worshipers of Lessing, Schiller, Goethe, Kant, Fichte, and Hegel were capable, and to this day are capable, of serving as submissive and even zealous tools for the execution of all measures, far from humane and anti-liberal, dictated to them by their governments. In general, one can even say that the loftier the ideal world of a German, the uglier and more trivial are his life and his deeds in the world of living reality.[33]

In all probability, Bakunin's vitriolic attack on "the worshipers of Lessing, Schiller, Goethe . . ." must be understood in the light

[32] Bakunin, *Poln. sobr. soch.,* ed. A. I. Bakunin, II, 128.
[33] Bakunin, *Poln. sobr. soch.,* ed. A. I. Bakunin, II, 160.

of his implacable but unsuccessful struggle with Karl Marx for the control of the international workers' movement. "An internationalist in the scope of his activities, he [Bakunin] was at heart a Slavic chauvinist who hated and loathed the Germans and the Jews."[34] Interesting, too, that Bakunin now places Schiller in one line with Goethe although previously he always had very carefully differentiated between the two, contrasting Schiller's subjective idealism with Goethe's majestic objectivism. The Soviet biographer of Bakunin affirms this observation:

Now, Bakunin does not separate Schiller from Goethe and does not set the one against the other as he did toward the end of the thirties at the climax of his enthusiasm with "rational reality" and during the period of his anathematizing any kind of opposition against the established order.[35]

In view of Bakunin's lumping of the representatives of German thought, one could almost have the impression that, by implication, he accuses them—including Schiller—of being in some obscure way responsible for the failure of the German educated classes to live up to their lofty ideals in the world of cold and hard reality. Bakunin, no doubt, appreciated the literary and aesthetic achievements of Schiller and the other German classicists, but he felt repelled by their abstract idealism, their dreamlike "hovering between heaven and earth," which divorced them from the social and political realities of their time and caused them to become obedient tools in the hands of their despotic governments.

On the other hand, it should be kept in mind that—at this late stage of his development—as an atheistic materialist who now believed only in the "elemental surge of the masses" and in the "creative power of destruction," any kind of idealism, by its

---

[34] Nomad, *Apostles of Revolution,* p. 147.
[35] Steklov, *M. A. Bakunin,* I, 55.

very nature and regardless of its nationality, had become equally hateful and disgusting to Bakunin. This fact illumines and, to a certain degree, mitigates his unusually harsh attitude towards the representatives of German idealism during the last years of his life.

Recapitulating, we may say that Schiller played an almost uninterrupted and, at the same time, very important role in the spiritual and ideological development of Bakunin. He studied and admired Schiller in his youth, as a member of the circle of Stankevich, and—apart from a short period in 1838 when he rose against "fair-souledness" and "abstractness"—remained under the spell of Schiller also as a mature man, as witnessed by his *Catechism of a Revolutionist* which, in many parts, echoes the revolutionary spirit of Schiller's "Storm and Stress" plays and, in particular, Karl Moor's denunciation of the tyranny of law and government, of church and social conventions.

Even later, towards the end of his life, Schiller, together with other German idealists, maintains a place in Bakunin's esteem and, in *State and Anarchy,* is hailed as the co-creator of a "magnificent literature." Bakunin died in Switzerland on July 1, 1876. He died as a sick and disillusioned man—badly shaken in his belief that something solid and durable could be built on a foundation of lawlessness, violence, hate, and deceit. In this, Bakunin is reminiscent of the pathetic figure of Karl Moor who —after years of ruthless war on society—"at the end of a terrible life," experiences the tragedy of final comprehension and utmost disillusionment.

V

Herzen

ALEXANDER IVANOVICH HERZEN (1812–70) IS ONE OF THE GREAT representatives of the nineteenth century—a man who has left distinct traces in the political and literary history of Russia and Europe both by his writings and his ideological activity. The illegitimate son of a rich nobleman and a German middle-class woman, he received, nevertheless, an excellent education which enabled him to attend the university and subsequently opened for him the way to the civil service. Organization of a radical student circle, imprisonment, exile, and, finally emigration to Western Europe, are milestones on the road of his development. Herzen's political career culminated in the founding of the weekly paper *Kolokol (The Bell)* which in the years 1857–61 was "the principal political force in Russia."[1] His eminent place in literature is secured by his masterly series of essays and dialogues *From the Other Shore* and by his monumental autobiography *My Past and Thoughts*.

For an important part of his education Herzen was indebted to his German mother. Although she herself could not boast of a "good education" in the conventional sense of the word she still endeavored to act upon the mind of her son by arousing and keeping alive his interest in the best of German literature and, especially, in Schiller:

Although she had had little education she [Herzen's mother] was

[1] D. S. Mirsky, *A History of Russian Literature* (New York, 1949), p. 210.

135

nonetheless an enthusiastic admirer of Schiller with whom she also acquainted her son by reading with him, in the original, the works of the celebrated German writer. The reading of Schiller had made a tremendous impression upon the young boy. During his entire life Herzen preserved a grateful memory and recognition of the merits of the German idealist.[2]

Hand in hand with Herzen's enthusiasm for Schiller went his enthusiasm for the poets and writers of classical antiquity. But the reading of the classical authors caused him to fall into a mood of profound melancholy. Looking at his uninspiring surroundings he could not help noticing their inferiority to the heroic world of the past. It was the reading of Schiller which freed him from this state of dejection and sorrowful despair. The reading of Schiller revealed to him that the modern world was not devoid of valor and grandeur, that the world in which he lived had also its aspects of beauty and virtue. "This discovery," says T. P. Passek, "caused a revolution in his [Herzen's] life."[3] Herzen's precocious bitterness and sorrow, his shame at having to live in a seemingly unheroic age, his contempt of a trivial and cruel humanity gradually gave way to a surge of fresh and tender sentiments. This is how a Soviet critic accounts for this change :

Schiller satisfied that demand for optimism which was so sharply contradicted by the real world surrounding young Herzen. Optimism was here identical with faith in man : that, sooner or later, man would triumph over barbarism and despotism, that human heroism was alive and never would die. Undoubtedly, Schiller could be such a source of optimism for his spirit was akin to that of the nobleman-revolutionary [Herzen].[4]

It was an exciting period in the spiritual development of the

[2] V. Ya. Bogucharsky, *Aleksandr Ivanovich Gertsen* (St. Petersburg, 1912), p. 15.

[3] *Gertsen v vospominaniakh sovremennikov* (Moskva, 1956), p. 40.

[4] *Literaturnoye Nasledstvo* (Moskva, 1941), XXXIX–XL, 120.

boy. Life was again bright and beautiful, full of ecstasies and thrilling hopes. As Herzen himself recalls in his *Sketch Book of a Young Man* (1840): "The bravery of Achilles and the aspirations of Posa filled my soul. It was a time of noble raptures, self-sacrifice, Platonism, ardent love of mankind, and boundless friendship. . . ."[5] Schiller's Marquis Posa appeared to his youthful and, as yet, uncritical mind as the embodiment of genuine, self-denying friendship. Herzen's heart yearned for a friend who would be to him as affectionate, as sympathetic, as faithful and steadfast as Posa had been to Don Carlos:

Posa, Posa! Where are you, friend of my youth, with whom we shall enter upon life hand in hand, strong in our love? In this question to the future there was hope and prayer, sorrow and rapture. I wanted sympathy because there was no room in one heart to contain all that agitated it. I needed another soul to which I could entrust my secrets. I needed eyes filled with love and tears which would be fixed upon me. I needed a friend into whose arms I could throw myself and in whose arms I would feel expansive and free. Posa, where are you? . . .

He was nearby . . . and as soon as a strong and genuine need for a friend had seized my soul he appeared : very handsome and young as I had dreamed of him and as Schiller had depicted him.[6]

This friend was Nikolay Platonovich Ogarev. The two boys met in Moscow and a lifelong friendship began—a romantic, passionate, and dedicated friendship under the auspices of Schiller's *Don Carlos*. This was in summer 1826 :

Panting and flushed we stood there [Vorobyovy Hills] wiping off our perspiration. The sun was setting, the domes of the cathedrals

---

[5] A. I. Gertsen, *Polnoye sobranie sochineniy i pisem,* ed. M. K. Lemke (St. Petersburg, 1919–25), II, 397. Hereafter abridged to "PSS."

[6] Gertsen, *PSS,* II, 402. "Mais, à côté de Karl Moor et du marquis de Posa apparurent pour Hertzen des héros plus réels. Son professeur de français lui apprenait à admirer les héros de la grande Révolution." P. N. Milioukov, *Le Mouvement Intellectuel Russe* (Paris, 1918), p. 194.

were shining, the city spread out in the vast space below the hills, a refreshing wind was blowing. We stood and stood leaning against each other. Then, suddenly, we embraced and swore before all Moscow to dedicate our lives to the struggle for freedom.[7]

The motif of self-sacrifice which pervades the works of Schiller found thus its living embodiment in the two noble-minded Russian idealists. Both Herzen and Ogarev fulfilled their solemn oath and dedicated their lives to the service of mankind.

Their friendship grew and prospered inspired by Plutarch, Rousseau, Ryleyev, and Schiller. Herzen saw with delight and amazement how much he had in common with his friend Nikolay and how similar their ideas were, particularly about poetry and history. Their favorite occupation in those years was reading aloud together from the works of Schiller. Ogarev knew much more about Schiller than his friend and was able to recite from memory the very passages Herzen loved best. After each such reading a discussion ensued which almost inevitably would lead them from the heroes of Schiller to the heroes of the Decembrist revolution and to the despotism of Tsar Nicholas I. In his memoirs Herzen conjures up the atmosphere of these readings and discussions:

From Möros sneaking with his dagger in his sleeve "to free the city from the tyrant" [Schiller, "Die Bürgschaft"], from Wilhelm Tell waiting for the Governor on the narrow path in Küssnacht, it was easy to pass to the Fourteenth of December and to Nicholas.[8]

The characters of Schiller's dramas were to Herzen and Ogarev living personalities whom they discussed, loved, and

[7] Gertsen, *PSS*, XII, 73–74. This friendship with Ogarev had "incalculable consequences for Herzen himself and for his wife." P. V. Annenkov, *Literaturnye vospominania* (Leningrad, 1928), p. 518. Incidentally, there are critics who have doubted the reality of this famous oath on the Vorobyovy Hills. Cf. M. E. Malia, *Alexander Herzen and the Birth of Russian Socialism* (Cambridge, Mass., 1961), p. 51.

[8] Gertsen, *PSS*, XII, 72.

hated not as poetic creations but as real human beings. Moreover, they actually identified themselves with some of the
dramatic figures of Schiller. In *My Past and Thoughts* Herzen
gives striking proof of this :

I wrote to Nik, somewhat worried because he loved Fiesco too
ardently, and warned him that behind "every" Fiesco stood his
Verrina. My own ideal was Karl Moor but soon I betrayed him and
began to identify myself with Marquis Posa. In a hundred ways I
imagined how I would speak to Nicholas [the Tsar], and how he
then would send me off to the mines and have me executed. It was
a strange thing that nearly all of our dreams ended with Siberia or
execution and almost never with victory. Could it be that this is the
Russian brand of imagination, or was it the impact of Petersburg,
with its five gallows and forced labor, upon the young generation?[9]

Young Herzen merely imagined how he, as Marquis Posa,
would speak to the Tsar, but history knows of a real Russian
Marquis Posa, Vasily Nazarovich Karazin (1773–1842), who
after having written a letter to Alexander I, actually had a conversation with the Tsar almost identical with that between Posa
and King Philipp. Herzen, inspired by the enthusiastic Posa—
dreams of his own youth, has saved this Russian Marquis Posa
from oblivion by dedicating to him an essay entitled "Emperor
Alexander I and V. N. Karazin."[10]

When Herzen left Moscow for Vasilyevskoye (1827) he did

[9] Gertsen, *PSS*, XII, 76–77.

[10] Gertsen, *PSS*, XV, 141 ff. In this connection, discoursing on the Russian
social reformers of the nineteenth century, Otto P. Peterson remarks : "Von
ihnen hat zuerst der erwähnte 'Russische Posa' Karasin den Versuch unter-
nommen, Russland auf der Grundlage von Schillers ästhetischem Staat aufzu-
bauen. Der Versuch misslang. Erst Alexander Herzen schuf unmittelbar aus
dem Geist seines 'Lehrers Schiller' die Grundlagen für sein Reformwerk, das
später von Tschernischewsky und Michailowsky weiterausgebaut wurde. Für
diese vier Sozialreformer war Schillers ästhetischer Staat keine Unwirklich-
keit, sondern eine Wirklichkeit, die nach den Worten Herzens 'einen unge-
heuren Schritt in der Entwicklung der geschichtlichen Idee' Russlands
bedeutete." *Schiller in Russland* (New York, 1934), p. 325.

not forget to take his Plutarch and Schiller with him. Once there, Alex used to get up early and wander off into the depths of the woods. There he would lie down under a tree, imagining that he was in the Bohemian forests and from a volume of Schiller's *Die Räuber* would "read aloud about myself. . . ."[11]

Herzen's enthusiasm for Schiller did not diminish in the following years. In the summer of 1828 he was "reading aloud from Schiller,"[12] and in 1829 and 1830 he "was writing a *philosophical* article on Schiller's *Wallenstein*."[13] Schiller's poetry and the beauty of the countryside made him put his school books aside even though he had to prepare himself for the university. In his *Sketch Book of a Young Man* Herzen nostalgically recalls the pictures and moods of his summer dreams in Vasilyevskoye :

An immense idyl lay unfolded before my eyes and I hardly could have enough of it : so new it was to me who had grown up on the third floor in Prechistenka [Moscow]. I read little and then only Schiller. On a high hill from which I could see five or six villages. I devoured *Tell*, and in a dark woods I read again Karl Moor—and it seemed to me that the courageous whistling of his band and the stamping of the cavalry which surrounded him resounded among the pines and firs.[14]

On December 31, 1829, Herzen secretly stole away from his home in Moscow to celebrate New Year together with Nik Ogarev in the house of the latter. There was also a very funny German who participated in the celebration, and there was a whole bottle of champagne which Ogarev had put on ice, and which accounted for the gay climax of this episode. After a while the conversation turned to literary matters and Herzen launched into a eulogy of Schiller. The German, on the other hand,

[11] Gertsen, *PSS*, XII, 66.
[12] Gertsen, *PSS*, I, 25. Letter to his nurse T. P. Kuchina.
[13] Gertsen, *PSS*, XII, 66. [Italics Herzen's.]
[14] Gertsen, *PSS*, II, 404.

praised Goethe and inveighed against Schiller. In defense of his favorite author, Herzen replied that a poet who had created *Wilhelm Tell* was deserving of great admiration. "What's so great about *Wilhelm Tell?*" the German exclaimed, "can you possibly compare him to *Wilhelm Meister!*"

This attack on Schiller was all that was needed to arouse the gaiety of the two others to the point of paroxysm. "After that," Herzen writes, "there was no more conversation, no more philosophizing but just guffaws of laughter."[15] An episode in the lighter vein—and yet revealing of Herzen's attitude toward Goethe and Schiller at this early stage of his development.

Herzen's friendship with Ogarev was soon followed by the experience of his first love. "But who was she?" Herzen asks in a letter to Ketcher and Sazonov, and answers: "All that the dream of Schiller could create in Thekla, a Beatrice leading to Paradise—nay, more than all that."[16] Herzen's mysterious reference is to his cousin Natalya Zakharina. A rapturous love story developed between the two which, very romantically, ended with a secret marriage. It was at this time that Herzen took up Rousseau's *New Heloise* only to drop it again. In an early autobiographical sketch Herzen explains his disappointment with the French novel:

Intoxicated with the heavenly maidens of Schiller who in their inviolable virginity and unearthly existence all bore a resemblance to his "Maiden from a Strange Country" ["Das Mädchen aus der Fremde"], I could not develop a liking for Julia's physically impetuous love, nor even for the style of her correspondence with her lover. Real life I did not understand very well at that time . . . I liked abstract figures in poetry, shadows hardly of human shape, since abstract ideas constituted my whole treasury of thinking. Schiller is thus the poet of youth par excellence for his imagination

[15] Gertsen, *PSS,* I, 47–48.
[16] Gertsen, *PSS,* I, 326.

expresses not the whole compass of human life, as does Shakespeare's, but only youth with its dreams and enthusiasms.[17]

One could take exception to the assertion of the twenty-year-old biographer that Schiller expresses not all of life but "only youth." While it is true that Schiller has always had a special power of attraction for the younger generation, it is no less true that many aspects of his genius are inaccessible to youthful and immature minds. Ironically, young Herzen himself may serve as an example for this inaccessibility with his rapturous misinterpretation of the ambiguous figure of Marquis Posa. Morever, there are elements of realism and of a mature view of life even in *Die Räuber*, in Karl Moor, for instance, and in his decision to give himself up to the courts. And there is a vast panorama of humanity in the *Wallenstein* trilogy and in *Wilhelm Tell*, to say nothing of Schiller's aesthetic and philosophical writings, the majority of which are not easily accessible to immature minds.

A rather humorous episode of May 1833 shows that Schiller was Herzen's faithful companion also in less serious moments of the latter's life. During a drinking-bout with merry fellow students Herzen suddenly jumped on a chair and cried:

Mylords et lords! le punch cardinal, tel que le cardinal Mezzofanti, qui connaît toutes les langues existantes et qui n'ont jamais existées, n'a jamais goûté; le punch cardinal est à vos ordres. Hommes illustres par vos lumières, connaissez que Schiller, décrété citoyen de la république une et indivisible . . . a dit, il me semble en parlant des prisonniers, lors du siège d'Anony par les troupes du roi-citoyen Louis Philippe:

Eh' es verduftet
Schöpfet es schnell.

[17] *Lit. Nasl.* (1953), LXI, 12. With reference to Herzen's love story, M. E. Malia remarks: "Less wise than Stankevic, Herzen and Ogarev tried to live Schiller's ideal of love in their marriages." "Schiller and the Early Russian Left," *Harvard Slavic Studies* (Cambridge, Mass., 1957), IV, 194–195.

Nur wenn er glühet,
Labet der Quell

Je propose donc de nous mettre à l'instant même dans la possibilité de vérifier les proverbes du citoyen Schiller—à vos verres, citoyens![18]

On June 30, 1833, Herzen revisited the Vorobyovy Hills together with his friend Ogarev and again, as on previous occasions, they read Schiller and the poems of a Decembrist writer :

I [Herzen] took out Schiller and Ryleyev. How clear and beautiful did these great poets appear to us at that moment! We read the first one and grasped his deep and thought-packed poetry; we read the second one and understood his unselfish soul of a martyr. We were overwhelmed by the sonorous powerful language of Schiller.[19]

What strikes one in this passage is Herzen's classification of Ryleyev as a "great poet" who can be placed on a level with Schiller. This overestimation of a relatively minor poet must, of course, be seen in the light of Herzen's and Ogarev's enthusiasm for the heroes of the Decembrist revolution of which Ryleyev was one of the principal leaders. Much later, in February 1858, in his article "The Russian Conspiracy of 1825," Herzen again honored Ryleyev by comparing him to Schiller :

Ryleyev was perhaps the most remarkable among the members of the Northern Society. He is the Schiller of conspiracy, a rhapsodical, youthful, poetic element, a Girondistic element in the best sense of this word.[20]

Schiller's rule over the hearts and minds of the two friends was so complete that they could not help looking at the Decembrist revolution with the eyes of Schiller's heroes. They did not realize "that the dekabrist program as they conceived it smacked

[18] Gertsen, *PSS*, II, 166–167.
[19] Gertsen, *PSS*, I, 112. Also Schelling had an influence on Herzen but it was "verschwindend kurz." W. Setschkareff, *Schelling's Einfluss in der Russischen Literatur* (Leipzig, 1939), p. 97.
[20] Gertsen, *PSS*, IX, 144.

rather of Schiller's *Don Carlos* than of historical reality."[21] But one thing seems to be certain : the fascination of Schiller's heroes —now of the robber Karl Moor in his struggle with the unjust old order, now of Marquis Posa audaciously demanding freedom of thought for all subjects—did not instill reconciliation but rather educated young Herzen in a spirit of social protest and struggle with reality.

In the summer of 1833, after a university examination, Herzen felt that he deserved a rest. For several days he slept and ate, bathed, and slept. But his restless mind could not remain inactive for a long time, and the first task which he assigned to himself was the study of Goethe. On the basis of his knowledge of Schiller, he draws a comparison between the tranquillity of Goethe and Schiller's tempestuousness :

Schiller is a turbulent torrent, from afar you can hear its thundering roar. Its waves rush on furiously, and the moment you set your boat afloat—it dances in a whirlpool. Not so Goethe, he is deep like the sea, there is no apparent current and calmly surge its big and mighty waves.[22]

These were prophetic words. Before long, Herzen floated in a dangerous whirlpool and Schiller who had swayed the idealistic youth to make "the realization of his, Schiller's, sublime types the religion of his life,"[23] was responsible for it—Schiller with *Die Räuber* and *Don Carlos,* with his love of freedom, and humanity, and truth.

In the university Herzen and Ogarev had organized a student circle in which political and philosophical questions were discussed, in particular the philosophical views of Schiller and the Utopian socialism of Saint-Simon. This interest of university students in Schiller and socialism appeared highly suspicious to

[21] T. G. Masaryk, *The Spirit of Russia* (New York, 1919), I, 386.
[22] Gertsen, *PSS,* I, 113.
[23] *Gertsen v vospom. sovremennikov,* p. 41.

the Russian police and in 1834 the members of the circle were arrested. Herzen was questioned about his correspondence with Ogarev. The authorities wanted to know why Ogarev, in one of his letters, had advised him to read *Wilhelm Tell* as often as possible. Herzen replied :

Wilhelm Tell is the best work of Schiller. This is how the Germans evaluate it, how Schlegel characterizes it. For this reason Mr. Ogarev, who has as high an opinion of the beauties of this tragedy, advises me to read it more often.[24]

That Herzen and Ogarev rated *Wilhelm Tell* as the best work of Schiller, at that time, one can readily believe. But the real reason for their infatuation with *Wilhelm Tell* was obviously Schiller's glorification in it of popular resistance to despotism. Furthermore, Schiller's *dramatis personae* had become merged for them with the heroes of the Decembrist revolution, sufficient reason why Herzen was urged by his friend to read *Wilhelm Tell* as often as possible. The police were also suspicious of the postscript which Ogarev had added to his advice :

This drama [*Wilhelm Tell*] depicts a period of crisis. Oh ! . . . what I felt when I was reading it. You simply cannot imagine; you will understand it when you read it again, but especially in a moment of bitterness, of anger and hatred. Yet these are thoughts of destruction, and I want to create; on the basis of my philosophy of history I shall work out the plan of an association.[25]

Herzen gave an evasive answer to the investigator :

The words of Mr. Ogarev I am not able to explain distinctly but I understand them in the following way : He likes the drama of Schiller about which he speaks, yet he would have liked it still better if it did not treat a period of crisis, of destruction, if it, in a word, did not have revolution for its subject matter.[26]

[24] Gertsen, *PSS*, XII, 344.
[25] Gertsen, *PSS*, XII, 345.
[26] *Ibid.*

As a result of the investigation and trial Herzen was exiled
to the provinces, not as a prisoner but as an employee in the
provincial administration. For some unknown reason he was
kept in prison even after the announcement of the verdict. Herzen was outraged by this illegal treatment. In a letter to his
sweetheart N. A. Zakharina he gives vent to his fury and indignation :

Who, indeed dares now to detain us any longer? The verdict was
announced to us and they do not take the trouble to let us out. Oh,
beasts, beasts, wild beasts, and not human beings! "People—progeny
of crocodiles, your tears are water, your hearts are iron," as Schiller
says.[27]

From his exile in Vyatka, near Perm, Herzen continued to
write bitter letters to Natasha Zakharina expressing his disgust
with humanity and quoting—with a certain melancholy satisfaction, as it were—Karl Moor's invectives against mankind, that
"brood of crocodiles." In the fall of 1835 the tone of his letters
began to change. Disillusioned with people in general, he concentrated all his affections on the distant image of Natasha
Zakharina, proclaiming her "an angel sent for his salvation" and
extolling her above Schiller's Thekla and all other extraordinary
characters of ancient and modern poetry. This same tone characterizes a letter of November 25, 1835, where Natasha is apostro-
phized as "that 'maiden from the foreign land' of whom Schiller dreams—that maiden who in her sublimity was stranger to
all earthly things."[28] In another letter Herzen urges Natasha to
study German so that she would be able to derive pleasure from
reading Schiller in the original :

Natasha! Try a little to occupy yourself with the German

[27] Gertsen, *PSS,* I, 173. Letter of April 2, 1835. The lines in *Die Räuber*
read : "Menschen–Menschen! falsche, heuchlerische Krokodilbrut! Ihre
Augen sind Wasser! Ihre Herzen sind Erz!" (I, 2).
[28] Gertsen, *PSS,* I, 208.

language. . . . I want to open to you the ocean of poetry of German literature. I want to acquaint you with that Schiller of whom Ogarev has said :

> With a tear like dew so clear
> He looks at the azure sky
> Seeking his home in heaven. . . .[29]

Imbued with Schiller, Herzen did not tire of recommending the study of the German poet both to his friends and to his children. Thus, in a letter to his daughter O. A. Herzen, he solicitously admonishes her to set about reading the works of the German poet :

Let me know, in detail, what you now are reading and whether you like what you are reading. It is time, also, for you to get around to working on Schiller. I recommended Tata [another daughter of Herzen] to read *Tell* and *Wallenstein* even for the second time : good books grow with us.[30]

When N. A. Ogareva asked him about suitable reading material for her daughter Liza, Herzen made a similar recommendation :

I have not been able to find *Die Jungfrau von Orleans* in French but I have found *Wilhelm Tell*. Give it to Liza after having aroused her interest and whether she understands it or not—make her read it. In the reading room of Viskovatov you will probably find translations of the other tragedies and also *Die Junfrau von Orleans*. At any rate, this is pure and wholesome nourishment.[31]

As can be seen, Herzen thought very highly of the didactic and moral value of Schiller's poetry and its beneficial influence on the mind of the young. He himself was experiencing the uplifting impact of Schiller's humane idealism and this exper-

[29] Gertsen, *PSS*, I, 263. Letter of March 28, 1836.
[30] Gertsen, *PSS*, XIX, 274. Letter of April 24, 1867.
[31] Gertsen, *PSS*, XIX, 275. Letter of April 25, 1867.

ience gave him the right to set him up as a model for children and adolescents.

In 1836 Herzen wrote a story entitled "The First Encounter." The characters in the story are a Philosopher, an admirer of Goethe, and a German, a follower of Schiller, who is the mouthpiece of Herzen himself. The German advances the thesis that there had never been a bond of sincere friendship between the two poets. But the Philosopher disagrees and maintains that they had really loved one another. To this the German replies: "I do not believe it. Goethe overwhelmed the timid Schiller by his genius and authority, but surely they could not have loved one another."[32] At the time Herzen did recognize the genius of the author of *Faust,* however, he intensely disliked Goethe for his egoism and also for his apathy in political affairs. As for Herzen's views on the friendship of Schiller and Goethe, it is safe to assume that he did not yet know the correspondence between the two poets which, in essence, is a monument to their remarkable relationship.

Herzen's letters to Natasha Zakharina continue to carry references to Schiller. Once more he compares her to the "maiden from a foreign land": "Read Schiller's 'Das Mädchen aus der Fremde.' This is again you, Natasha, my sister."[33] Also the comparison to Thekla reappears: "Read also 'Thekla, Eine Geisterstimme.' Thekla is akin to you. . . ."[34] On another occasion, Natasha appears to him like an embodiment of Joan of Arc: "Have you read Schiller's *Die Jungfrau von Orleans* in the translation of Zhukovsky? Do read it, by all means: also there . . . all is you, is sublime and heavenly."[35] Natasha evidently took

[32] Gertsen, *PSS,* I, 297.
[33] Gertsen, *PSS,* I, 468. Letter of September 10, 1837.
[34] Gertsen, *PSS,* I, 470. Letter of September 16, 1837.
[35] Gertsen, *PSS,* I, 357–358. Letter of December 5, 1836.

Herzen's advice to heart for in another letter he exclaims joyfully :

With delight I have seen excerpts from Schiller's *Jungfrau* in your letters. If you can read the *Jungfrau,* even though with difficulty, then success has been attained and I shall send you the complete text.[36]

At times the tone of Herzen's letters to Natasha becomes extremely rapturous. In a *billet d'amour* which sounds like a hymnal prayer he again compares her to Joan of Arc :

Natasha, Natasha, my savior! Schiller says of the Maid of Orleans : "And the Lord chose a dove to fulfill His will." Holy dove that flew down from Heaven, angel of the Lord, rule over me! Before a messenger of God I am not ashamed to bend my head.[37]

The motif of the "dove" reappears several months later in a letter to Ogarev in which, in glowing terms, he pays tribute to the "strength" and "sublimity" of Natasha Zakharina :

Two people have strongly influenced me during my life : you and she; no other person has influenced me besides. But her influence has been a hundred times stronger than yours.

   . . . Eine weisse Taube

   Wird fliegen. .

   . . . .

   Durch eine zarte Jungfrau wird er sich

   Verherrlichen, denn er ist der Allmächtige.

             (Schiller, *Die Jungfrau von Orleans*)

Before her strength and sublimity I have bent my proud head. Some time in future you will read her letters—and you too will bend your head.[38]

---

[36] Gertsen, *PSS,* I, 386–387. Letter of February 10, 1837.

[37] Gertsen, *PSS,* I, 417. Letter of April 30, 1837.

[38] Gertsen, *PSS,* II, 27. Letter of January 19, 1838. This letter is addressed to Zakharina. The above quotation is an excerpt from a letter to Ogarev which Herzen adduces in his message to Natasha.

As can be seen, Herzen attributes to his Natasha the supernatural qualities of Schiller's Johanna. But after that he abruptly recalls his mission of a teacher and educator and he adds: "I hope you will understand these lines from the *Jungfrau,* they are very simple. . . . I will send you also Schiller's tragedies,—work on the German language."

In his correspondence with his sweetheart Herzen repeatedly compares his own happiness in his love for Natasha with Schiller's unhappiness:

Do read, do read Schiller. He was dreaming all his life long of a maiden who would be in part Johanna and in part Thekla. All his life long he was evoking an angel from heaven; he did not belong to this world,—but this angel never descended to him, and his life of dreams ended with a melancholy note. In a melancholy poem ("Resignation") he says that he has not found the cup of enjoyment. Natasha, could I possibly say such a thing, having you? I am terribly happy, more, much more than I deserve. The sublime soul of Schiller almost withered because his prayers found no echo. . . . Do read Schiller. If it should be difficult in the beginning do not become discouraged, I will get you some of his works.[39]

This theme of Schiller's unhappiness and melancholy resignation in contrast to his own infinite happiness is further elaborated in a subsequent letter to Natasha:

So Schiller and Byron demanded greater, more colossal, more refined things of life than I did, and for that reason I am happy and they are not? But this is very unjust for I demanded even greater things! The demands of Schiller, for instance, are clear: it is easy to reconstruct from his works that ideal the realization of which his soul was craving. It is Joan of Arc and Thekla combined; even the external appearance of his ideal can be envisioned. I demanded no less—oh no! and I have found in you more, and more than I demanded.[40]

[39] Gertsen, *PSS,* I, 386–387. Letter of February 10, 1837.
[40] Gertsen, *PSS,* I, 388. Letter of February 14, 1837.

Throughout the year 1837 Herzen is preoccupied with the motif
of Schiller's "Resignation" and Natasha's "celestial" sublimity.
Again and again he encourages Natasha to learn German and
enjoy Schiller in the original :

> Read Schiller's "Resignation,"—his soul too was tender, he too was
> a sufferer [like Herzen], but he knew loftiness of purpose. . . .
> Natasha, Natasha . . . I am happy again; no, you are not a human
> being, you are a divinity—let me dissolve in the light of your
> splendor.[41]

Even of his future happiness with Natasha, Herzen can conceive
only in connection with Schiller :

> Oh, how beautiful our life will be; if only we could begin it sooner,
> sooner ! All will be a poem to us—we ourselves, and nature, and
> Schiller, and the noon mass, and winter evenings in a cold room, and
> summer nights stifling like an ominous presentiment.[42]

Herzen's repeated references to Schiller as unhappy dreamer
whose "life of dreams ended with a melancholy note," call for
some criticism and comment. That Schiller "did not belong to
this world" seems, in the light of Schiller's correspondence, a
dubious allegation.[43]

Herzen gives also a much too gloomy interpretation to the
poem "Resignation." It was not really Schiller's "life of dreams"
which ended with his writing this poem but rather the unhappy
episode of his stay in Mannheim (1783–85) after which he
immediately started hoping and dreaming again.[44] Finally, Schiller's cordial friendship with Körner and Goethe entirely con-

[41] Gertsen, *PSS,* I, 470. Letter of September 16th, 1837.

[42] Gertsen, *PSS,* II, 99. Letter of February 26th, 1838.

[43] Even a short time before his death Schiller was giving much thought to
business and financial affairs. Cp. letter to Humboldt of April 2, 1805.

[44] Cp. Schiller's letter "An die Leipziger Freunde" of February 22, 1785 :
"Bei Ihnen will ich, werd ich alles doppelt, dreifach wieder sein, was ich
ehemals gewesen bin, und mehr als das alles, o, meine Besten, ich werde
glücklich sein."

tradicts the assertion of Herzen that "the sublime soul of Schiller almost withered because his prayers found no echo . . ." Obviously, the ecstatic character of his love for Natasha did not permit Herzen to see and grasp the whole Schiller but only that part of Schiller which corresponded to his own exalted state of mind. Herzen's image of an "unhappy" Schiller is thus not borne out by the facts. While there were undoubtedly many unhappy moments in the poet's life, there were, on the other hand, also long periods of high satisfaction and genuine happiness.[45]

With the coming of winter Herzen tried to diversify his readings but his attempt was not very successful:

I started twenty books and each one of them I threw away—trivial, false, unnatural. Cold books, rational books I didn't even take into my hands—of course. Schiller alone, the friend of my childhood whom I read with Ogarev with the innocent lips of a boy, he alone is magnificent—and he knows our love. Terrible is Shakespeare, colossal, great, but I did not want to be astounded. I was looking for harmony and Schiller gave it to me. I did not so much read as reflect on his tragedies elaborating each character in my imagination.[46]

At times Herzen was overcome by anxiety, being afraid to remain alone. In such moments, when his "soul was overwhelmed by the black present," he took refuge in the house of an under-standing friend, Polina Trompeter, whose simple and refreshing personality had a soothing influence on his anguished state of mind. In an essay entitled "To 'Sympathy,'" Herzen pays tribute to his benevolent and warmhearted friend:

Her simple tales, her sympathy—strong and pure like mountain air—breathed health into my suffering soul, and when nothing

---

[45] Cp. Schiller's letter to the painter Grass of April 2, 1805: "Viel Freude habe ich in diesen zwölf Jahren erlebt, wiewohl auch viel durch Krankheit gelitten; aber der Geist ist doch immer frisch geblieben."
[46] Gertsen, PSS, I, 501. Letter to Natasha of November 18, 1837.

would help, she quieted me with the songs of her Germany, with the songs of her Schiller—she sang for me Thekla, das Mädchen . . . das Freude . . . [sic!], and many times my soul was healed and the heart-rending tempest was stilled.[47]

Indeed, Schiller was "the ruler of his thoughts," the poet who was able "to move him to tears of tender emotion,"[48] and it is therefore not very surprising that at that time he cared little or nothing for other poets and writers—not even for the "colossal" Shakespeare.

In July 1837 Herzen began to take German lessons from the theologian Böttger who also had been exiled to Vyatka. It was Herzen's avowed aim to attain the same fluency in written German as he had in Russian. At the same time he carefully watched the progress Natasha was making in her study of German and Schiller:

Once you are able to understand it [Schiller's drama *Don Carlos*] you will find very much in this drama : an unhappy love, the love of a stepson for his stepmother, a pure love as it could spring forth only from the pure heart of Schiller; and friendship—Marquis Posa.[49]

The reader is here struck by the fact that Herzen thinks of Don Carlos in terms of a tragedy of love and completely ignores its political aspect which, undoubtedly, is the dominant element in the drama as a whole. It would be difficult to imagine that Herzen was not aware of the eminently political character of this play, but at that time he was so engulfed in his love for Natasha that he was apt to forget or neglect everything else.

[47] Gertsen, *PSS*, XXII, 149. Manuscript (which is lost) was written on January 18, 1838, in Vladimir on Klyazma. By "das Mädchen . . ." Herzen probably means "Das Mädchen aus der Fremde," and by "das Freude . . ." the song "Das Lied an die Freude."
[48] N. S. Derzhavin, *A. I. Gertsen* (M.–L., 1947), p. 7.
[49] Gertsen, *PSS*, II, 33. Letter to Zakharina of January 27, 1838.

In September 1838, speaking of his dramatic experiment *William Penn,* Herzen makes another reference to *Don Carlos:*

The William Penn of my historical scenes bears no resemblance to the historical Penn. I knew the history of England of that time inadequately and had the most nebulous ideas about Penn who settled Pennsylvania. In my sketch one must look for another truth, not the historical one; in Schiller's *Don Carlos* it is as difficult to find the Don Carlos of the Spanish chronicles as in my colorless *William Penn* the clever Quaker described (with partiality for the other side, perhaps) by Macaulay.[50]

Herzen defends himself here against the harsh criticism of Belinsky who had "mercilessly killed" his two dramatic experiments, that is to say, *Licinius* and *William Penn,*[51] and Schiller is his excuse for having portrayed, not the historical figures, but imaginary figures of his own making. When he writes: "In my sketch one must look for another truth, not the historical one," Herzen evidently refers to the "poetic truth" of Schiller about which he had read in the latter's essay "Über die tragische Kunst." Agreeing with Schiller, Herzen felt that the poet had the right to subordinate historical truth to the demands of poetry and to deal with his subject matter according to its needs.

During his exile in Vladimir (1838) Herzen wrote his *Sketch Book of a Young Man* the second chapter of which is initiated by a motto from Schiller's *Don Carlos* (IV, 21): "Respekt vor den Träumen deiner Jugend." In this work Herzen affectionately recalls the time when he gained consciousness of being a spirited youth and demanded for the first time a share in everything human. It was the time when he "fell into the hands of Schiller's *Die Räuber,*" the time when the band of Karl Moor carried him off, for a long time, "into the Bohemian woods of romanticism."[52]

[50] Gertsen, *PSS,* II, 208–209.
[51] Cp. Gertsen, *PSS,* II, 205 (note).
[52] Gertsen, *PSS,* II, 392.

In his *Sketch Book of a Young Man* Herzen pays high tribute to Schiller, the inspiration of his youth :

Schiller! I bless you, to you I am obliged for the bright moments of my early youth! How many tears flowed from my eyes upon your poems! What an altar did I build for you in my heart! You are the poet of youth par excellence. Yours is that youthful dreamy look directed toward the future—"thither, thither!" those noble, powerful, aspiring sentiments, that love of humanity, and that sympathy for the present . . . Having once taken Schiller in my hands, I did not abandon him, and also now, in moments of sorrow, his noble songs restore my soul.[53]

Herzen then tells of his attitude toward Goethe whom he ranked below Schiller for a long time. He sees the reason for his inability to understand Goethe in his youthful lack of experience and purifying suffering. In contrast, striving for virtue and love of the sublime were sufficient to awaken sympathy for and understanding of Schiller. At a later time, however, the author of *Faust* strongly captivated the imagination of Herzen, and Schiller appeared to him in a less favorable light. But this cooler and somewhat indulgent attitude toward Schiller did not last very long :

At all events, I quickly returned to my senses, blushing because of my ungratefulness, and with burning tears of repentance I threw myself into the arms of Schiller. The world was not too narrow for the two of them—there will be room for them in my heart; they were friends; as such they shall go down to posterity.

But at that time of which I am speaking I was absolutely unable to understand Goethe : in his breast did not beat such a humane and tender heart as in Schiller's. Schiller with his Max, Don Carlos, lived in one sphere with me, how could I possibly not understand him?! Barren is the soul of that man who did not love Schiller in

[53] Gertsen, *PSS,* II, 400.

his youth, withered is the soul of him who once loved him and stopped loving him.[54]

Herzen thereupon calls to mind the tragedies of Schiller he read as a very young boy and how, at a more mature age, he re-read the same tragedies with different eyes.

The years of my first youth passed, and over Moor and Posa rose the dark and pensive shadow of Wallenstein, and still higher hovered the Maid of Orleans; more years passed—and Isabella, the wonderful mother, took her place beside the proud Maid. Where had Isabella been before? The passages which caused me, a fifteen-year-old, to rave in ecstasy have faded, the sallies of the students and the sententiousness in *Die Räuber*—and those which had scarcely aroused my attention, now move my soul. Yes, it is necessary to read the great poets anew, and especially Schiller, the poet of noble aspirations, in order to revive one's soul whenever it begins to wither.[55]

The interesting point in this passage is Herzen's reference to the figure of Isabella (from Schiller's tragedy *Die Braut von Messina*). Why does he call her "the wonderful mother," and why does he rank her with the Maid of Orleans? His admiration for Joan of Arc, the savior and liberator of her country, the chosen "dove and angel from heaven," appears completely natural and does not raise any questions. His high esteem of Isabella, on the other hand, seems at first glance both puzzling and surprising.

Contrary to Joan of Arc, Isabella is the ruin of her children and of her country—her character becomes one of the principal sources of the final catastrophe. Why then does Herzen call her "the wonderful mother"? Did he look at her exclusively from an aesthetic point of view? Did he appreciate in her only the genius of Schiller's portrayal of character? Perhaps—but a more convincing answer may be derived from his prevailing emotional attitude at the time, toward the dramatic figures of Schiller. Accordingly, it will be safe to assume that Herzen saw in her not the principal cause of the final catastrophe, but rather the loving mother who courageously rebelled against a cruel and inhuman tyrant. Furthermore, a note of freedom resounds in the words of Isabella which could not but appeal to the lonely exile who himself was the vicitm of tyrannical oppression: "Glaubt mir! Es liebt ein jeder, frei sich selbst / Zu leben nach dem eigenen Gesetz. . . ." Finally, the hypothesis is not to be discarded that Herzen regarded Isabella's revolt against her tyrannical husband as an analogy to Natasha's revolt against the severe restrictions imposed on her by her despotic family.[56]

In the same *Sketch Book of a Young Man* Herzen retraces also the story of his friendship with Ogarev and how it developed under the auspices of Schiller:

Our friendship which had begun to grow with the blessing of Schiller also bloomed with his blessing: Indeed, we assimilated the characters of all his heroes. I am unable to express the whole ecstasy of that time. Life opened before us triumphantly, majestically; we candidly swore to dedicate our life to the welfare of humanity; we pictured to ourselves an unattainable future without the smallest admixture of selfishness or personal considerations. These glorious days of youthful dreams and sympathies accompanied me far into life.[57]

[56] Natasha was forbidden to read the works of Schiller, moreover, she had to hide her love for Herzen. Cp. Herzen's letter to Natasha of February 26, 1838, in which he tells her to read *Don Carlos* in defiance of her family, "what will be, will be." Gertsen, *PSS,* II, 99–100.

[57] Gertsen, *PSS,* II, 403. N.B.: Herzen clearly speaks here of his dedication to the "welfare of humanity." Herzen's Soviet biographer, however, specifies only the Russians as the beneficiary of his plans and lofty dreams: "Reading Schiller, Herzen dreamed of unselfish deeds for the welfare of Russia." Ya. Elsberg, *Gertsen* (Moskva, 1956), p. 26.

In 1839 Herzen began to clash with Belinsky who—as we have seen—had turned into a bitter foe of idealism and Schiller during his period of "reconciliation with reality." Herzen resented especially Belinsky's attacks on the noble-minded heroes of Schiller's tragedies, on Karl Moor, Don Carlos, Marquis Posa, and all the other characters who, after the Decembrist revolt, had appeared to him like an embodiment of truth and justice inspiring him with a passionate longing for brotherhood and freedom. Another topic of dissension between Herzen and Belinsky was the question whether Goethe and Schiller ought to be considered as "objective" or as "subjective" poets. However, in this regard their quarrel was not a very serious one. In *My Past and Thoughts* Herzen gives the following account of it :

A long as our controversy revolved around the issue that Goethe was objective but that his objectivity was subjective whereas Schiller was a subjective poet but his subjectivity was objective and vice versa, everything proceeded peaceably. Nevertheless, more exciting problems were not long in arising.[58]

The reference to "more exciting problems" concerns Herzen's violent quarrel with Belinsky about Hegel and his famous thesis "What is real is rational, what is rational is real," which Belinsky, during the period of his "reconciliation with reality," interpreted in the most reactionary way as a justification of the despotic form of government in Russia and elsewhere. Herzen, whose ideology had formed under the influence of Schiller and Saint-Simon and who was steeped in the ideas of the French Revolution, immediately rose as a champion of the revolution and an implacable enemy of the conservative views of Belinsky. Goethe's rejection of the French Revolution was one of the reasons why, for a long time, the author of *Faust* was ranked lower by Herzen than Schiller, the author of *Wilhelm Tell* and honorary citizen of the

[58] Gertsen, *PSS,* XII. 14.

French Republic.[59] In fact, Schiller and the French revolution were so closely interwoven in Herzen's mind that in an essay on N. Kh. Ketcher (in *My Past and Thoughts*) he compares the French revolution to a tragedy by Schiller:

The Nineties, that stupendous, colossal tragedy in the manner of Schiller, with their philosophy and bloodshed, with their sinister virtues and bright ideals, with their Schillerean mood of sunrise and rebellion—the Nineties tore him [Ketcher] to pieces.[60]

After his return from exile, in 1840, Herzen immediately became an outstanding figure in Russian literary circles. Time and again, the names of Schiller and Goethe reappear in his numerous articles on progress, natural sciences, and literature. Thus, in his article "Dilettantes–Romanticists" (1842), he pays tribute to Schiller and Goethe for having replaced the narrowly national element in German literature by the universal-human one. Then, turning to the controversy of romanticism vs. classicism, he remarks, alluding to the two German poets:

Schiller and Goethe are exemplars of how to treat the romantic and classical elements in our own age. As a matter of fact, Schiller had more sympathy for romanticism than Goethe, but his principal sympathy was for the present, and his last and most mature works are purely *humanistic* (if I may use this term) and not romantic. And was there anything strange to Schiller in the classical world—to him who had translated Racine, and Sophocles, and Virgil?[61]

Whether Schiller's principal sympathy was for the present, as Herzen maintains, appears somewhat problematical. In favor of such an assumption speak Schiller's socio-political dramas and

---

[59] Ricarda Huch observes in this connection: "Schiller hatte die Französische Revolution begrüsst, Goethe sie abgelehnt. Herzen, der für Schiller schwärmte, war erfüllt von den Ideen der Französischen Revolution." *Michael Bakunin und die Anarchie* (Leipzig, 1923), pp. 50–51.

[60] Gertsen, *PSS*, XIII, 207.

[61] Gertsen, *PSS*, III, 189. [Italics Herzen's.]

his "Das Lied von der Glocke," against it—the historical and romantic tragedies and *Die Braut von Messina*. Against it is Schiller's overwhelming preoccupation with history, philosophy, and aesthetics. Schiller's "sympathy for the present" was, in reality, limited to the "Storm and Stress" period of his literary career—that is the period extending from the revolutionary *Die Räuber* to the liberal-philosophical *Don Carlos* (1781-87). It is only after the completion of *Die Braut von Messina* in 1803 that Schiller suddenly turns to the political and timely subject matter of a people's struggle for freedom and independence (*Wilhelm Tell*, 1804.)

Herzen's use of the terms "humanistic" and "romantic" is very interesting. The word "romantic" calls, almost as a matter of course, for its antonym "classical." But Herzen sets the word "romantic" in opposition to the word "humanistic," using the latter quite obviously in its original, etymological meaning and thus showing himself to be a critic of understanding and acumen. Speaking of Schiller's last and most mature works *(Die Braut von Messina, Wilhelm Tell, Demetrius)*, it would indeed be difficult to apply to them without heavy reservations, either the term "romantic" or the term "classical."

Herzen comprehended this difficulty, nay, impossibility, and understanding that Schiller in his last works had progressed far beyond the limits of the romantic and classical drama, very felicitously used the term "humanistic" in order to emphasize the fact that Schiller's principal concern in these dramas is man (homo) and not the ghosts of a romantic past.

Herzen's critical attitude toward romanticism becomes intelligible in the light of his gradual turn from romantic idealism to scientific positivism in the early forties. But this turn, it must be added, was never complete: "In love and in friendship, in his letters to his wife, in all things in general that concerned women,

Herzen remains an extreme romanticist."[62] He becomes critical of the romanticism of the past to be sure, yet Schiller's romantic–revolutionary dream of the future, which in Herzen's mind is inseparable from his "sympathy for the present," remains dear to his heart.

In the same article, "Dilettantes–Romanticists," Herzen then turns to an analysis of the nineteenth century which he finds remarkable for its spiritual independence :

In fact, the autonomous character of the nineteenth century revealed itself from its very first beginnings. It started with the sweeping development of the Napoleonic epoch, it was greeted by the poems of Goethe and Schiller, by the powerful philosophy of Kant and Fichte. Replete with memories of the events of the last decade, full of presentiments and questions, it was unable to trifle as did its predecessor. Schiller, in a cradle song, reminded it of its tragic destiny :

> Das Jahrhundert ist in Sturm geschieden,
> Und das neue öffnet sich mit Mord.[63]

The quoted lines are from a poem entitled "Am Antritt des neuen Jahrhunderts" (1801) in which the author asks where there is still a refuge for peace and freedom. In the last stanza Schiller gives the answer to this question :

> In des Herzens heilig stille Räume
> Musst du fliehen aus des Lebens Drang,
> Freiheit ist nur in dem Reich der Träume,
> Und das Schöne blüht nur im Gesang.

Herzen's choice of these lines from Schiller's poem seems to be indicative of a mood of resignation and disappointment pervading the Russian's mind during those years. In a letter to Passek,

---

[62] Ivan Tkhorzhevsky, *Russkaya Literatura* (Paris, 1950), p. 221. Cf. "Neizdannye pisma Gertsena," ed. L. Dogmer, *Novy Zhurnal*, XLIX (New York, 1957), 121–136.
[63] Gertsen, *PSS*, III, 190.

dated June, 1843, he relates how he sought refuge in the countryside, hoping to find comfort and relief in the familiar places of
his childhood :

With Pokrovskoye, Vasilevskoye, with their woods, and hills,
and river are connected my childhood, my boyhood, the time when
I believed in the sunrise of happiness, when I was carried away by
the ancient republican ideas and the ideals of Schiller . . . and
here I am, disillusioned and exhausted, looking for sympathy from
the very same places.[64]

Caprices and Musings is the title of a series of articles Herzen
wrote in Moscow in October, 1842. In his third article he finds
occasion to comment upon the two different aspects of the
German national spirit :

In Germany, Kotzebue and Schiller were at the same time
acclaimed with bursts of applause because in Germany, by a strange
coincidence of circumstances, sentimentality and conventionality
were the crust under which a powerful and healthy seed was stirring.
Schiller and Kotzebue are perfect and worthy representatives : the
former of everything sacred and human that originated in this
epoch, the latter—of everything filthy and repulsive that was decay-
ing at the very same time.[65]

All but simultaneously Herzen's friend Ogarev criticized the
conventionality and sentimentality of the German people. To be
sure, he went much farther than Herzen, including into his
criticism even what he called the "Philistine aspects" of Goethe
and Schiller.[66] Herzen did not raise a similar reproach against the
two German poets, on the contrary, at least in the case of Schiller,
he did not hesitate to speak of a "worthy representative of everything sacred and human."[67]

[64] Gertsen, *PSS,* III, 242.
[65] Gertsen, *PSS,* III,, 248.
[66] See following chapter, pp. 198–200.
[67] Incidentally, Herzen shows himself a more severe judge of Kotzebue

Very interesting is Herzen's appraisal of Goethe's *Die Leiden des jungen Werthers*. Adducing *Werther* as a striking example of German sentimentality, Herzen confesses that he shed "bitter tears" over the hero's last letters and over the details of his death, but then he critically adds:

One feels sorry for him—and yet Werther was an empty little boy. Compare him or Eduard [*Wahlverwandtschaften*] and all similar sufferers with characters that are extensively developed and who give a large share to their subjective Caesar without forgetting their universal-human share; compare them with Karl Moor, with Max Piccolomini, with Tell, finally, that kindly patriarchal *pater familias,* that energetic liberator of his fatherland. Notwithstanding all poetic escapades of Werther you understand that this good and tender soul is unable to step out of himself; that nothing enters into his lyricism except the little world of his heartfelt relationships! He has nothing, neither within nor without himself, except his love for Charlotte, in spite of the fact that he reads a little Homer and Ossian. One feels sorry for him![68]

There is not much to be added to these words of Herzen except, perhaps, that he somewhat overestimated the "universal-human share" of such figures as Max Piccolomini and Tell. Also Max knows little more than the "little world of his heartfelt relationships" with Wallenstein and Thekla; and Tell, "that kindly patriarchal *pater familias,*" does not, by any means, think of liberating his fatherland when he lies in wait for the Governor: "Des Feindes Leben ists, worauf er lauert.—Und doch an *euch* nur denkt er, liebe Kinder. . . ."[69]

From the standpoint of his new sympathy for positivism Her-

than even Schiller had been. In a letter to Kotzebue of October 1803, Schiller very generously admitted that Kotzebue's drama *Die Kleinstädter* had value "as theater." Cp. *Friedrich Schiller—Briefe,* ed. R. Buchwald (Leipzig, n.d.), p. 824.

[68] Gertsen, *PSS,* III, 262.

[69] *Wilhelm Tell,* IV, 3. [Italics Schiller's.]

zen declared war on sentimentality and romanticism. In the third part of his *Caprices and Musings* he ridicules the concept of love of some unnamed romantic poets:

Platonic, unhappy love harmonized with romanticism as well as romanticism with the Middle Ages. But its time has passed, yet the romantic poets do not want to admit it. Imagine, however, instead of the stately figure of Knight Toggenburg, iron-clad and with a cross on his breast,—imagine Sir Toggenburg, in a coat and with rubber galoshes, living somewhere in Paris, London, Brussels, waiting on the street for the "clatter of the window,"—and you will realize how awfully ridiculous this is. . . ."[70]

Herzen may have been right in his attack on a specific out-growth of exaggerated romanticism, but he probably did not completely understand its essence which is so rooted in human nature itself that its time can pass only with the passing of humanity. Whether it be called Pythian, bacchantic, sentimental, or romantic—it is one of the fundamental elements in the soul of man; and the positivist, the realist whose eyes are glued to the things of the earth will forever be challenged by the visionary who raises his eyes to the glory of the sunrise.

Summer, 1843, was the time when, during a stay in the village Pokrovskoye, Herzen plunged into the study of Schiller's *Briefe über die ästhetische Erziehung des Menschen*. The treatise produced a strong impression on him and on July 13, 1843, he made the following entry in his *Diary:*

I read *Von der ästhetischen Erziehung der Menschheit* by Schiller. A great and prophetic work! It was ahead of its time in many respects—just as Lessings *Die Erziehung des Menschenge-schlechts*. But the merits of Schiller were not duly appreciated in recent years. These letters [*Briefe über die ästhetische Erziehung des Menschen*] were written in 1795 or so—at that time Schelling had

---

[70] Gertsen, *PSS,* III, 265.

scarcely begun to write. Schiller started out from the position of Kant, but behold his fruits : full of juice, vivifying, magnificent— he progressed far beyond the horizon of the critical school. Here, as in some pages of Goethe, one hears the first sonorous and poetic chords of the new science.[71]

Herzen was still a boy when the reading of Schiller convinced him that the beauty of human exploits had not disappeared with the vanished ancient world, that also this world in which he was living was not divested of valor and grandeur. "This discovery caused a revolution in my life," Herzen acknowledges in his memoirs.[72] Now, in the Forties, Herzen's attention is again directed towards Schiller's unshakable faith in the progress and betterment of humanity, in the existence of the heroic traits in man and in the ultimate realization of his best potentials.

In Schiller's *Briefe über die ästhetische Erziehung des Menschen* Herzen found the philosophical justification for the belief that man was free and noble by his very nature. At the same time, however, he found there also Schiller's disbelief in the liberation of man by means of bloodshed and revolution. Here we approach an important idiosyncrasy in the aesthetic views of Herzen. Analyzing revolution in all its multiformity, Herzen discovered also its aesthetic aspects, and he was able to instill revolutionary spirit into aesthetics: "To him beauty is always inseparable not only from the idea of human freedom but also from the actual process of liberating humanity."[73] To be sure, by connecting the idea of beauty with the idea of revolution Herzen obviously deviates from the aesthetic views of Schiller who, in his treatise, forswears his previous faith in revolution. Paradoxically, in spite of Schiller's patent disbelief in the liberation of man by means of revolution, his *Briefe über die ästhetische Erziehung des*

[71] Gertsen, *PSS*, III, 126.
[72] Gertsen, *PSS*, II, 399.
[73] *Lit. Nasl.* XXXIX–XL, 120.

Menschen "were, in the interpretation of Herzen, a justification of this revolutionary struggle."[74]

Another interesting reference to Schiller's *Briefe über die ästhetische Erziehung des Menschen* is contained in Herzen's article "The Public Lectures of Mr. Granovsky" (1843). In the opinion of Herzen, Granovsky defined too narrowly the influence of Kant upon the science of history while overemphasizing the importance of Herder :

Kantianism has had an effect on all spheres of thought, and everywhere it has caused a revolution. History could not be an exception, and, in fact, Schiller started out from Kantianism and developed it further in his *Briefe über die ästhetische Erziehung des Menschen*. And this dissertation, cast in the form of letters, is a gigantic step forward in the development of the idea of history.[75]

This represents an incisive and far-sighted appreciation of Schiller's contribution to the idea of history and of his relationship to Kant which is borne out by contemporary literary theory.[76]

It is not often that a word of criticism is heard in Herzen's pronouncements on Schiller. Yet, in a letter to Ogarev, dated November 14, 1839, he does point to a serious shortcoming in his idol :

[74] *Lit. Nasl.*, XXXIX–XL, 121. It should be remembered, however, that after 1848 Herzen's revolutionary enthusiasm cooled considerably and that he often oscillated between revolution and liberal reform. According to M. E. Malia, Herzen's disappointment in the West was "aesthetic quite as much as political. Europe was morally as well as socially 'bourgeois' — petty, uninspiring, and lacking in spiritual grandeur." "Schiller and the Early Russian Left," p. 197.

[75] Gertsen, *PSS*, III, 282–283.

[76] Cp. Fritz Martini, *Deutsche Literaturgeschichte* (Stuttgart, 1952), p. 269: "Schillers Lehre [*Briefe über die ästhetische Erziehung des Menschen*] bedeutete den Höhenpunkt der klassischen Humanität. Kants Philosophie gab ihm die Grundlagen, aber er dachte weit über sie hinaus, und sein dichterisch-philosophisches Weltbild blieb nicht im Bereich der analytisch-logischen Erkenntnis, sondern drängte zur aktiven, sich entscheidenden Bildung des Zeitalters."

. . . love Schiller as much as you wish, he does not have the universality that is in Shakespeare and Goethe. Schiller conceived life one-sidedly, for this reason he incessantly aspired to the future, that's why it seemed to him : "Und das Dort wird nimmer hier," *but it is hier.*[77]

Herzen here quotes inaccurately from Schiller's poem "Der Pilgrim,"—in reality the line reads : "Und das Dort ist niemals hier !" Regarding Schiller's "one-sidedness" and incessant aspiration to the future, Herzen changed his opinion three years later when he declared that Schiller's "principal sympathy was for the present," and that "in these giants Goethe and Schiller conflicting and clashing tendencies merged, in the fire of genius, into a conception of astounding amplitude,"[78] only to reverse himself once again in a *Diary* jotting of February 6, 1844 :

I recall how I, surmounting a heavy fit of boredom, compelled myself to read the correspondence between Goethe and Schiller where there is an occasional flare-up of ideas worthy of a genius which, however, are lost in conventionality and Gellertean [Gellert, 1715–69, author of *Fabeln, Geistliche Lieder*] trifles; and when I compare it with the extraordinary fascination of these letters [by Georg Forster, 1754–94, traveler and politician]—then I get a very strange feeling. The fullness of life is more sublime than the one-sidedness of a genius.[79]

To be sure, Goethe himself had a higher esteem of the letters of his friend. In a conversation with Eckermann he said : "Seine [Schiller's] Briefe sind das schönste Andenken, das ich von ihm besitze, und sie gehören mit zu dem Vortrefflichsten, was er geschrieben. Seinen letzten Brief bewahre ich als ein Heiligtum unter meinen Schätzen." Obviously, Herzen was not in the right frame of mind ("heavy fit of boredom") when he forced himself

[77] *Lit. Nasl.* LXI, 388. [Italics Herzen's.]
[78] Gertsen, *PSS,* III, 189.
[79] Gertsen, *PSS,* III, 306.

to read the correspondence between Goethe and Schiller, and as a result he was unable to appreciate it. The letters of Georg Forster may be very interesting, indeed, but one can hardly compare them to the stylistic brilliance and profundity of thought by which the letters of Goethe and Schiller are distinguished.

Herzen's attack on the "conventionality" (Spiessbürgerlichkeit) of the Germans, including Goethe and Schiller, which had begun in 1842 reaches here its high point. But his sallies continue in the following years and in 1846 he strikes another blow at the "German Philistine." In an article of "Caprices and Musings" Herzen defines the Philistine as an "old youth" who has been unable to reconcile his adolescence with maturity, and who can be recognized by his hatred of Goethe and his enthusiasm for Schiller. Citing Goethe's Egmont as an outstanding literary example of an "old youth," Herzen turning to Schiller, continues:

Don Carlos, Marquis Posa, Max Piccolomini had to die in the springtide of life, but their images have remained for us inseparable from the features of their adolescent beauty, and how magnificent they are! . . . Had Piccolomini lived to become a general, Don Carlos—to the death of Philipp II, they would have outlived themselves. They would have played a grotesque role, or they would have been forced to change completely; yet the trouble is that you can perceive in them but little strength to accomplish any change. They are highly artistic as they are, but in order to preserve them in this quality it was necessary to save them by cutting short their lives.[80]

There was a time when Herzen himself came close to fitting his definition of a Philistine—a time when he was full of enthusiasm for Schiller and full of fear and misgivings about Goethe (Sketch Book of a Young Man). But in 1846 Herzen had

[80] Gertsen, PSS, IV, 405–406.

already arrived at an understanding of Goethe's genius, and his heart was not too narrow to contain "the two of them." This estimation of the German poets' superior place in literature made him sensitive to encroachments upon their poetic dignity. Thus, when the journalist and critic Pogodin dared to parallel Khomyakov and Yazykov with Goethe and Schiller, Herzen reacted sharply :

One may appreciate the talents of Messrs. Khomyakov, Yazykov, and one can value their poems highly, but there is a recognized feeling of decency and modesty which forbids placing one's friend or brother on the same level with Goethe and Schiller from a feeling of personal affection. There is something provincial in such an attitude.[81]

In 1847, having gained financial independence after the death of his father, Herzen left Russia for Western Europe and openly declared himself in favor of the European revolutionary movement.

For Russia itself Herzen envisaged a kind of agrarian socialism which he considered as the *sine qua non* of a rational and unhampered development of the Russian people. With regard to the mutual relationships between Western and Eastern Europe, Herzen expressed the belief that the world of the East would take the initiative in offering friendship and brotherhood to the proud and tradition-bound West :

The Slavic world, less acquainted with the arrogant, aristocratic point d'honneur, will give in first and extend its hand to its older brothers [Western Europe] like that tyrant of Syracuse who, stopping the executor, asked the self-sacrificing friends for one thing—to accept him as *the third:*

---

[81] Gertsen, *PSS,* XXII, 156. Khomyakov and Yazykov were both outstanding representatives of Slavophilism, and Herzen's polemical tone reflects his general hostility towards a movement which, in his opinion, was nothing but a "literary disease." Cp. Gertsen, *PSS,* III, 362.

So nehmet auch mich zum Genossen an,
Ich sei—gewährt mir die Bitte—
In Eurem Bunde der Dritte.

This place of *the third* is unusually fitting for the receptive Slavic world sympathizing both with the East and the West, a world diffuse and wide open, less rigidly defined and concentrated in its thought and in its geography, not fragmentized by high mountains or insurmountable traditions.[82]

The lines quoted by Herzen are taken from the last stanza of Schiller's ballad "Die Bürgschaft,"—a significant quotation which shows that Schiller, in spite of Herzen's turn to Saint-Simon, Feuerbach, and Hegel, has not lost his grip over Herzen's mind, continues as an influence even in his political thinking and in his dreams of a united European family of nations. Incidentally, Herzen's definition of the Slavic world as "receptive, sympathizing, diffuse," etc., involuntarily calls to mind Grillparzer's prophetic drama *Libussa* (1848) where the world of the Slavs has been described in analogous terms.[83]

Herzen's profound disillusionment with the failure of the revolution of 1848 is reflected in his writings. Banished from France after the victory of reaction, he did "not know where to escape, where to rest his head." In "Western Arabesques" *(My Past and Thoughts),* discoursing on the sorrowful restlessness of Byron, Herzen remarks:

Goethe, the realist, as well as Schiller, the romanticist, have not experienced that being torn to pieces [as Byron did]. The former was too religious, the latter—too much of a philosopher. Both could find reconciliation in the spheres of abstraction. If the "spirit of negation" is a jester like Mephistopheles, then the tear is not yet terrible; his derisive, eternally contradictory nature merges in a

[82] Gertsen, *PSS,* XIV, 824. [Italics Herzen's.]
[83] Cp. "Grillparzer and the East," *Monatshefte* (October 1955), pp. 273–284.

higher harmony, and in its own time the whole world is notified : sie ist gerettet.[84]

Herzen's reference to Byron is, of course, an allusion to his own devouring restlessness. That Schiller ranks here as a romanticist may seem interesting in the light of Herzen's earlier claim that Schiller principally was a realist. However, this ranking need not be in the nature of an inconsistency. Already in "Dilettantes-Romanticists" (1842) he had written that "Schiller had more sympathy for romanticism than Goethe," and the expression "Schiller, the romanticist," could simply be a shift of emphasis due to the comparison with Goethe.

The degree and intensity of Herzen's spiritual disquietude during the years of his forced migrations through Western Europe (1848–52) can be inferred from the passage in *My Past and Thoughts* where the frustrated revolutionary exclaims :

The "men of faith, men of love," as they call themselves in contrast to us, the "men of doubt and negation," have nevertheless known the tender plant with its root of hope nurtured throughout life; they do not know the *disease of truth,* they never had to leave behind a treasure with that "heart-rending wail" of which the poet speaks :

> Ich riss sie blutend aus dem wunden Herzen,
> Und weinte laut und gab sie hin.
>
> (Schiller, "Resignation")

Happy lunatics who never sober—inner struggle is unknown to them, they suffer from external causes, from evil people and accidents; internally all remains intact, their conscience remains calm and they rest contented.[85]

The "plant rooted in hope nurtured throughout life" was

---

[84] Gertsen, *PSS*, XIII, 387–388.

[85] Gertsen, *PSS*, XIII, 493. [Italics Herzen's.] The quotation from "Resignation" is not precise. In reality, Schiller says : "Und weinte laut, und gab sie ihr" (that is, Laura to Truth).

Herzen's dream of political freedom and social justice which had been shattered by the failure of the revolution in 1848. The parallel between Herzen's state of mind, at that time, and the state of mind of Schiller, as expressed in the poem "Resignation," appears to be very close. There is, in particular, in both the same obsession with the idea of "truth" in the name of which all personal happiness is sacrificed. Four years earlier, on July 9, 1844, Herzen had spoken as a fanatic of absolute "truth" when, in a letter to Granovsky, he solemnly declared : "Truth is always truth, and if it is true that Schiller made Kassandra say 'Und der Irrthum ist das Leben,' then, of course, every decent man would contemptuously reject such a gift [the gift of life]."[86] In 1848, standing before the ruins of his revolutionary dreams, Herzen may have unconsciously realized that there was, after all, some truth in Kassandra's affirmation : "Nur der Irrthum ist das Leben. . . ."[87]

In this mood of profound disillusionment and sorrow Herzen wrote a series of essays and dialogues entitled *From the Other Shore* (first published in German as : *Vom andern Ufer*). In one of the articles, dedicated to his son Alexander, Herzen voices deep pessimism regarding the future destinies of Europe : "This world [Europe] has outlived the epoch of its glory, the time of Schiller and Goethe has passed away, as has the time of Raphael and Buonarotti, the time of Voltaire and Rousseau, as the time of Mirabeau and Danton. . . ."[88] And one of the dialogues is preceded by a significant motto from Goethe's drama *Tasso:* "Der Mensch ist nicht geboren frei zu sein." The dialogue itself— a conversation between a gentleman and a lady—touches upon

---

[86] Gertsen, *PSS*, III, 410.

[87] Also Stankevich used to intersperse his letters with quotations from Schiller, and in one of his letters written in 1834, he quotes the very same line from the poem "Kassandra" : "Nur der Irrthum ist das Leben. . . ."

[88] Gertsen, *PSS*, V, 425.

the problem raised in Goethe's "Vorspiel auf dem Theater."[89] The lady, evidently expressing the views of Herzen himself, makes the following point :

Goethe represents in all his grandeur precisely your way of thinking : he alienates himself, he is content with his own greatness, and in this respect he is an exception. Did Schiller and Fichte behave like that, Rousseau and Byron, and all those men who were torturing themselves in order to lift the multitude, the masses, up to their own level? To me the poignant and desperate sufferings of these men which accompanied them sometimes to their graves, sometimes to the executioner's block or to the madhouse, are much more valuable than the tranquillity of Goethe.[90]

Schiller, with his sympathy for humanity, takes again the first place in Herzen's heart while the lack of this sympathy makes him see Goethe in a less favorable light although he was able to understand his genius "better than many enthusiastic admirers of the great poet and thinker."[91] To be sure, Herzen's antipathy for the "tranquillity" of Goethe was not entirely new— in one form or another it went back to the thirties when he criticized Goethe for his indifference to political affairs.

It was in the thirties too, in his *Sketch Book of a Young Man,* that Herzen had written of his friendship with Ogarev :

We were drawn to each other by some kind of mysterious urge, as two atoms of a homogeneous substance in a solution are drawn to each other by an affinity which is incomprehensible to them.[92]

These words apply with equal force to Herzen's singular relation-

---

[89] *Faust:* for whom shall the poet write?—for the many and the present, or for the few and the future?

[90] Gertsen, *PSS,* V, 466. Cp. Ogarev's dialogue "The Crowd" (1833–34) in which the theme of the "lifting up" of the uneducated masses plays a central role. Ogarev, *Izbrannye proizvedenia* (Moskva, 1956), II, 322–323.

[91] *Lit. Nasl.,* XXXIX–XL, 121.

[92] Gertsen, *PSS,* II, 402.

ship with Schiller. It is a rare spectacle to observe how the mind
of the Russian is again and again attracted by Schiller's powerful
genius. In 1853, after more than two decades of enthusiasm for
the German poet, Herzen writes in his memoirs :

> Schiller has remained our favorite; Schiller's poetry has not lost
> its influence upon me. Several months ago I read *Wallenstein* to my
> son—this is truly a gigantic work ! He who loses his taste for Schiller
> is either an old man or a pedant, has either become apathetic or
> forgetful of his own better self.[93]

This passage reflects Herzen's development as a social reformer
and revolutionary who went beyond the limited program of the
Decembrists in many regards, yet continued to oscillate between
Karl Moor and Marquis Posa, between a revolutionary Utopia
and a liberal-democratic Utopia :

> Often the Posa in Herzen recognized that Moor was a Utopian
> and supplanted the revolutionary Utopia of the robber by his own—
> liberal—Utopia. Yet often, Herzen realized this and understood
> Moor's profound truth and hostility toward a proprietary society,
> and together with this—the hopelessness of the robber's way. . . .[94]

In 1852 Herzen found a haven in England and opened there
the first free Russian printing shop abroad. Five years later, he
started publishing a periodical which he called *Kolokol (The
Bell)*. On the title page, under the name of the paper, Herzen

[93] Gertsen, *PSS*, XII, 76. Malvida von Meysenbug corroborates this confession of Herzen in her *Memoirs of an Idealist* where she writes that Herzen
read *Wallenstein* to his son and to her "with particular enthusiasm," "loved
this drama very dearly and regarded it as Schiller's best." *Gertsen v vospom.
sovremennikov*, p. 362.

[94] *Lit. Nasl.*, XXXIX–XL, 120. What the Soviet critic Lavretsky means
by Moor's hostility toward a "proprietary society" is not quite clear. Schiller
does not emphasize the fact that the society against which Karl Moor
rebelled was organised on the basis of the sanctity of private property, and
the impression prevails that Moor's revolutionary struggle was directed at
mankind as such: "Menschen—Menschen ! falsche, heuchlerische Krokodilbrut !" *Die Räuber*, I, 2.

placed the battle-cry "Vivos voco!" which he took from the motto of Schiller's poem "Das Lied von der Glocke." The voice of Herzen's *Bell* penetrated deep into the hearts of the Russian people raising the lonely exile in a suburb of London to one of the most powerful political figures of Russia.

The one hundredth anniversary of Schiller's birth, on November 10, 1859, was commemorated by celebrations throughout Europe and the rest of the civilized world. Commenting on the preparations for such a celebration in England, Herzen writes in a letter to the historian Michelet, under the date of November 4, 1859 :

On se prépare (même ici) [à] fêter le jour de naissance de *Schiller* —dans le Crystal Palace. C'est bien que les grands hommes de l'Allemagne sont morts—et qu'ils ne peuvent assister eux mêmes à leur jubilés.[95]

London's Crystal Palace was, at that time, a meeting place for fanatical revivalists whom Herzen, in his essay on Robert Owen, sarcastically characterized as :

. . . those crowds which fill to the last seat the colossal aisle of the Crystal Palace listening with avidity and hand-clappings to the preachments of some insipid medieval bachelor who, I don't know how, has appeared in our century and who threatens the multitudes with heavenly chastisements and earthly calamities in the vulgar language of Schiller's Capuchin in *Wallenstein's Lager*.[96]

Thence Herzen's irony and indignation in his letter to Michelet : ". . . fêter le jour de naissance de *Schiller*—dans le Crystal Palace." In spite of his disgust, Herzen prevailed upon himself to attend the celebration. A letter to his son reflects his disappointment with the whole affair :

[95] Gertsen, *PSS*, X, 146. [Italics Herzen's.] For the value of the *Fest* for all the Germans in London at that period see K. H. Schaible, *Geschichte der Deutschen in England* (Strassburg, 1885), p. 458.
[96] Gertsen, *PSS*, XIV, 481.

How did *you* celebrate your Schiller? Here a crowd of fourteen thousand participated in the festivities, but without *entrainement;* the address by Kinkel was boring, the bust by Grass well done. The rest Tata [Herzen's daughter] will describe to you.[97]

A few days later, in a leter to Ogarev, Herzen makes yet another reference to a Schiller commemoration : "Herwegh was the hero of the Schiller festivities in Zürich."[98] A name to arouse bitter thoughts in Herzen : Herwegh, the German revolutionary poet, was the man who had eloped with his wife Natasha and thus shattered his romantic belief in the celestial nature of woman.

Having lost his faith in the success of a socialist revolution in Europe, profoundly shaken by the betrayal of his wife, long since disbelieving in the charity of Divine Providence, Herzen went through a severe spiritual crisis. To save himself from utter despair, he concentrated his love and faith and enthusiasm on Russia and the Russian People. Herzen returned to the land of his fathers—not physically but in sentiment and spirit. His fast growing periodical *Kolokol* became his bridge to Russia and his link with the Russian people. Every week an enormous stream of copies of the *Kolokol* surged over the Russian frontiers. The Russian police, unable to stem this flood of illegal literature from London, thought of the most desperate measures to silence its author. Agents of the Third Division were dispatched to England to abduct or assassinate Herzen—but their scheme was thwarted. In a letter to the Russian ambassador in London, written in October, 1861, Herzen indignantly denounced the murderous plot of the Russian police : "How disgraceful that it [the Russian government] will be suspected of setting up snares

[97] Gertsen, *PSS*, X, 151. [Italics mine.] Letter of November 15, 1859.
[98] Gertsen, *PSS*, X, 153. Letter of November 19, 1859.

and sending out secret service Bruti across seas and mountains, 'den Dolch im Gewande.' "[99]

Even in a moment of acute danger to his life, there flash through Herzen's mind lines of Schiller, terms of Schiller's poetry! The Russian government deemed it wise not to reply directly to the embarrassing charge of murderous complicity with its secret police leveled at it by Herzen, but it responded indirectly through the mouth of one of its representatives who called himself D. K. Chédo-Ferroti (pseudonym), contesting all charges and accusing Herzen of lunacy and megalomania :

In the same letter [Herzen's letter to the Russian ambassador in London], speaking of assassins sent out "across seas and mountains, den Dolch im Gewande," you compare yourself, by quoting Schiller, to a ruling monarch, viz. to Dionysus of Syracuse.[100]

After the liberation of the serfs, in 1861, Herzen's political influence declined. Large sections of the Russian population became estranged from him by his pro-Polish sympathies during the Polish insurrection in 1863–64. Moreover, a new generation had grown up in Russia to whom the reformist theories of Herzen appeared old-fashioned and even reactionary. When the young radicals published their manifesto, in May, 1862, Herzen rebuffed it as un-Russian. In his opinion, it was a hotchpotch of ill-digested Schiller, Gracchus, Babeuf, and Feuerbach. An article of July, 1862, entitled "Young and Old Russia," reflects this negative attitude. In an indulgent tone of gentle irony Herzen "politely calls the young revolutionaries' attention to the fact that your costumes of Karl Moor, Gracchus, and Babeuf look on the Russian scene not only old-fashioned but downright like a masquerade." And he continues :

[99] Gertsen, *PSS,* XI, 249. Cf. Schiller's ballad "Die Bürgschaft" from which Herzen took the German quotation.
[100] Gertsen, *PSS,* XI, 295.

In "Young Russia" [title of the proclamation of the young radicals] there is really as much of Schiller as of Babeuf. The noble and somewhat rapturous and metaphysical transports of Schiller disguised themselves very often as the sanguinary locutions of Moor, Posa, and Ferdinand, but behind them beat his loving and eternally young heart.[101]

Herzen's reference to the "sanguinary locutions" of Moor *(Die Räuber)* and Ferdinand *(Kabale und Liebe)* is well founded in Schiller's text—less clear is his allusion to Marquis Posa *(Don Carlos)* whose mode of expression can scarcely be called "sanguinary."

The intervention of Napoleon III in Italy was watched closely by Herzen who had not lost his interest in Western European affairs. After Garibaldi's defeat in the Battle of Mentona (November 3, 1867), Herzen, with his intuitive insight into the process of historical development, exclaimed : "Holy father, now it is your turn!" What he meant by "Holy father," Herzen explains in his article "After the Attack," dated December 31, 1867 : "These words I really feel the urge to reiterate to Bismarck. The pear is ripe and without his Excellency the affair cannot be settled. Do not stand on ceremony, Count!"[102] Already on a previous occasion Herzen had made reference to the same scene in Schiller's *Don Carlos,* namely when he received the news that Prince Golitsin was heading a commission for the criminal persecution of radical students in Kharkov. Noting that the very same Prince Golitsin had sentenced him and his friends to prison and exile more than a quarter century ago, Herzen makes the wistful comment : "All political surgeons . . . have a life-span of

[101] Gertsen, *PSS,* XV, 315.

[102] Gertsen, *PSS,* XIV, 763. Herzen's quotation from Schiller's *Don Carlos* (V, 11), "Holy father, now it is your turn," is not accurate. In reality, King Philipp says to the Grand Inquisitor: "Kardinal, ich habe das Meinige getan. Tun Sie das Ihre."

two centuries; in Schiller's *Don Carlos* the inquisitor is depicted as a senex, a hundred years old, blind and grey."[103]

As a disciple of Schiller, Herzen did not believe that man is evil by nature. Following the author of the *Briefe über die ästhetische Erziehung des Menschen,* Herzen put his trust in the capability of the human race to grow spiritually and progress morally, and he rejected historical determinism and any theory that would have extraneous forces mysteriously directing the course of human history.

In a letter to his oldest daughter, Herzen called Schiller "a great propagandist" who "made propaganda of everything."[104] As a matter of fact, in a certain sense Schiller was just that—yet with a basic difference: his "propaganda" did not, as did Herzen's, deviate from the disinterested pursuit of truth, beauty, and virtue; pure humanity was his aim, not the realization of a party program or doctrine. Conceiving of revolution and human freedom in terms of Schiller's aestheticism, Herzen strongly believed in the power of propaganda and persuasion. So much so that almost all of his political essays are "primarily propaganda [tracts] and written not in the disinterested pursuit of truth for itself, but with the aim of influencing other men's actions and opinions."[105]

Herzen's rejection of historical determinism also throws a new light upon his high esteem for Schiller's historical tragedies in which, side by side with the influence of "destiny" or "the stars," room is given to the spontaneous and incalculable play of human psychology.[106] Herzen himself strove for a long time to incor-

---

[103] Gertsen, *PSS,* X, 344. "Prince A. F. Golitsin," article of June, 1860.

[104] Elsberg, *Gertsen,* p. 67. Herzen wrote his letter in 1867.

[105] Mirsky, *A History of Russian Literature,* p. 212.

[106] Cp.: "In deiner Brust sind deines Schicksals Sterne." *Die Piccolomini* (II, 6); "Der Zug des Herzens ist des Schicksals Stimme." *Die Piccolomini* (III, 8). Cp. also the concluding line of *Die Braut von Messina*: "Der Übel grösstes aber ist die Schuld."

porate his concept of history as an unfathomable creative process
into his more serious writings. Sometimes, however, his confi-
dence in the perfectibility of mankind led him to be over-opti-
mistic about the "spontaneous and unpredestined stream of
history." Such is the case in his article "Journalists and Terrorists" in which he peremptorily declares: ". . . the May of
death, like the May of life, blooms only once und nicht wieder.
The terror of the Nineties [French revolution] cannot be repeated."[107]

To the last days of his life, Herzen preserved for Schiller an
undiminished sentiment of veneration. When Herzen was criticized by a friend for being dry-as-dust in his "Views from Switzerland," he parried with a reference to his beloved poet:

I stick to my old teacher Schiller. "Musst ins Weite dich entfalten
Soll sich dir die Welt gestalten," says Schiller. Well, and if little can
be derived by drawing from various streams and pools—then, of
course, the fault is mine : either my bucket is too small, or my hand
trembles.[108]

Herzen, very significantly, quotes here from Schiller's poem
"Sprüche des Konfuzius" the principal thought of which is epitomized in its concluding lines:

Nur Beharrung führt zum Ziel,
Nur die Fülle führt zur Klarheit,
Und im Abgrund wohnt die Wahrheit.

In his youth, Herzen had been obsessed by the idea of truth.[109]
Now, at the close of an eventful life, he may have sensed the
exasperating wisdom of the dictum: "Und im Abgrund wohnt
die Wahrheit,"—in depths inaccessible to human vision. All his

---

[107] Gertsen, *PSS*, XV, 373. The quotation is from Schiller's "Resignation":
"Des Lebens Mai blüht einmal und nicht wieder. . . ."
[108] Gertsen, *PSS*, XXI, 486. "To the Other Side," article written in
September 1869.
[109] Cp. letter to Granovsky of July 9, 1844. Gertsen, *PSS*, III, 410.

life he strove with tireless perseverance to come closer to truth as he understood it, all his life he struggled against heavy odds to see the dawn of a humane and rejuvenated civilization. Yet after a brief intermezzo of unparalleled political success his noble striving terminated in loneliness and disenchantment. In 1870 Herzen closed his eyes forever. Faithful to his solemn oath on the Vorobyovy Hills, he had dedicated his life to the welfare of humanity. A remarkable Russian—writer, thinker, man of action who often wavered between skepticism and idealism but who never relinquished his "respect for the dreams of his youth."

VI

Ogarev

THE NAME OF NIKOLAY PLATONOVICH OGAREV (1813–77) IS intimately connected with that of Herzen. From their romantic childhood friendship under the auspices of Schiller developed later a firm political alliance which culminated in the co-founding and editorship of the periodical *Kolokol* (1857). It is to Ogarev that Herzen dedicated his memoirs, *My Past and Thoughts*. But this friendship proved a heavy burden on the shoulders of Herzen, both politically and financially. As a Russian critic says: "He [Ogarev] was to a great extent Herzen's evil angel, not on account of any evilness of his intentions, but because he was entirely devoid of that genius of political tact which was so prominent in his great associate."[1]

For a long time Ogarev's political activity overshadowed his small yet noteworthy literary production. As a poet—a very subjective one—he ranks high among the followers of Lermontov. Reflection, critical introspection, dissatisfaction with the world and with his own self are the characteristic features of his poetry, the best part of which is dedicated to melancholy recollections of an irretrievable past. In a great measure this poetry of wistful

[1] D. S. Mirsky, *A History of Russian Literature* (New York, 1949), p. 139. Note, however, that Herzen himself never thought of his friendship with Ogarev in terms of a "burden." Cf. in this connection "Neizdannye pisma A. I. Gertsena k N. I. i T. A. Astrakovym," ed. L. L. Dogmer, *Novy Zhurnal*, XLVII (New York, 1956), 73–74, and XLIX (1957), 121, 126, 131, 136. See also P. V. Annenkov, *Literaturnye vospominania* (Leningrad, 1928), p. 518.

longing and sorrowful disillusionment has to be regarded as a transcript of Ogarev's own ill-fated biography: "Ogarev was twice unhappily married, lived in exile, lost all his immense property in Russia, trustful, deceived, disappointed."[2]

As a child Ogarev became acquainted with the works of Byron, Rousseau, Voltaire, and Schiller, and when he first met Herzen his mind was already impregnated with the revolutionary romanticism of Schiller's poetry. But his first contacts with Herzen did not immediately lead to a cordial relationship:

Real friendship began with an encounter in February 1826. On that morning Ogarev's grandmother died and he was brought to Herzen . . . Then a serious conversation developed—about the unprinted poems of Pushkin and Ryleyev, about Schiller, about the liberation "from the tyrant" (Nicholas I).[3]

In a later autobiographical sketch, entitled "My Confession" (1860-62), Ogarev recalls the importance of his acquaintance with Herzen for his spiritual evolution: "The compass of my life increased, everything conspired to tune it ever higher: Schiller, the Russian literature of the decembrists, their annihilation. . . ."[4] The concepts and ideals of the forbidden decembrist literature merged thus in Ogarev's heart with the socio-critical pathos of Schiller's revolutionary tragedies—a process that was closely paralleled by the subsequent spiritual development of his newly-won friend Herzen.

Very early, too, Ogarev felt an urge to occupy himself with philosophy. In his quest for philosophical reading matter he turned to C. A. Tiedge's *Urania*. Before long his searching mind was satiated with this author and he started looking for a more substantial thinker. Schiller, the philosopher, entered his spiritual horizon:

[2] Ivan Tkhorzhevsky, *Russkaya Literatura* (Paris, 1950), p. 333.
[3] *Literaturnoye Nasledstvo* (Moskva, 1953), LXI, 668.
[4] N. P. Ogarev, *Izbrannye proizvedenia* (Moskva, 1956), II, 416.

But soon my need for philosophical knowledge found much more nourishment in the philosophical letters of Schiller. Schiller was for me everything : my philosophy, my spiritual fatherland, my poetry. Not the Germans should celebrate his one hundredth anniversary but we.[5]

There can be little doubt that Ogarev played an important role in acquainting Herzen with philosophy in general and German philosophy in particular, a fact which helps to explain Herzen's rapid acceptance of the German idealistic philosophy once his friendship with Ogarev had developed. A Soviet critic remarks :

Ogarev had a more extensive knowledge of German culture than Herzen, specifically, he called Herzen's attention to the philosophical principles of Schiller's revolutionary aesthetics during their common reading of Schiller's "Philosophical Letters."[6]

Ogarev's youthful passion for Schiller made it difficult for his French teacher to introduce him to the beauties of Racine. In his autobiographical sketch Ogarev recalls: "Racine did not

[5] *Lit. Nasl.*, LXI, 686, "My Confession." Cp. also Martin Malia, *Alexander Herzen and the Birth of Russian Socialism* (Cambridge, Mass., 1961), p. 38 ff.

[6] L. Piper, *Mirovozzrenie Gertsena* (Moskva–Leningrad, 1935), p. 43. It is not quite clear what the critic means by "Schiller's revolutionary aesthetics." There appears to be nothing "revolutionary" in the accepted sense of the word, about Schiller's aesthetical views in his "Philosophical Letters." In fact, their quintessence is downright counter-revolutionary : "Lasst uns helle denken, so werden wir feurig lieben. Seid vollkommen, wie euer Vater im Himmel vollkommen ist, sagt der Stifter unsers Glaubens. Die schwache Menschheit erblasste bei diesem Gebote, darum erklärte er sich deutlicher : liebet euch untereinander." [*SW*, XI, 128.] In the love of God and man human knowledge achieves its highest completion — this is the core of the philosophical deliberations of Julius–Schiller. Nor can the aesthetical and philosophical writings of the mature Schiller be termed "revolutionary" by any stretch of the imagination. Not revolution but harmonious education toward beauty and freedom is the message of Schiller's *Briefe über die ästhetische Erziehung des Menschen*. They signify the apex of his humanism and the culmination of his philosophical thinking.

exist for me beside Schiller."[7] To be sure, his German teacher Aller was "a fool" but in the eyes of Ogarev he had one advantage :

He read with me Schiller, in the way of a habit, of course, not out of sympathy—directing my attention at the *beauties of the poetry* with a tender emotion which did not suit him. But I did not notice that; I saw Schiller and not Aller. The string of a poetical and civic-philosophical [filosofsko-grazhdanskogo] mood was plucked. Its tone harmonized with the tone of the contemporary prohibited Russian literature. I was touched to the quick, and Aller's lessons became to me an essential nourishment.[8]

How did it happen that Aller became the mainspring of his pupil's freethinking? He, a "bureaucrat in his spirit, in his methods, and in everything—even in his dark-green coat which was buttoned up to the two lower buttonholes."[9] How did this tedious schoolmaster manage to interpret Schiller and to kindle Ogarev's enthusiasm? In his autobiographical sketch Ogarev frankly admits : "I do not know." The answer, of course, is— and Ogarev must surely have subconsciously felt it—that there was a spiritual affinity between the pupil and the author and that the teacher's function was merely the "mechanics" that provided the occasion and the materials.

Schiller is mentioned frequently in Ogarev's prose and many of his poems also are pervaded by a characteristic mood of melancholy distinctly reminiscent of the German poet : ". . . a note of resignation in the sense of Schiller's sounds throughout his poetry, amongst which fierce poems of revolt and of masculine energy are few."[10] It is precisely for this lack of revolutionary

[7] Ogarev, *Izbr. proizved.,* II, 417.
[8] Ogarev, *Izbr, proizved., II,* 408. [Italics Ogarev's.]
[9] *Lit. Nasl.,* LXI, 687. Cp. V. Putintsev, *N. Ogarev* (Moskva, 1959), p. 8.
[10] P. Kropotkin, *Ideals and Realities in Russian Literature* (New York, 1925), p. 275. See also *Opisanie rukopisey N. P. Ogareva,* ed. A. Z. Chernyak (Moskva, 1952), pp. 16, 49.

ardor and masculine energy that Ogarev was dubbed a "meek revolutionary Oblomov" by another of his countrymen.[11]

From one of his later poems, in hich Ogarev looks back at the happy days of his childhood in his usual mood of sweet sorrow, it can be inferred that Schiller's *Wallenstein* had a special place among his favorite books. At the same time the poem gives a vivid self-characterization of Ogarev as a boy:

> You will remember that by temper
> I was quiet, gentle, even tender,
> I loved green fields,
> And the dark woods, and the slope of the bank,
> The talk of my friends, the rustle of the brook,
> Songs of rebellion amidst the peace of night,
> And Schiller's Thekla, and my dreams,
> And the wistful rays of the moon![12]

Ogarev's reference to Thekla, this embodiment of tender and spiritualized love, throws light not only upon his youthful conception of ideal love but also upon his attitude toward women in general. In contrast to his sister, who gave him the shocking spectacle of a very unspiritual and earthly-minded passion, Ogarev—in this regard similar to Herzen—yearned for ideal love. So intense was this yearning that even the now unsublimated affairs of his sister assumed with him the celestial "glow of Schiller's heroines."[13] But, as Ogarev says in his autobiographical sketch, at that time he had not yet found an object for his

[11] Tkhorzhevsky, *Russkaya Literatura*, p. 332.

[12] Ogarev, *Izbr. proizved.*, II, 55. Reporting on his visit to Wallenstein's castle in Eger (1841), Ogarev lovingly recalls Thekla whom he regards as "Schiller's best creation." Cp. M. Gershenzon, *Obrazy proshlago* (Moskva, 1912), p. 405. For a characterization of Ogarev's poetry see Gershenzon's *Istoria Molodoy Rossii* (Moskva, 1908), pp. 294–315. An interesting analysis of Schiller's *Wallenstein* is given by B. M. Eichenbaum, "Tragedii Schillera v svete yego teorii tragicheskogo," Sbornik *Iskusstvo staroye i novoye* (St. Petersburg, 1921), pp. 113–127.

[13] Ogarev, *Izbr. proizved.*, II, 419.

love. He did not know then that he was destined never to find
the heavenly love of his dreams. With the passing years, however,
Ogarev began to sense that he would not find the image of his
reveries upon this earth. In a letter to Herzen he writes with a
touch of discouragement: "Still another passion devours me:
love of a woman. From pole to pole I search for this heavenly
love, but instead of a dreamlike Louise [Schiller, *Kabale und
Liebe*], a Faustian Gretchen or a bayadere crosses my path."[14]

When Ogarev conceived the idea of writing down the memorable events of his childhood and adolescence he described to his
friend Herzen the difficulties of such an undertaking and traced
the history of their spiritual development. Speaking of the factors
and forces which influenced him most in the years of his intellectual growth, Ogarev mentions Schiller as one of the great and
decisive inspirations of his youth:

To begin writing reminiscences from one's childhood or
adolescence is perplexing: Everything is so confused and vague. But
I cannot help pausing upon a few paramount aspects, those moments
of sublime pleasure which influenced all my later development.
Thus, I cannot forget the first impressions which shook me profoundly (and, soit dit en parenthèse, also you)—that is to say, the
reading of Schiller and Rousseau, and the Fourteenth of December.
Under these three influences, so very similar to one another, we
accomplished our transition from childhood to adolescence.[15]

As strange as it may seem, it was in these idealistic influences
par excellence that lay the hidden seed of Ogarev's later realism
—a realism, to be sure, which never could completely rid itself

[14] N. P. Ogarev, *Izbrannye sotsialno-politicheskie i filosofskie proizvedenia*
(Moskva, 1952), II, 274. Cp. also Martin Malia, "Schiller and the Early
Russian Left," *Harvard Slavic Studies* (Cambridge, Mass., 1957), IV,
194–195.

[15] Ogarev, *Izbr. sots.–polit. i filos. proizved.*, II, 22. Cp. also M. T.
Iovchuk, *Filosofskie i sotsiologicheskie vzglyady Ogareva* (Moskva, 1957),
p. 39.

of romantic hues and overtones. Schiller played an important and very special role in this development toward realism :

What has the high-minded Schiller given to us? Noble aspirations. But these noble aspirations were filled with doubts and with negation of the rationality and justice of contemporary society. What became important to us in Schiller's heroes and in his philosophical letters was not the idealization, not the spirituality of his concepts. This was transitory. Important was the fact that to justify his idealization and spirituality we had to touch real society and point out the lie, point out the sore, point out the suffering. . . . The combination of these influences [Schiller, Rousseau, the Decembrist revolution] had this effect that our first step in the sphere of thought was not the quest of an abstract, not a beginning from an absolute, but a collision with real society which aroused in us a passion for analysis and criticism.[16]

Ogarev's "collision with real society" soon brought him also into conflict with the guardians of that society—the Russian bureaucrats and the Russian police. His enthusiasm for Schiller, his activity in the political circle of Herzen, and, finally, an incautious letter which he wrote to Herzen on July 30, 1833, prepared the ground for a catastrophe. Ogarev's letter contained a passage which incriminated him heavily in the eyes of the Okhrana :

In a moment of murderous boredom which was consuming me I took to reading *Wilhelm Tell*. Friend, if you have not read it for a long time, for heaven's sake, read it and read it often, as often as possible. This drama portrays an epoch of crisis. Oh! what I felt when I was reading it, you simply can't imagine! You will understand when you read it again, especially if you read it in a moment of hatred, anger, and bitterness.[17]

Among the social concepts of Rousseau, Ogarev and his friend

[16] *Literaturnoye Nasledstvo* (Moskva, 1941), XXXIX–XL, 358–359.
[17] Ogarev, *Izbr. sots-polit. i filos. proizved.*, II, 266.

had been struck by the sonorous and challenging sentence: "l'homme est né libre et partout il est dans les fers." What impressed them most was not so much the statement that "l'homme est né libre"—this was accepted by them on faith—but the soul-stirring sequel that "partout il est dans les fers." This was a fact of which the young Russian generation of the thirties was only too painfully aware, growing up as they did under the gallows which cast their ominous shadows across Russia. No wonder then that the revolutionary poetry of Schiller should evoke such a resounding echo in the hearts of the young Russians: The ideas of Schiller's champions of freedom and humanity were to them a confirmation of their own patriotism and that lofty concept of civic liberty for which the Decembrists had died or had to suffer exile.

This is the reason why *Wilhelm Tell,* that drama of an oppressed people's struggle for dignity and liberty, produced such an overwhelming impression on young Ogarev. The figure of the independent and energetic tyrant-killer Tell who despite his individualism personifies the innermost hopes and wishes of the whole people merged in the mind of Ogarev with the images of the Decembrist heroes, those brave and lonely fighters for freedom who had given expression to the inarticulate aspirations of the Russian people.

There may have even been moments when Ogarev projected *himself* in the role of a Tell and yearned to strike a daring blow for his fatherland as Tell had done for the Swiss confederation. Such, at any rate, was the interpretation given to Ogarev's letter by the investigating commission when, after his arrest in 1834, he and his friends were questioned about his reference to Schiller's drama *Wilhelm Tell:*

The investigating commission saw in Ogarev's reference to the famous drama by F. Schiller proof of the existence of a conspiracy within the [Herzen] circle to assassinate the Tsar. The letter, with part of it underlined by the commission, (from the words "read it" to the end of the paragraph), was presented to Ogarev, Herzen, and the other prisoners with the demand of explanation.[18]

The accused denied the existence of any regicidal plans and we may believe them even though, at one time or another, both Ogarev and Herzen had identified themselves with some of the freedom-loving heroes of Schiller.[19] But this identification had been practiced by a group of romantic-utopian youths which had not the slightest resemblance to a realistical hardbitten terroristic organization.

From the time of Ogarev's collision with the realities of Russian society dates his sketch "The Crowd" (1833–34). Written in the form of a dialogue between two friends, Voldemar and Leonid, who have met on a busy square in Moscow, it reflects Ogarev's Schillerean attitude toward the uneducated masses of Russia. Voldemar-Herzen, who is here portrayed in the role of a skeptic, sarcastically ridicules the feverish activity of the multitude. "Isn't it funny," he asks, "to watch all these people?— They are busy all their life long and accomplish nothing!" But Leonid-Ogarev, the idealist and dreamer, disagrees with his friend. A feeling of pity and sorrow seizes him at the sight of the crowds. In terms reminiscent of Schiller's *Briefe über die*

---

[18] Ogarev, *Izbr. sots.-polit. i filos. proizved.*, II, 590 (notes).

[19] In *My Past and Thoughts* Herzen says in reference to their common reading of Schiller: "From Möros sneaking with his dagger in his sleeve 'to free the city from the tyrant' ["Die Bürgschaft"], from Wilhelm Tell waiting for the Governor on the narrow path in Küssnacht, it was easy to pass to the Fourteenth of December and to [Tsar] Nicholas." See A. I. Gertsen, *Polnoye sobranie sochineniy i pisem,* ed. Lemke (St. Petersburg, 1919–25), XII, 72. Cp. also the following passage: "I wrote to Nik [Ogarev], somewhat worried because he loved Fiesco too ardently, and warned him that behind 'every' Fiesco stood his Verrina." *Ibid.,* XII, 76–77. For an outline of the Russian government's attitude toward the plays of Schiller see A. Altshuller and V. Tsinkovich, "Schiller v Rossii," *Teatr,* V (Moskva, 1955), 143–145.

ästhetische Erziehung des Menschen he demands that the masses be led to a recognition of their responsibilities as autonomous human beings and public-spirited citizens and that they be taught how "to work for the common weal."[20]

As the years passed Ogarev did not become oblivious of the "moments of sublime pleasure" which Schiller had bestowed upon him in the questing days of his adolescence. In a letter to Herzen, Ogarev conjures up the time when they both, with pounding hearts, used to read aloud from the works of Schiller on the Vorobyovy hills near Moscow:

Soon it will be decided whether I shall go to that place [a health resort in the Caucasus] or not. I believe that I shall go. Then we will recall our glorious youth on the Vorobyovy hills, we will grapple resolutely with the present and fearlessly confront the future. Friend! There are many, many great and wonderful things in this future, many thunderstorms and clouds, but these thunderstorms will sweep away the dust, and out of them beneficial rain will pour.

> Du musst glauben, du musst wagen,
> Denn die Götter leihn kein Pfand.
> Nur ein Wunder kann dich tragen
> In das schöne Wunderland.[21]

Reading these lines, it is hard to believe that twelve years have passed since the two friends read Schiller on the Vorobyovy hills, and that Ogarev has become a realist in the meantime—as he himself affirms in "My Confession"—dedicated to the study of natural sciences and mathematics. Reading the verses from Schiller's "Sehnsucht," one seems to be in the presence of an adolescent Ogarev, still in his teens, an exalted youth dreaming

[20] Ogarev, *Izbr. proizved.*, II, 322–323. Cp. also D. Chizhevsky, "Schiller v Rossii," *Novy Zhurnal*, XLV (New York, 1956), 119.

[21] Ogarev, *Izbr. sots-polit. i filos, proizved.*, II, 293. Letter to Herzen of the end of April, 1838. For the "glorious youth on the Vorobyovy hills" cp. Gertsen, *Poln. sobr. soch. i pisem*, XII, 73–74. See also Otto P. Peterson, *Schiller in Russland* (New York, 1934), p. 112.

of struggles for the welfare of mankind and embodying his
dreams in the images of Schiller.[22] At approximately the same
time, in 1837 or 1838, Ogarev made another reference to Schiller which sheds light on a certain aspect of his attitude toward
the German poet:

Ich liebe . . . die Philosophie—das ist die Poesie des Intellektes,
grosse, allumfassende Dichtkunst; auch einem Philosophen, wie
einem Dichter, ist die Begeisterung nötig. Descartes und Schiller,
Goethe und Spinoza sind gleicherweise Dichter.[23]

This passage reveals the Schiller who gains Ogarev's enthusiastic
admiration. It is Schiller, the philosopher, the impassioned and
inspired "poet of the intellect," who evokes Ogarev's sympathy
and veneration alongside of Schiller, the creator of soul-stirring
tragedies and rebellious ballads. This predilection for the "poet
of the intellect" was characteristic not only of Ogarev but also
of Herzen, Stankevich, Bakunin, and many other representatives
of the philosophically-minded Russian youth of the Thirties.

On April 18, 1839, Ogarev wrote a letter to his wife Maria
which is interesting because in it a polemical element makes its
appearance in Ogarev's hitherto uncritical attitude toward Schiller. Discoursing on the nature of true poetic inspiration and
quoting Homer, Shakespeare, and Goethe as illustrative examples, Ogarev remarks:

Note that all great poets are naïve. Schiller once divided poetry
into sentimental and naïve (romantic and classical). It seems to me
this is wrong. In poetry naïveté and truth are identical things.
Homer is naïve in his delineation of the linen-washing princess, but
so is Goethe in his portrayal of Werther.[24]

[22] Cp. F. F. Nelidov, *Ocherki po istorii noveyshey Russkoy Literatury*
(Moskva, 1907), p. 81 ff.
[23] Boris V. Yakovenko, "Aus dem Briefwechsel vor kurzem tätiger Personen," *Der Russische Gedanke,* IX (1889), 161 (notes).
[24] *Lit. Nasl.,* LXI, 857.

This is certainly a curious passage. One could ask if Ogarev would also consider Dante a "naïve" poet. But apart from this, his remark about Schiller's division of poetry into sentimental and naïve raises a number of challenging and very pertinent questions. For instance, when Ogarev says that "all great poets are naïve," one wonders whether Schiller should be placed into the category of the great, naïve poets together with Homer, Shakespeare, and Goethe? The question arises, too, how Ogarev would have solved the problem of the division of poetry, having rejected Schiller's solution. Should we infer from his letter that he rejected all categorizing and recognized only one type of poetry, that is the naïve, relegating all other literary productions to the limbo of inferior writing? Unfortunately, Ogarev himself did not elaborate on that point. In the absence of more substantial clues it may seem permissible to favor this last supposition, namely, that he recognized only the naïve type of poetry.

Much more revealing is a letter to Herzen, written on November 6, 1839, in which Ogarev speaks of his relationship with the poet N. M. Satin:

Yes, Ritter [nickname of Satin] is a man before whom I am ready to bend my knee because of his capacity for loving. It seems to me that none of us can boast such force of love. He all but has the nature of a woman, so tenderly does he love. But as for me—I like this trait in a man.

> Jetzt mit des Zuckers
> Linderndem Saft
> Zähmet die herbe
> Brennende Kraft.[25]

Thus, with a quotation from Schiller's "Punschlied," Ogarev—himself the kindliest imaginable of men—recommends us to sweeten the tartness of manly vigor by the admixture of some

[25] Ogarev, *Izbr. sots.-polit. i filos. proizved.*, II, 302–303.

feminine tenderness. Schiller's "Punschlied," incidentally, seems to have been popular in Russian student circles in spite, or should we say because, of its merry insignificance. It was translated into Russian by Pushkin (oddly enough, the only poem by Schiller which he deemed worthy of this distinction), it was well known to Küchelbecker, and it was quoted by Herzen in his sketch "About Myself" (1838),[26]

Of considerable value for an insight into Ogarev's attitude toward Schiller are his letters to his secret lady-love Yevdokia V. Sukhovo-Kobylina which among other things, reveal the scope of his intellectual interests and occupations in the early Forties. Particularly noteworthy in these letters are his references to Pushkin and Goethe and his remarks on Schiller's "romanticism." Apparently in mental anguish, Ogarev writes to his sweetheart on June 14, 1842 :

I allow you to suffer only the anguish of Schillerean *Sehnsucht,* to suffer the pangs of yearning for the beautiful. I have grown old. I can no longer sympathize with Schiller, I cannot content myself with his flights *ins Blaue.* Give me real life and real happiness, right here, and not *jenseits,* not in some far-off distance. Schiller seems like a radiant youth whom I love, whom I cannot help loving but for the appreciation of whom I have grown too dreadfully old. Yet when you said that it would be delightful to read him together on the bank of the river, in your favorite place, I suddenly felt deep sorrow that we had not done it. To become young again with you would be so marvellous,—to become young and to escape again into some kind of wonderful dream ! And why did I depart so soon? whither do I hurry?[27]

A very characteristic and self-revealing letter ! Here we have the whole Ogarev—the man and the poet. All the principal themes of his poetry which he began publishing in 1840 are

[26] Gertsen, *Poln, sobr. soch i pisem,* II, 166–167.
[27] *Lit. Nasl.,* LXI, 862.

already present in a remarkable degree : wistful memories of missed happiness, paralyzed longing, dissatisfaction with himself, melancholy disenchantment, rueful retrospection. "I have grown old," Ogarev writes with an innuendo of self-pity. But in reality he is a young man of twenty-nine on the point of setting out on a grand tour of Western Europe (1842–46). His hitherto unequivocal admiration for Schiller has become lost in the maze of a typical father-son complex. Aversion struggles with love : "I can no longer sympathize with Schiller. . . ." Yet a few lines farther the admission is wrung from him : "I cannot help loving him. . . ."

Ogarev's allusions to Schiller's "flights *ins Blaue*," to a supernatural happiness beyond the limits of human experience, are undoubtedly references to poems like "Hoffnung," "Sehnsucht," "Der Pilgrim," "Thekla,"—but they also reflect his gradually increasing criticism of Schiller's alleged indifference for humanity's "real life" and "real happiness, right here, and not *jenseits,* not somewhere far off." In a less antagonistic mood Ogarev might have recalled the poet's *Briefe über die ästhetische Erziehung des Menschen,* intended not as an abstract treatise on beauty and happiness but as a guide and program of action designed to save a humanity resigned to despotism, anarchy and the horrors of revolution.

However, at the time of writing the letter, Ogarev apparently was involved in his personal unhappiness rather than concerned about the welfare of mankind, and at the bottom of his love–hate for Schiller lurked bitter disillusionment caused by his failure of becoming a happy lover in "real life,"—a disillusion which drove him to seek a scapegoat and to find it in Schiller. But although on the one hand Ogarev seems to say : "Schiller, with his 'flights *ins Blaue,*' made me miss real life and real happiness," on the other he shows himself more than ready to

undertake another "flight *ins Blaue*," together with his sweetheart, under the aegis of the very same Schiller at whom he had
pointed an accusing finger. In the end one cannot help asking :
What *does* Ogarev want? "Real life and real happiness," or
"escape into some kind of wonderful dream"? Weighing the
pros and cons, one is left with an impression that it was Ogarev's
yearning for "real life and real happiness" that was the dominant
drive in his life at the time.

In another passage of the letter Ogarev gives advice to Sukhovo-Kobylina on how to widen her literary horizons :

You don't know very much about Goethe. Read a few of his
works, perhaps this universal spirit will arouse your interest. Read
his *Wahlverwandtschaften* in memory of me. It is a pity that I have
not read *Wallenstein* with you. In this work there are already real
human beings, real life. By the way, you have told me of Toggenburg
so many times that I sing continuously in different tunes :
> Ritter, treue Schwesterliebe
> Widmet Euch dies Herz. . . .[28]

Perhaps under the influence of Belinsky who during his
"reconciliation with reality" extolled Goethe at the expense of
Schiller, Ogarev too begins to express admiration for the "universal spirit" of Goethe. This new attitude toward Goethe, his regret
at not having read *Wallenstein,* and his reference to the realistic
character of the tragedy corroborate the impression that Ogarev
now tends to reject his long-cherished romantic attachment to
the idealism of Schiller. By saying that in *Wallenstein* there are
"already real human beings, real life," Ogarev, by implication,
denies their existence in Schiller's earlier dramatic production.
On the whole, such an opinion is borne out by the facts, but it
fails to do complete justice to such figures as the musician Miller
in *Kabale und Liebe* and the King with his poignant suffering

---

[28] *Lit. Nasl.,* LXI, 863.

in loneliness in *Don Carlos*. In strange contrast to Ogarev's new preference for realism stands his undiminished enthusiasm for the sentimental romanticism of Schiller's poem "Ritter Toggenburg." And yet, this need not surprise in view of his Toggenburg-like personal experiences of amorous longing and woeful disappointment.

Imbued with wistful memories of bygone happiness is a poem, dated January–October, 1843, and written on an excursion near Rome. Amidst the splendors of the Italian landscape Ogarev recalls a spring day in his native Russia:

> I do not know! Perhaps you think no more of days of old,
> And I alone still cherish in my memory
> The quiet morning and your tranquil face,
> The brightness of your dress suggesting festive days,
> And this that with your lips, oh breath of spring!
> You breathed in me the airy dreams of Schiller.[29]

Considering the date of this poem we must regard it as a relapse into a very extravagant kind of Schiller-inspired romanticism. At the same time, it is also one of the very few poems by Ogarev in which he makes a direct reference either to Schiller himself or to his works. The identity of the lady who read to him from the writings of Schiller has not been established but his sweetheart Sukhovo-Kobylina would be a logical guess.

During a stay in Berlin in the summer of 1844, Ogarev entered into friendly relations with Professor Karl Werder, a follower of Hegel, who also lectured on Schiller and was popular among the Russian students in the Prussian capital. In a letter of June 11, 1844, addressed jointly to Herzen and Granovsky, Ogarev reports on a conversation he had with Werder:

We spoke of contemporary literature. We got to *Reflexionspoesie*. I was very pleased that we thought alike in this regard. I have long

[29] Ogarev, *Izbr. proizved.*, I, 213.

since stopped being an enemy of *Reflexionspoesie*. However, I do not like a poetry of reflection which does not express the human soul and the drama unfolding in its innermost depth. I cannot enjoy a ready-made theory, for no good reason wrapped up in poetry, where inner feeling is replaced by some sort of very spurious *Schwung*. Schiller's or Byron's poetry of reflection is certainly very different from the poetry of reflection of Rückert and of the contemporary political poetry.[30]

Charging a certain type of contemporary German poetry of reflection with "spurious *Schwung*," Ogarev gives credit between the lines to Schiller for having "genuine *Schwung*." But the sharp edge of criticism he directs at a poetry of reflection which is just a "ready-made theory, for no good reason wrapped up in poetry" could be turned against Ogarev himself. Though, as has been said before, Ogarev ranks as one of the principal representatives of the poetry of reflection in Russia, his verse is a far cry from that spiritual buoyancy and profundity by which the philosophical poems of Schiller are distinguished. The drama unfolding in the depths of Ogarev's self is the monotonous drama of a soul chronically dissatisfied with its own impotence whereas the reflection of Schiller effortlessly transcends the bounds of his individual self making it, as it were, transparent by the incandescence of his all-embracing sentiments.

Ogarev was a keen observer of the German scene. In another letter from Berlin written several months later, he vents his anger at the Philistine traits in the German people and their national poets :

Oh ! Germans, Germans. Indeed, I love them very much, but they enrage me more than any other nation in the world. The fantastical rules here everywhere impregnated with *Mehlspeise*, beer,

[30] Ogarev, *Izbr. sots.-polit. i filos. proizved.*, II, 337. For a characterization of Professor Werder see P. N. Sakulin, *Iz istorii russkago idealizma* (Moskva, 1913), I¹, 384.

and bad tobacco. After having eaten ten times a day the German wanders off into his world of fancy, that is, he imagines things which do not exist and completely loses sight of real life.

> Morgens, wenn ich aufstehe,
> pfleg' ich Goethe zu lesen;
> Abends, wenn ich schlafen gehe,
> Schiller! les' ich in dir! . . .[31]

Ogarev was probably only half serious in this sarcastic sally against the German Philistine. At any rate, he must have been aware of the fact that it was not Goethe and not Schiller who were the favorite authors of the German Philistine but rather Kotzebue and Iffland, or, even worse, Gemmingen and Vulpius. Yet in those years, developing the ideas of Belinsky, Ogarev liked to satirize the various kinds of flight from reality in literature (for instance, the works of Zhukovsky, Ludwig Tiedge, Karamzin), and occasionally did not even spare Schiller and Goethe. Following Belinsky, he denounced that "duplicity" which, in his opinion, was a distinguishing mark of both great German poets.:

Like Belinsky, Ogarev pointedly condemned the Philistine features inherent in Goethe and subjected to criticism the weak sides of Schiller—that "romanticist in the sense of the Middle Ages," according to the expression of Belinsky.[32]

Ogarev's critical attitude toward the "Philistine features" in Goethe and Schiller is epitomized in his *Letters of a Country Dweller*, dedicated to Iskander (pseudonym of Herzen), where he remarks:

Keep in mind that even Schiller, in contrast [to Goethe] depicted as a man taking an ardent part in the affairs of humanity, that even Schiller himself—like Goethe—was unable to detect a "cause for songs of joy" in face of very important historical events. The reason

[31] Ogarev, *Izbr. sots.-polit. i filos. proizved.*, II, 343–344. Letter to Herzen of September 25, 1844.

[32] *Lit. Nasl.*, LXI, 528.

for this attitude lies in the fact that both poets, despite their dynamic inspiration, were Germans of a time when a writer considered it a great honor, almost a memorable event, to play boston with some Count Hoch Prififalp Haus Ritzkreuzburg Sonderbrügen.[33]

With his expression "very important historical events" Ogarev undoubtedly alludes to the French Revolution. In Goethe's and Schiller's negative attitude toward the event Ogarev saw a manifestation in them of Philistine narrow-mindedness, a submissive retreat before the aristocratic forces of reaction. This is harsh criticism which should not be accepted without reservations. Neither Schiller nor Goethe—both free and independent spirits— would have considered it a particular "honor" to "play boston" with a high-titled member of the feudal aristocracy. On the other hand, it is a fact that many an illustrious nobleman did eagerly seek the opportunity of making the poets' acquaintance. In the case of Schiller, the names of Count Schimmelmann and the Prince of Augustenburg may be adduced.

Although Ogarev spoke sharply at times of the "weak sides" of Schiller, developing the ideas which Belinsky had set forth in his article "The Works of Derzhavin" (1843), on the whole he regarded him as a progressive poet and as a "herald of a progressive Germany." In the world-weariness of the spiritual fathers of the French Revolution, the encyclopedists, in Byron's struggle with the sluggishness and conservatism of Tory England, in the criticism of the bourgeoisie with which Goethe's *Wahlverwandtschaften* are imbued, "in the powerful voice of Schiller, Ogarev divines the stirrings of a progressive Europe, recognizes the pledge and prophecy of the salvation of Europe from the predominance of the bourgeoisie."[34] Ogarev saw Schiller as the typical product of his native Germany, but at the same time he recognized and

---

[33] *Lit. Nasl.*, LXI, 532–533.
[34] *Lit. Nasl.*, LXI, 530.

appreciated the fact that the poet—despite his Philistine and romantic "blemishes"—fundamentally was not altogether un-critical of the national spirit of his land, just as Byron had been in opposition to his native England.

More than once a feeling of homesickness and loneliness over-whelmed Ogarev during his stay abroad. In such moments he took refuge in his memories of happy childhood days in Russia and in the poetry of Schiller to whom he always returned, not-withstanding his new sympathy for the realistic point of view. In Berlin where, to be sure, he had acquaintances and friends, he must nonetheless have also felt the pangs of loneliness as can be seen from his letter of January 8, 1845, written to his sweetheart Sukhovo-Kobylina :

An idea will find sympathy everywhere provided that it be an animated, substantial idea and not an empty thought about one's own self and a lament that life has deceived us. Life does not deceive us. We do not understand it and thus deceive ourselves. Deceit is only the retribution for our having sinned against real life.

> Aber flüchtet aus der Sinne Schranken
> In die Freiheit der Gedanken
> Und die Furchterscheinung ist entflohn,
> Und der ew'ge Abgrund wird sich füllen;
> Nehmt die Gottheit auf in euren Willen,
> Und sie steigt von ihrem Götterthron.
> Des Gesetzes strenge Fessel bindet
> Nur den Sklavensinn, der es verschmäht;
> Mit des Menschen Widerstand verschwindet
> Auch des Gottes Majestät.
>
> (Schiller, "Das Ideal und das Leben")

Now I am no more afraid of the loneliness in which I live. It is necessary for my spiritual remaking.[35]

Ogarev, it appears, has finally succeeded in making his way out

[35] *Lit. Nasl.,* LXI, 876.

of the labyrinth of melancholy frustration in which he was lost
due to his passion for Sukhovo-Kobylina. Like Schiller in his
poem, he bravely resolves to face the demands of real life: "Nur
der Starke wird das Schicksal zwingen,/Wenn der Schwächling
untersinkt." In the eternal contradiction between aspiration and
duty he decides to follow Schiller on the arduous path which
leads away from the bondage of the sensual world up to the freedom of spiritual harmony and moral reconciliation: "Aber
flüchtet aus der Sinne Schranken/In die Freiheit der Gedanken
. . ." It is the gallant acceptance of reality on the one hand
and the dissolution of the contrast between sensual nature and
ethical law on the other which makes Schiller's thought-packed
poem so fascinating for the lonely Russian: "Mit des Menschen
Widerstand verschwindet/Auch des Gottes Majestät." What is
more, under the circumstances it could not fail to impress him as
a challenging reflection of his own state of mind, as a revealing
and admonishing picture of his personal deficiencies and personal
guilt:

> Wenn ihr in der Menschheit traur'ger Blösse
> Steht vor des Gesetzes Grösse,
> Wenn dem Heiligen die Schuld sich naht,
> Da erblasse vor der Wahrheit Strahle
> Eure Tugend, vor dem Ideale
> Fliehe mutlos die beschämte Tat.

And Ogarev accepts the challenge: "Nehmt die Gottheit auf
in euren Willen . . . Und die Furchterscheinung ist entflohn. . . ."
Now he is "no more afraid of the loneliness" in which he lives.
Once more, as in the far-off days of his youth, he identifies himself with Schiller and "sympathizes" with Schiller's "animated,
substantial idea" of transcending the narrow limits of "one's own
self" in the service of an all-embracing "sacred compassion":

> Wenn der Menschheit Leiden euch umfangen,

....
Da empöre sich der Mensch! ....
Und der heil'gen Sympathie erliege
Das Unsterbliche in euch!

Apparently at the threshold of a spiritual rebirth, Ogarev resolves
to put an end to egoistical "empty thoughts" and self-pitying
"laments" and resolutely sets out to "remake" his innermost self
in the spirit of his teacher Schiller.

But there is often a discrepancy between thinking and doing.
On paper it was quite easy to envision a "spiritual remaking,"
in practice, however, the problem proved much more complicated and difficult. In fact, after his return to Russia, in the
spring of 1846, Ogarev continued to struggle for inner harmony
and a philosophy of life which would be a synthesis of realism
and romanticism. His critical intellect urged him to view the
world with the eyes of a cool and sober natural scientist, but
his heart seduced him time and again to listen to its insinuations
of undefined longing and sorrowful melancholy. Ogarev's letter
to Granovsky is a striking example of such a contradictory mood,
where his innate romanticism clashes with the rational insight of
his abstract thinking:

To love and to live *dans le vague* (in which there is a dangerously
fascinating poetical charm) becomes with every day more impossible.
Thus melancholy with its *Mondscheinfarbe* turns perhaps into
bitter sorrow but somehow one feels moved to bear it bravely and
unflinchingly. In fact, in the poetry of this sorrow there glitters
some kind of a rational *Sonnenlichtfarbe*. Maybe this is the romanticism of our time which is closer to real life, *aber die Harmonie des
Lebens ist noch nicht errungen.*

> Forward, forward, my History!
> Nur Beharrung führt zum Ziel,
> Nur die Fülle führt zur Klarheit
> Und im Freien wohnt die Wahrheit.

Forgive my making such a poor verse but I wanted to avoid the word *Abgrund* which does not mean anything to my mind except morass. I will also explain why I have replaced it by the word *das Freie:*

Zwischen Realität und Wahrheit ist ein grosser Unterschied. Die Realität ist bloss sagend, ohne sich zu bekümmern, ob sie wahr oder falsch ist. Nur das frei hervorgebrachte, d. h. das bewusste Wirken, nur das Menschliche, das aus der Indifferenz der Realität sich befreite, kann eine Wahrheit sein.[36]

The quoted quatrain represents a curious mixture of Pushkin and Schiller. The first line is borrowed from *Yevgeny Onegin* (VI, 4), the other three lines are taken from Schiller's poem "Sprüche des Konfuzius" with a change in the last line as indicated by Ogarev. By declaring with Schiller (not literally but in his spirit): "Und im Freien wohnt die Wahrheit," Ogarev apparently takes issue with the thesis of the conservative Hegel: "Was wirklich ist, ist wahr." Ogarev conceives of reality as something indifferent or neutral which, depending on the circumstances, may turn out to be either "true" or "false." The decisive factor to him is, in contrast to Hegel, the human element, or, in other words, the conscious and self-determined activity of an autonomous humanity rising above the unconscious indifference of reality.

The deeply democratic and humanistic roots of Ogarev's revolutionary thinking become here discernible as also his indebtedness to Schiller's concept of the "schöne Seele." In Ogarev's insistence on the development of a harmonious reconciliation between duty and inclination ("Harmonie des Lebens") and in his eloquent defense of the full autonomy of a freely creative mankind ("das bewusste Wirken") it is not difficult to

---

[36] Ogarev, *Izbr. sots.-polit. i filos. proizved.*, II, 395–396. Letter to Granovsky of January 17, 1847. See also N. M. Mendelson, "N. P. Ogarev," *Zvenya*, I (Moskva, 1932), 119.

recognize the influence of Schiller's *Anmut und Würde* and of
his *Briefe über die ästhetische Erziehung des Menschen.*[37]

The task Ogarev had set for himself in his above-mentioned
letter to Granovsky : harmony of life, definiteness of purpose,
fulness of experience, proved to be an arduous one, and more
than once he relapsed into a state of melancholy frustration and
profound pessimism :

I have small faith in the importance of literature, and now[38] I
have equally small faith in the importance of practical activity and
feel overwhelmed by a kind of chaos in which I find myself
caught. . . .[39]

As the years passed it became more and more difficult for him
to live in a country whose atmosphere weighed heavily upon
his soul. At last, in 1856, Ogarev resolved to turn his back on
Russia and to follow the example of his friend Herzen who had
gone abroad nine years earlier. But before he embarked, he
inscribed his name with indelible letters in the hearts of his serfs :

He [Ogarev] was a thorough lover of freedom, who, before he left
Russia, set free his ten thousand serfs, surrendering all the land to
them, and who, throughout all his life abroad remained true to the
ideals of equality and freedom which he had cherished in his youth.[40]

That Ogarev remained true to the ideals of his youth and that
he was ready to sacrifice his personal happiness in the name of

[37] Cp. in this connection Bakunin who "covets truth as it is and not truth
at is is adapted to certain conditions." D. I. Chizhevsky, *Gegel v Rossii*
(Paris, 1939), p. 89. Incidentally, as an example of the parallelism of their
intellectual interests, the fact may be mentioned that Ogarev's friend Herzen
also quotes from the "Sprüche des Konfuzius" in his article "To the Other
Side" (1869). See Gertsen, *Poln. sobr, soch. i pisem,* XXI, 486.

[38] In January 1847, after Ogarev had witnessed the "painful spectacle" of
a recruits' levy in the village of Insar.

[39] N. Mendelson, "Iz proshlogo," *Novy Mir,* V (Moskva,, 1931), 180.
Letter to Granovsky of January 17, 1847.

[40] Kropotkin, *op. cit.,* p. 275. Cp. also *Arkhiv N. A. i N. P. Ogarevykh*
(Moskva, 1930), p. 297.

humanity and freedom, is evidenced by his letter of September 19, 1860, written to Herzen :

At any rate, if the common cause should require of me another personal sacrifice, for instance, participation in an uprising in Russia, I would of course tear out any sentiment of tenderness [for persons dear to him]

>   . . . blutend aus dem wunden Herzen
>   Und weinte laut und gab sie hin.
>   (Schiller, "Resignation")[41]

As a contributor to Herzen's periodical *Kolokol* Ogarev kept a watchful eye on the development of literature in Western Europe and in Russia giving particular attention to that part of literature which did not reach the public because of difficulties with the censor. Thus, in his introduction to the collection *The Forbidden Russian Literature of the Nineteenth Century* (1861), he wistfully reflects on English, German, and Russian literature and its difficulty in reaching the public :

Everywhere literature is inaccessible to the masses. Byron is hated by the higher social classes in England but unknown to the common people, Shakespeare is known to the city dwellers because they see him in the theatres. Goethe and Schiller are known to the university-educated Germans but not to the Germans laboring six days and reading the Bible and the catechism on the seventh. Everywhere literature is the property of the townspeople and not of the masses. Pushkin has as few readers among our people as does Koltsov. Evidently, the hour of the people has not yet struck.[42]

As far as Schiller is concerned, Ogarev's assertion should not be accepted without criticism. Such plays, for instance, as *Die*

---

[41] Ogarev, *Izbr. sots.-polit. i filos. proizved.*, II. 448. Incidentally, this is another parallel to Herzen who quoted the same two lines from Schiller's "Resignation" in *My Past and Thoughts* with reference to the year 1848 when he had to give up his dreams of a revolutionary and socialistic Europe. Gertsen, *Poln. sobr. soch. i pisem*, XIII, 493.

[42] Ogarev, *Izbr. proizved.*, II, 462.

Räuber and *Kabale und Liebe* enjoyed a huge popularity which was by no means limited to the "university-educated Germans," and *Wilhelm Tell* became, soon after the poet's death, a real "people's drama" in the widest sense of the word both in Germany and Switzerland.[43]

At another point of his introduction to *The Forbidden Russian Literature of the Nineteenth Century,* discoursing on the position of Pushkin in European literature, Ogarev observes with reference to Goethe and Schiller:

If world-wide significance means in general influence on the contemporary world, then the influence of Pushkin on the Russian world was not inferior to the influence of Goethe and Schiller on the German. The reason why he [Pushkin] had no influence on Europe is obvious : for European eyes we are obscure; a little handful of people in our midst reads Western literature whereas Europe does not read ours at all; our interests are either strange or hostile to her.[44]

It would be difficult to quarrel with Ogarev in this regard. As a matter of fact, Europe began to be interested in Russian literature only with the appearance of Dostoyevsky when several of his novels had become available in German translations. A man like Friedrich Bodenstedt who tried to acquaint the German public with Pushkin, Lermontov, and other Russian writers about the middle of the nineteenth century is a striking exception.

[43] Schiller's biographer Berger remarks in this connection: "Nachdem der Schillersche *Tell* auf den ziemlich im argen liegenden Schweizer Kunstbühnen Eingang gefunden hatte,—zuerst in Luzern am 4. November 1804— nahm mehr und mehr das Volk selbst, Alt und Jung, das Stück in seine Hand. Aus der Enge der Bühnenkulissen und dem Schein erborgten Lichtes ward es hinausgeführt in die freie Gottesnatur und in die Sonnenhelle des Tags, 'auf offenen Dorfgassen, auf Matten und luftigen Höhen' mit stetig zunehmender Veredlung der Darstellung überall im Lande, besonders auch an den durch die Dichtung selbst geweihten Stätten gespielt." Karl Berger, *Schiller* (München, 1909), II, 697.

[44] Ogarev, *Izbr. proizved.,* II, 463.

In March 1863, two months after the outbreak of a great anti-Russian insurrection in Poland, Ogarev turned to V. S. Pecherin, a Moscow university professor, with the proposal of immediate revolutionary action: "But where, in all conscience, is our real field of action? Where is it that you will 'take the oriflamme into your hands?' "[45] The implication was that Pecherin should prove his loyalty to the Russian people by taking an active part in the struggle of the Polish revolutionaries. The expression "you will take the oriflamme into your hands" is a quotation from Schiller's drama *Die Jungfrau von Orleans* (Prologue, fourth scene: "Dann wirst du meine Oriflamme tragen") and very characteristic of Ogarev's attitude toward the Polish uprising which he thus placed on a level with the rightful and sacred war of the French people against the English invaders.[46] To be sure, Ogarev's enthusiasm for the Polish revolution diminished gradually and half a year later his attitude had become somewhat less

[45] Ogarev, *Izbr. sots-polit. i filos. proizved.*, II, 477. For details see A. Jzjumov, "Der Briefwechsel V. S. Pecerins mit A. I. Herzen," *Jahrbücher für Kultur und Geschichte der Slaven*, N. F. IX, Heft IV (Breslau, 1933), 493–517. Cp. also M. Gershenzon, *Zhizn V. S. Pecherina* (Moskva, 1910), pp. 179–184.

[46] In reference to Ogarev's quotation from *Die Jungfrau von Orleans* a Soviet critic supplies the following commentary: "Oriflamme (from orflamme — golden flame) — the battle gonfalon of the French kings of red silk on a gilded staff. 'You will take my oriflamme into your hands — words of Joan of Arc from Schiller's tragedy *Die Jungfrau von Orleans* signifying that Joan of Arc will move in front of the army." Ogarev, *Izbr. sots.-polit. i filos. proizved.*, II, 626 (notes). To be precise, the words about the oriflamme are spoken by the Lord, and Joan of Arc only repeats to herself what the voice of God commanded her to do from behind the branches of the tree. Furthermore, the oriflamme is clearly not the battle gonfalon of the French kings but the battle flag of God a description of which is given by Joan herself:

Und eine weisse Fahne lass mich tragen,
Mit einem Saum von Purpur eingefasst.
Auf dieser Fahne sei die Himmelskönigin
Zu sehen mit dem schönen Jesusknaben,
Die über einer Erdenkugel schwebt,
Denn also zeigte mirs die Heilge Mutter.
(*Die Jungfrau von Orleans*, I, 10)

than fervent. When Bakunin was on the point of departure for Poland to carry military assistance to the revolutionaries, Ogarev wrote to him almost reproachfully :

Sous l'influence des agents polonais tu t'es laissé entraîner trop loin dans l'union polonaise; après cela il ne te restait qu'à prendre la direction du bateau de l'expédition; c'était pour toi une de ces nécessités que l'on rencontre dans sa vie. Lorqu'on n'a plus de choix, "kann ich nicht mehr zurück, weil ich es gewollt," dit Wallenstein. Et la *Cloche* elle-même ne put se maintenir dans son équilibre.[47]

Ogarev quotes here from *Wallensteins Tod*.[48] Perhaps he did so on purpose to remind Bakunin of the highly ambiguous, in fact, treacherous role played by Wallenstein with regard to the German people. The quotation could thus be interpreted as a hint and warning to Bakunin not to play a similar treacherous role with regard to the Russian people. Be this as it may, there can be no doubt that Ogarev's enthusiasm for the Polish revolution declined strikingly in less than a year. Participation in the Polish struggle for freedom seemed to him no longer a sacred duty but "une de ces nécessités que l'on rencontre dans sa vie."

At best, his reference to Wallenstein is therefore indicative of his torn state of mind, of his doubts whether or not sympathy for the Polish cause was compatible with the conscience of a Russian patriot. Ogarev's critical allusion to the pro-Polish position of Herzen (in the periodical *Kolokol*—"la *Cloche*") is significant in this regard.

Enthusiasm for the revolutionary romanticism of Schiller's poetry had been the starting point of Ogarev's relationship to

[47] "Correspondence de Michel Bakounine," *La Société Nouvelle*, II (Paris, 1895), 595. Letter to Bakunin of October 12, 1863.

[48] *Wallensteins Tod*, I, 4. Ogarev obviously quotes from memory, for in the original the corresponding passage reads as follows:

Wärs möglich? Könnt ich nicht mehr, wie ich wollte?
Nicht mehr zurück, wie mirs beliebt? Ich müsste
Die Tat *vollbringen,* weil ich sie *gedacht* . . . [Italics Schiller's].

the German poet. This early influence of Schiller tended to stress
and develop Ogarev's own sentimental, wistful, romantic incli-
nations. It was in the happy days of his childhood that he loved
"Songs of rebellion amidst the peace of night, / And Schiller's
Thekla, and my dreams, / And the wistful rays of the moon."
Schiller was the great and decisive inspiration of his youth. From
his poetry and philosophy he derived "moments of sublime
pleasure which influenced all his later development." So profound was the impression made on him by Schiller that he still
vividly remembered it when he was an old man. Under the
threefold influence of Schiller, Rousseau, and the Decembrist
revolt Ogarev accomplished his transition from childhood to
adolescence.

Paradoxically enough, it was in these idealistic influences that
was hidden the seed of Ogarev's later realism. The reading of
Schiller had imbued him with "noble aspirations" but these
noble aspirations were filled with gnawing doubts about the
justice and rationality of contemporary society. To justify Schiller's idealism Ogarev had come into contact with real society
in which, however, he discovered nothing but falsehood, iniquity,
and suffering. The result of these experiences was a "collision
with real society" which aroused in him a passion for social
analysis and criticism. Under the conditions of political terror
prevailing in Russia at that time such an attitude was bound to
bring him into conflict with the authorities. An over-enthusiastic
letter about Schiller's drama *Wilhelm Tell* precipitated his arrest
and imprisonment on grounds of an alleged conspiracy to assassinate the Tsar.

Schiller thus played a great role in awakening Ogarev's revolutionary tendencies. Equally important, however, was Schiller's
role as a great influence in consummating Ogarev's friendship
with Herzen. This friendship grew and flourished under the

auspices of Karl Moor and Marquis Posa. It was a remarkable
relationship—reminiscent of the friendship between Schiller and
Körner—which deepened and widened as the years went by, out-
lasting all storms and vicissitudes of life. After his emigration to
England, Ogarev wrote to his wife :

Maria ! My friendship with A. [Alexander Herzen] is something
particular and unusual and not many will understand it. Look, in
what an amazing way destiny has brought me together with the idol
of my heart ! I was beginning to read Schiller and something had
just begun to bud in my soul—and exactly at that moment Sonnenberg appeared and acquainted me with A.[49]

In his youth, on the eve of their first separation, Ogarev
brought a volume of Schiller containing his "Philosophische
Briefe" and with tears in his eyes began to read the passages
which expressed the state of their souls : "Du bist fort, Raphael—
und die schöne Natur geht unter. . . ." As an old man, worn
out by life and disillusioned, he is still Julius and Herzen is still
his Raphael, and the memory of happy childhood days restores
his weary heart. This is what Ogarev wrote to Herzen on the
occasion of another separation :

Du bist fort, mein Raphael ! How many glorious memories echo
in these words ! Let me repeat them before the fall of the curtain—
and let me tell you that they have remained the same; perhaps they
have been revived by the trial of this separation. Your departure
has grieved me beyond all my worst expectations.[50]

The dominant characteristic of the Ogarev-Schiller relationship in Ogarev's later years was an intricate maze of a paradoxical father-son complex. The first signs of such an attitude can

---

[49] Gertsen, *Poln. sobr. soch. i pisem,* XIII, 241 (notes). Sonnenberg was
Ogarev's German tutor. See also P.-N. Milioukov, *Le Mouvement Intellectuel Russe* (Paris, 1918), p. 194.

[50] *Lit. Nasl.,* XXXIX–XL, 425. Letter to Herzen of December 18, 1866.

be discerned toward the end of the thirties. In the forties his
hitherto unlimited enthusiasm for Schiller gives way to bursts
of criticism interspersed with protestations of sympathy and love :
"I can no longer sympathize with Schiller . . . Schiller seems
like a radiant youth whom I love, whom I cannot help loving
. . . ." It was in the forties too that Ogarev came under the influence of Belinsky who, at that time, was extolling Goethe and
realism at the expense of Schiller. Ogarev's tendency toward
Belinsky's "reconciliation with reality" explains to a large extent
his stiffening attitude toward Schiller and his sallies against the
"flight from reality" in literature. Ogarev also revealed himself
as a faithful follower of the views of Belinsky in his attacks on
the "Philistine features" in Goethe and Schiller.[51]

In spite of these occasional bursts of criticism Ogarev remained, on the whole, attached to his adolescent admiration of
Schiller. As a social revolutionary he appreciated the fact that
the German poet was not uncritical of German society and the
German national spirit. Accordingly, he recognized him as a
"progressive poet" and as a "herald of a progressive Germany."
At the height of a spiritual crisis, in the pangs of despair and
loneliness, he took refuge in his memories of a happy childhood
in Russia and in the poetry of Schiller : "Aber flüchtet aus der
Sinne Schranken / In die Freiheit der Gedanken. . . ." Torn
by the contradiction between his sensual nature and his ideal
aspirations, he ultimately resolved to follow Schiller on the
arduous path toward spiritual harmony and moral reconciliation.
A note of anguished resignation reverberates in the correspondence of the old Ogarev. Like Schiller in the poem "Die Ideale,"

[51] But cp. Martin Malia : "Herzen and Ogarev, while always more at
home with the ideal than Belinskij, never used it to become 'reconciled with
reality' and consistently construed it in a radical sense. Their whole effort
was to make the ideal impinge on the real, and not to seek refuge in it
as did Schiller." *Loc. cit.*, p. 199. Cp. also A. Anikst, "O kharaktere realizma
Schillera," *Teatr*, V (Moskva, 1955), 53–67.

he had not found happiness in life—but he had found a true and faithful friend.[52] At the end of his sufferings and strivings, "before the fall of the curtain," Ogarev could nonetheless derive comfort from the soothing words of his beloved Schiller:

> Von all dem rauschenden Geleite,
> Wer harrte liebend bei mir aus?
> Wer steht mir tröstend noch zur Seite,
> Und folgt mir bis zum finstern Haus?
> Du, die du alle Wunden heilest,
> Der Freundschaft leise, zarte Hand,
> Des Lebens Bürden liebend teilest,
> Du, die ich frühe sucht' und fand.
>
> (Schiller, "Die Ideale")

---

[52] Cp. T. P. Passek, *Iz dalnikh let* (Moskva–Leningrad, 1931), p. 173.

VII

Dostoyevsky

WHILE PUSHKIN MARKS THE BEGINNING OF A TRULY NATIONAL Russian literature, it was Fyodor M. Dostoyevsky (1821–81) who, together with Tolstoy, did more than any other Russian writer to elevate Russian literature to the status of world literature. Dostoyevsky's genius had already won general recognition toward the end of the nineteenth century. After the turn of the century a wave of enthusiasm for the author of *The Brothers Karamazov* became irresistible not only in Russia, but throughout Europe, and even in America. But this posthumous upward flight of Dostoyevsky's fame was suddenly interrupted by the Bolshevik revolution. It laid bare the erroneousness, the illusiveness of many of Dostoyevsky's fundamental conceptions. Nevertheless, as a towering literary figure he remains unsurpassed, and he continues to be read the world over, including the Soviet Union where, after years of official rejection, he is now being once more celebrated as one of the greatest of the Russian writers.[1]

Dostoyevsky and his work represent a striking example of Schiller's influence on Russian literature. Dostoyevsky's first contact with the German poet occurred when he was still a child.

[1] Cf. Fan Parker, "The Revival of Dostoevskij on the Soviet Stage," *SEEJ*, XVI (Spring 1958), 33–41. Regarding the bankruptcy of Dostoyevsky's national and political conceptions, see Ivan Tkhorzhevsky, *Russkaya Literatura* (Paris, 1950), p. 367.

In a letter of August 18, 1880, addressed to his friend N. L. Osmidov, he vividly recalls that memorable occasion :

At ten I saw in Moscow a performance of *Die Räuber* with Mochalov acting one of the principal roles. I can justly say that the strong impression of this performance has acted as an enormous stimulation for my entire spiritual development.[2]

Dostoyevsky was a lonely and unhappy child. Books meant much more to him than real life and real people. Pushkin, Lermontov, Scott, Hoffmann, and Shakespeare were his favorite authors—but still stronger was Schiller's attraction for him. Schiller is the principal source of his youthful exaltation; he is the poet whom Dostoyevsky idolizes during his student years.

It is in 1840, in the School of Engineering at St. Petersburg, that Dostoyevsky begins his serious study of Schiller. Here I. N. Shidlovsky, the later romantic poet, initiates him into the works of the German. Shidlovsky's sensibility, his poetic inclination, "everything about this tall, ascetic-looking youth enchanted the lonely boy [Dostoyevsky]. Here was 'the proper image of a man,' such as Shakespeare and Schiller had painted."[3] In a letter to his brother Mikhail, dated January 1, 1840, Dostoyevsky gives an impassioned account of his enthusiasm for Schiller and his association with an unnamed friend :

You wrote to me, dear brother, that I have not read Schiller. You are wrong, my dear brother ! I have learned Schiller by heart, I have talked in his language and have raved about him; and I think fate never did me a greater favor in all my life as when it allowed me to get to know the great poet at that period of my life; I could never have gotten to know him so well at any other time. Reading Schiller with him [Shidlovsky?], I saw *in him* the noble ardent Don Carlos, and Marquis Posa, and Mortimer. This friendship has caused

---

[2] F. M. Dostoyevsky, *Polnoye sobranie sochineniy* (St. Petersburg, 1883–1904), I, 119 (Appendix).

[3] Avrahm Yarmolinsky, *Dostoevsky* (New York, 1934), p. 26.

me much sorrow and much joy! But my lips shall remain sealed about this forever. To be sure, the name of Schiller has become dear to me, a kind of magic formula that conjures a host of dreams; bitter dreams, dear brother; this is the reason why I have never spoken to you of Schiller and the impressions he produced on me : it hurts me when I hear his very name.[4]

In another passage of the same letter Dostoyevsky defends himself against the reproach that he had "assorted" the great poets according to their "quality" although he, allegedly, did not know them at all : "I have never paralleled Pushkin with Schiller. . . . There is not the slightest resemblance between the two." This last, very peremptory, statement calls for closer scrutiny and comment. Pushkin, it is true, did not fully sympathize with Schiller—a fact which may be ascribed to the bent of his genius. Nevertheless, in this connection it is interesting to note that the dramatic works of Schiller, in a French translation, were "the first books he [Pushkin] insistently demanded from his brother while working on his *Boris Godunov*."[5]

Another interesting point in Dostoyevsky's letter is his reference to Schiller as a "thoroughly Christian poet," especially when we consider that Dostoyevsky's compatriot Vyacheslav Ivanov held a diametrically opposed view, regarding Schiller as "the pagan and dithyrambic poet par excellence."[6] Dostoyevsky's conception

[4] Dostoyevsky, *op. cit.,* I, 15–16. [Italics Dostoyevsky's.] Dostoyevsky's biographer Kirpotin thinks the mysterious friend was Berezhetsky.

[5] *Schiller,* ed. S. A. Vengerov (St. Petersburg, 1900), I, i. In addition his poem "October 19, 1825" shows that Pushkin had a not altogether superficial knowledge of Schiller and that his works were read and discussed by him and his friend Küchelbecker. Finally, evidence of Schiller's influence on Pushkin can also be found in *Yevgeny Onegin,* especially in the figure of Lensky and in Tatyana's farewell which undoubtedly was inspired by Johanna's famous farewell to the places of her childhood (cp. *Yevgeny Onegin,* VI, 20, 21; VII, 28). See also Rudolf Fischer, "Schiller und Puschkin," *Weimarer Beiträge,* III (Weimar, 1960), 603–611.

[6] Vyacheslav Ivanov, *Po zvezdam* (St. Petersburg, 1909), 81–82. See following chapter.

of Schiller is indicative of the Russian's preoccupation with the relationships between Christianity and art. In view of his youthful enthusiasm for the German poet there can be little doubt that it was Schiller who, with his aestheticism and his unshakable faith in the essential identity of the Good and the Beautiful, had inspired him to occupy himself with these problems of aesthetics.

It was in these early years that Dostoyevsky, then still a student in the School of Engineering, began to try his hand at literature and poetry. Nothing but the titles have been preserved of these first poetic experiments, yet even these scant remnants leave little doubt that Dostoyevsky was writing in those early days under the direct influence of Schiller : one of these early experiments was entitled *Maria Stuart* and the other *Boris Godunov*. The latter title, of course, makes one think of Pushkin's *Boris Godunov*. Yet Schiller's *Demetrius* may also have contributed to the genesis of Dostoyevsky's drama.[7]

When Dostoyevsky's brother Mikhail, having passed his examinations, was departing from St. Petersburg, Fyodor gave a farewell party at which he recited passages from his two plays. He was still at work on *Maria Stuart* in 1842 "attracted to the subject both by his passion for Schiller and because he had seen Lily Loewe in the title role of the German drama."[8]

In 1844 the brothers Dostoyevsky conceived the idea of publishing a complete translation of the works of Schiller. Fyodor, flushed with grand projects, hoped that a Russian Schiller edition would be the road to financial success and literary glory. Prompted by his brother, Mikhail translated *Die Räuber* and *Don Carlos,* while Fyodor himself assumed the role of critical

[7] Cp. D. Chizhevsky, "Schiller v Rossii," *Novy Zhurnal,* XLV (New York, 1956), 121–122.

[8] Yarmolinsky, *Dostoevsky,* p. 35.

adviser and occasional editor. Fyodor was well pleased with the work of his brother :

Upon receiving *Die Räuber* I began to read immediately; here is my opinion of the translation : The songs are rendered incomparably—the songs alone are worth money. Also the prose is translated magnificently—as far as power of expression and precision are concerned. You complain about Schiller's language; but note, my friend, that this language could not possibly be different. I noticed, however, that frequently you were carried away by the colloquial language and often, very often, sacrificed the correctness of a Russian word for the sake of colloquial fluency.[9]

When the translation of *Don Carlos* was completed, Fyodor was likewise satisfied though not as completely as he had been with the translation of *Die Räuber*:

I have received *Don Carlos* and hurry to reply as promptly as possible (I have no time). The translation is quite good, in some passages amazingly good, in a few lines bad; but only because you translated in a hurry. However, there are perhaps only five or six poor lines altogether. I have been so bold to make a few corrections, also, in some places, to make the verse more melodious.[10]

The drama *Don Carlos* remained the last work of Schiller translated by Mikhail, and nothing came of Fyodor's grand plans for quick and easy cash. Yet it was with great reluctance that Fyodor finally turned away from this cherished project and even after his first literary triumph, the publication of his novel *Poor Folk* (1846), he continued dreaming of the edition of a Russian Schiller. It was only toward the end of 1847 that he definitely abandoned the project.

Incidentally, there is a reference to the German poet in the first novel by Dostoyevsky. Makar Devushkin, confessing to

⁹ F. M. Dostoyevsky, *Pisma,* ed. A. S. Dolinin (Moskva–Leningrad, 1928–59), II, 553.
¹⁰ *Ibid.,* I, 72.

Varvara that he is not a learned man, mentions Schiller's poem "Die Kraniche des Ibykus" as the only poem he has ever read in his life.[11] Two other poems of Schiller, "Der Handschuh" and "Ritter Toggenburg," are named in Dostoyevsky's tale *A Little Hero* which was written in the Peter and Paul fortress during his detention there in 1849.[12]

Through Belinsky, who was enthusiastic about the young author's first novel, Dostoyevsky became acquainted with socialistic ideas (1846). Yet the path to this ideology was well prepared, for it was but a short road from the poet of freedom, Schiller, to the apostle of socialism, Fourier. Dostoyevsky started frequenting the radical circle of Petrashevsky in which the works of Fourier were read and discussed and the shortcomings of the Russian government severely criticized. In April, 1849, the members of the circle were arrested and some of them, including Dostoyevsky, sentenced to death. Later Dostoyevsky's sentence was commuted by the tsar to hard labor in Siberia. While confined in the Peter and Paul fortress Dostoyevsky read Schiller's *Geschichte des Dreissigjährigen Krieges* which his brother Mikhail had managed to smuggle in to him.[13] This reading did not remain without influence on Dostoyevsky's intellectual development and some of his essays written in the sixties and seventies show distinct traces of his preoccupation with the historical ideas of Schiller.[14]

The cruel years of penal servitude in Siberia were a profoundly sobering experience to Dostoyevsky—an experience that dealt a severe blow to his youthful illusions and Schiller-inspired idea-

---

[11] F. M. Dostoyevsky, *Polnoye sobranie khudozhestvennykh proizvedeniy* (Moskva–Leningrad, 1926), I, 53. Hereafter abridged to "PSKP."

[12] Dostoyevsky, *PSKP*, II, 161.

[13] Cp. Chizhevsky, "Schiller v Rossii," p. 122.

[14] About Dostoyevsky's youthful Schiller enthusiasm cf. V. Ya. Kirpotin, *F. M. Dostoyevsky* (Moskva, 1960), pp. 125–129, and J. A. T. Lloyd, *Fyodor Dostoevsky* (New York, 1947), p. 263 ff.

lism; they could not, however, shake Dostoyevsky's high admiration for Schiller the man. This paradoxical attitude is clearly reflected in Dostoyevsky's literary activities. While Schillerean idealists continue to play an important role in such novels as *The Injured and Oppressed, Crime and Punishment,* and *The Youth,* they are now treated with caustic irony. However, such irony is never directed at Schiller himself. In fact, when after Dostoyevsky's return from Siberia (1859) an attack on Schiller was published by the periodical *Vek,*[15] he gave an indignant reply in his journal *Vremya.* Dostoyevsky opens his defense of Schiller with a quotation from Pushkin's poem "October 19, 1825":

> We shall talk of the stormy Caucasian days,
> Of Schiller, of glory, of love . . .

and continues by countering the blow dealt to the greatness of the author of *Don Carlos* in a most effective manner:

Vek has attacked Schiller on the occasion of the edition of his works by Mr. Gerbel. Yet the very existence of this edition should have reminded the periodical [*Vek*] that Schiller is the chief favorite of our young writers as well as of our reading public. But for this evident fact Gerbel's edition would never have appeared.

Obviously, *Vek* chooses to look with disfavor on this love of our reading and writing public—a love beginning with Zhukovsky and continuing to our own day. Thus, if we look at our literature with attention, we cannot but call for a very different attitude toward the German poet! *We* [the Russians] *ought to regard Schiller in a very special manner, for he was not only a great universal writer, but—above all—he was our own national poet.*

The poetry of Schiller appeals more directly to the heart than does the poetry of Goethe and Byron. It is on this fact that his outstanding merit rests. Precisely for this reason is Russian literature so deeply indebted to him.[16]

---

[15] "We do not have a very high esteem of Schiller as a poet." "Nechto o Schillere," *Vremya,* I (St. Petersburg, 1861), 113.

[16] "Nechto o Schillere," pp. 113–114. [Italics mine.]

Many years later, in his *Diary of a Writer* (1876), Dostoyevsky returned once more to the theme of Schiller's profound influence on Russian society:

. . . in Russia, together with Jukovsky, he [Schiller] soaked into the Russian soul, left an impress upon it, and almost marked an epoch in the history of our development.[17]

Problems of art and literature are the main content of the essays written by Dostoyevsky in the Sixties and published by him in the periodicals *Vremya* and *Epokha*. Here Dostoyevsky continuously stresses the importance of the "idea" which to him represents the basis of any work of art, determining its real significance and value. Affirming the necessity of artistic generalization of the individual phenomena and striving to discover the universal in the individual, Dostoyevsky proceeds from the standpoint of Schiller's idealistic aesthetics, frequently using definitions and formulations derived, through Grigoryev, from the theories of Schiller (but also from Schelling and Hegel). Thus he attempts to illuminate a basic problem of the creative process —the problem of generalization and typification.

In terms of his own literary production these attempts resulted in the creation of the "higher man" (Schiller's "schöne Seele" : Alyosha Karamazov!) From the standpoint of Soviet literary criticism such a development constitutes a betrayal of reality, a dangerous deviation into the sphere of abstract idealism. "Typification," remarks a Marxist scholar reproachfully, "proved to Dostoyevsky possible only at the cost of tearing the phenomena away from social reality and by subordinating them to an abstract 'idea.' "[18]

[17] F. M. Dostoyevsky, *The Diary of a Writer*, transl. Boris Brasol (New York, 1949), I, 343. Dostoyevsky's biographer Lloyd is bewildered by the Russian's "curious faithfulness" to Schiller. He considers Schiller "a strange influence for a Russian realist." Cf. *op. cit.*, pp. 287, 263.

[18] *Russkie pisateli o literature* (Leningrad, 1939), II, xxi.

In his article "Former Agriculturists—Future Diplomats,"[19] Dostoyevsky extends the dominant role of "ideas" from art and literature to the whole realm of human history. Considering the problem whether history is made by great personalities or by superpersonal forces he arrives at the conclusion that it is great ideas which determine its course.

World history, he argues, is but a part of the greater Cosmic history which begins with the creation of the universe by God and remains under the direction of God. In this conception of history Dostoyevsky comes very close to that held by the Fathers of the Greek Orthodox Church. Other aspects of his historical views bear resemblance to the ideas of Rousseau and Schiller. Like the German poet, Dostoyevsky takes an intermediate position between the historical optimism of Enlightenment and the historical pessimism of Rousseau. Although Dostoyevsky admits that the development of civilization has been accompanied by many evil and pernicious symptoms he does not claim that this development has brought about a complete corruption of mankind :

Wie Kant und Schiller erkennt Dostojewski einen Sündenfall. Doch ist die menschliche Natur, nachdem sie dem Reiche des Naturtriebes entwuchs, nicht radikal böse geworden, wie Kant meint, sondern sie ist nur vom Bösen überschattet. Dem arkadischen Zustand, wie Schiller ihn nannte, ist der Mensch seitdem entwachsen, er tut nicht mehr mit instinktiver Nötigung das Rechte, sondern er kann bewusst zwischen Gut und Böse wählen. Es kommt nur darauf an, wie Schiller richtig gesehen hat, dass der Mensch seine Natur so veredelt, dass er das Sittengesetz natürlich erfüllt, dass er seine Natur zu einer sittlichen macht, aus der die moralische Handlung wie selbstverständlich hervorgeht. Wenn dieses Ziel gänzlich erreicht sein wird, dann tritt die Menschheit in das zweite paradiesische Stadium ein, das Schiller das elysische nennt. Dostojewski

---

[19] *The Diary of a Writer*, 1877.

hätte sich hingegen scharf gegen die Theorie Kants gewandt, dass die sittliche Freiheit nur gegen den Naturtrieb errungen werden kann, und dass der Mensch notwendig durch sie unglücklich wird, dass er also zwischen Glück und Freiheit zu wählen habe.[20]

While paying tribute to Schiller the philosopher and defending the greatness of Schiller the poet, Dostoyevsky can be seen in the paradoxical situation of satirizing and ridiculing Schillerean idealism in some of his central works. This is strikingly illustrated in his novel *The Injured and Oppressed* (1861) where Schillerean characters appear in the role of sentimental cranks and fools. Dostoyevsky mercilessly derides his "hero" who is characterized as a "little brother of Schiller" and whose very name, Pfefferkuchen, appears as a deliberate mockery and insult.

In the nocturnal conversation between the prince and Ivan Petrovich the name of Schiller is mentioned several times. The villainous prince feels an irresistible urge to give vent to his disgust with his Schilleresque surroundings which have become unbearable to him :

Don't be amazed at me : I've become so fed up with these innocent doings, with all these pastorals of Alyosha [the prince's son], with all these Schillerean raptures, with all that loftiness in this cursed love-affair with this Natasha (by the way, a darling of a girl) that I, so to speak, am only too grateful for the opportunity of making faces at all this humbug.[21]

Then the prince recalls how it was one of his most piquant pleasures to pretend that he, too, was an ardent follower of Schiller, how he would at first encourage a certain youthful idealist and then suddenly disconcert him by lifting before him the mask, "to make him a grimace and show him the tongue exactly at the moment when he least expected such a surprise."

[20] R. Lauth, *Die Philosophie Dostojewskis* (München, 1950), p. 519.
[21] Dostoyevsky, *PSKP*, III, 210.

Dostoyevsky seems to be speaking about himself when he has the prince confess to Ivan Petrovich :

Do you know that I once was a metaphysician and philanthropist out of caprice and moved almost in the same circle of ideas as you? . . . now one must make grimaces; now we all make grimaces—such are these times. . . .[22]

A clear echo of Dostoyevsky's Siberian experiences, his profound disenchantment with the Schillerean idealism of his youth, resounds in these words of the prince who insistently repeats that he "cannot stand pastorals and Schillerean doings" and scornfully laughs at the sentimental stupidity of "Schillerean characters."[23] It seems as if Dostoyevsky were struggling to liberate himself from his rapturous enthusiasm for the German poet by deriding that which he had adored. But as a result of this struggle the whole novel is overshadowed by the figure of Schiller, who actually assumes the role of the hero. Therefore, Dostoyevsky's derision of Schillerean idealism is not an episode in the novel but, on the contrary, a basic and essential element in the structure of the whole work. The prince, far from being its real hero, is nothing but a substitute and subterfuge, improvised by the author for a very special purpose : the implacable and fundamental analysis of Schillerean idealism and of his personal relationship to Schiller in the light of his Siberian experiences.

Allowing for some exaggeration, one could say that *The Injured and Oppressed* in its salient aspects, is but a prose version of Schiller's drama *Kabale und Liebe*. It is easy to single out several striking parallels between the two works : the musty atmosphere in Natasha's house recalls the narrowness and dull-

---

[22] Dostoyevsky, *PSKP*, III, 211.
[23] Dostoyevsky, *PSKP, III,* 218. According to de Michelis, the prince's sarcasm is directed against the "rhetoric of the Twenties." See *Dostojevskij* (Firenze, 1950), p. 101. Cf. also C. M. Woodhouse, *Dostoievsky* (New York, 1951), p. 19.

ness reigning in the family of the musician Miller. Natasha bears a great resemblance to Louise and the countess can easily be recognized as Lady Milford. Natasha's mother nourishes as ambitious plans with regard to her daughter as does Louise's mother, and Natasha's father, in his pedantic honesty and stubbornness, appears as a perfect match for his German counterpart, the musician Miller. The prince, who wants to marry his son Alyosha to the rich and influential countess, comes very close to the figure of wicked President Walter in Schiller's drama. Only Alyosha bears no resemblance to Ferdinand. It would seem that for this very reason he is condemned to a shadowy existence in the limbo of inactive and helpless sentimentalism. Summarizing this affinity between *The Injured and Oppressed* and *Kabale und Liebe,* a critic aptly remarks: "Die Ähnlichkeit des Stofflichen ist greifbar; noch überzeugender die ungreifbare Kongruenz. Wir schwimmen in der gleichen Sentimentalität. Nur hat es Schiller besser gemacht."[24]

Dostoyevsky continues his scoffing at Schillerean idealism in his *Memoirs from the Underground* (1864) in which, full of fierce despair, he mercilessly demolishes the idols of his youth. On the lips of the philosopher "from the underground" the name of Schiller becomes an insulting epithet which he throws "like a fool's cap into the face of every enthusiast and dreamer."[25] With caustic sarcasm he refers to the Schillerean concept of the Beautiful and the Sublime: "The more I became conscious of the Good and of all that 'Beautiful and Sublime,' the deeper I sank into the morass and the more likely I was to become completely

[24] Julius Meier-Graefe, *Dostojewski* (Berlin, 1926), p. 127. It may seem strange that Dostoyevsky uses the villainous Prince as his mouthpiece. Perhaps others would not have chosen such a villain but Dostoyevsky did. As for the dramatic structure of his novels, cf. Thomas Mann, "Dostojewski —mit Massen," *Ges. Werke* (Berlin, 1955), X, 630.
[25] Leonid Grossman, *Tvorchestvo Dostoyevskogo* (Moskva, 1928), p. 167.

mired in it."[26] On another occasion, the hero of the *Memoirs* remarks no less sarcastically:

Oh, if I were doing nothing just because of laziness, heavens, in how high an esteem would I hold myself! I would esteem myself precisely for being able to have at least laziness to my credit; . . . And then I would make a career of it: I would become an idler and a glutton, yet not an ordinary one but, for instance, one sympathizing with everything beautiful and sublime. How do you like that? I have been dreaming of it for a long time. This "Beautiful and Sublime" has awfully gotten stuck in my throat now that I am forty; but that's now that I am forty. . . ."[27]

Recalling his unbridled debaucheries which inevitably were followed by a feeling of miserable dejection, the "underground" philosopher slyly remarks that, nevertheless, he always managed to overcome that unpleasant feeling by taking refuge in the realm of "everything Beautiful and Sublime": "Of course, only in my dreams. And how much I did dream. Why, I could dream for three months on end."[28] These surges of "everything Beautiful and Sublime" used to overwhelm him during his vile excesses, at the very moment when he had sunk to the lowest depths. Yet their appearance could not induce him to give up his debauchery: "On the contrary—they revivified it by contrast, as it were, and occurred exactly as often as was necessary to make a savory dressing."[29]

The irony of the prince in *The Injured and Oppressed* and of the "underground" philosopher about Schiller's concept of the Beautiful and the Good inaugurates Dostoyevsky's ambiguous

---

[26] Dostoyevsky, *PSKP*, IV, 112.

[27] Dostoyevsky, *PSKP*, IV, 120.

[28] Dostoyevsky, *FSKP*, IV, 145. Cf. E. Wasiolek, "A Study of Dostoevsky's Moral Dialectic," *PMLA*, LXXVIII (March 1963), 96.

[29] Dostoyevsky, *PSKP*, IV, 146. The "underground" philosopher must not be identified with Dostoyevsky. He was a mouthpiece of Dostoyevsky but no more.

and complex attitude toward this concept in the great works of his artistic maturity. In this regard, Rodion Raskolnikov, Versilov, and Dmitry Karamazov are projections of the "underground" philosopher. Particularly Dmitry Karamazov appears almost as his reincarnation, especially in his long and impassioned conversation with Alyosha in which he gives vent to his tormented doubts about Schiller's concept.[30] Like the "underground" philosopher, Dmitry takes refuge after his unbridled debaucheries in the realm of the "Beautiful and Sublime," trying to overcome his feeling of shame and guilt by immersing himself in the reading of Schiller's philosophical poems. But, as is the case with the philosopher "from the underground," Schiller's aestheticism proves ineffectual to "cure" him from falling back into the lowest depths of vice and shame.

Ironic references to Schiller's concept of the Beautiful and Sublime abound also in *Crime and Punishment* (1866–67). Speaking of his mother's and sister's unrealistic attitude toward Mr. Luzhin, the future husband of his sister Dunya, Rodion Raskolnikov reflects:

It's always like that with these Schillerean beautiful souls: up to the last moment they dress a person with peacock feathers hoping for the good and not for the bad; and although they foresee the turn of the coin, they will not, not for anything, tell the truth when it is still time; they shudder at the very thought; with both hands they wave the truth away until the idealized person makes complete fools of them.[31]

The thoroughly disillusioned Raskolnikov has nothing but an ironic smile for Porfiry Petrovich's assertion that a man's soul is the only thing in life that really matters:

What of it if perhaps you will not be seen by the world for a very

[30] Cp. Dostoyevsky, *PSKP*, IX, 108–109.
[31] Dostoyevsky, *PSKP*, V, 37–38.

long time? It is not time that matters but your own soul. Be a sun
and the whole world will see you. The sun must above all be the
sun. Why do you smile again—because I am such a Schiller?[32]

It is easy to see that the name of Schiller stands here for
"dreamer" or "idealist"—for a man, in short, who has lost contact with life and reality. Dostoyevsky had been brought into
"contact with life and reality" in his Siberian "House of the
Dead," and now, having lost his youthful exalted delusions under
the hard hammer blows of reality, he takes a cruel vengeance on
the author of *Don Carlos* in the mordant irony of his "underground" philosophers and Raskolnikovs. Paradoxically, Rodion
Raskolnikov who derides the naïveté of "Schillerean Beautiful
souls" is in turn ridiculed by Svidrigaylov as a "Schiller" and an
"idealist" :

Now you surprised me, Rodion Romanych, although I knew in
advance that it would be like that. You talk to me about debauchery
and aesthetics! You are a Schiller, you are an idealist! All this, of
course, is as it should be and it would certainly be surprising if it
were otherwise, but, nevertheless, it strikes one as strange when it
becomes palpable reality . . . Oh, too bad I have so little time, for
you are a most interesting individual! But, by the way, do you love
Schiller? I do an awful lot.[33]

Svidrigaylov's expression "debauchery and aesthetics" is
reminiscent of the musings of the "underground" philosopher and
the reflections of Dmitry Karamazov on Schiller's philosophy and
especially on his concept of the Beautiful and Sublime. In fact,
both Svidrigaylov and Dmitry may be taken as "underground"
philosophers in disguise, as figures under whose mask the real
problem, Dostoyevsky's struggle with Schiller's idealism, is hiding.
Very revealing in this connection is Svidrigaylov's confession that

[32] Dostoyevsky, *PSKP,* V, 374.
[33] Dostoyevsky, *PSKP,* V, 383.

he "loves" Schiller "an awful lot." At first glance this confession appears to be fraught with mockery, but if we think of Dostoyevsky's own paradoxical love–hate of Schiller we will be inclined rather to see in these words a reflection of the Russian's profoundly contradictory and agonizingly torn state of mind.

The same is true of the figure of Raskolnikov who ironizes Schillerean idealism although at heart he continues to be a Schillerean idealist. Additional proof of this dual nature of Raskolnikov can be derived from some other passages in *Crime and Punishment* as, for instance, when he bids Svidrigaylov to stop telling him his base anecdotes. In reply to this "fair-souled" exhortation Svidrigaylov exclaims mockingly: "That's Schiller, that's our Schiller, that's Schiller! Où va-t-elle la vertu se nicher?"[34] And once again the name of the German poet appears when Svidrigaylov sarcastically comments on Rodion's continual sighing and moaning:

The Schiller in you is always troubled. . . . If that is so, then go and give yourself up to the authorities declaring that : so and so, such and such a particular case has happened to me; my theory has proved somewhat faulty.[35]

Some important points of contact with Schiller can be found in *The Possessed* (1871–72), that powerful and penetrating novel on the character and life of Russian terrorists who have been sidetracked by their ideas into a morass from which they are unable to extricate themselves. The figure of Kirillov, for example, bears considerable resemblance to the young Schiller, especially in his philosophical conviction that "man is the only God of man." Very similar ideas had been expressed by Schiller in his poem "Resignation" where the faith in God is called a "Wahn, den nur Verjährung weiht" and where eternity is

[34] Dostoyevsky, *PSKP*, V, 392.
[35] Dostoyevsky, *PSKP*, V, 394.

characterized as "der Riesenschatten unsrer eignen Schrecken/Im hohlen Spiegel der Gewissensangst."

Yet young Schiller had not drawn the last and inevitable conclusions from his God-defying anthropocentric philosophy. It is Dostoyevsky who, through the mouth of his hero Kirillov, proclaims the inexorable corollary that suicide is the ultimate and most powerful link in the chain of this philosophy, tending toward self-deification. The "great freedom" of which Kirillov dreams can be achieved only through an act of premeditated self-annihilation which, in the eyes of the atheist, is the supreme proof that he has blotted out his will to live, that he has triumphed over his instinctive fear of the unknown. If man is able to throw away his life in full consciousness and proud fearless serenity of the mind, then and only then, according to Kirillov–Dostoyevsky, has he furnished proof that God does not exist;—then man himself has become God and may rightfully occupy the empty throne of the Almighty. Kirillov, obsessed by the idea of attaining the "great freedom," draws the consequences of his rejection of God and actually commits suicide.

Yet his is a pitiful death; he dies not at all as the self-deifying conqueror of the "great freedom" but rather as a profoundly tragic desperate mortal *in extremis.* From this inglorious end of the haughty atheist it may be deduced that Dostoyevsky, at the time of writing *The Possessed,* had to a large extent dissociated himself from the anthropocentric philosophy of the young Schiller and moved toward an orthodox position. However, this was only a temporary dissociation and before long, as *The Brothers Karamazov* show, he was again tormented by skepticism and the temptation to put himself on the "empty" throne of God.

Schiller exercised an irresistible power of attraction for Dostoyevsky's torn and ambivalent mind even though this attraction often manifested itself in the negative form of repulsion : As irony and sarcasm, scorn and derision. While ridiculing Schillerean idealism through the mouth of his "underground" philosophers and Svidrigaylovs he still remained attached to the philosopher of the Beautiful and Sublime and the "incomparable" *Räuber* remained his favorite reading throughout the seventies.[36] In his enthusiasm for this tragedy Dostoyevsky went so far as to read it to his children when they were only about five and seven years old, "a performance that had the natural, if unintended, effect of putting them to sleep."[37] Moreover, references to the German poet appear again and again, both in his poetic and journalistic writings, to reach a final climax in *The Brothers Karamazov,* his last and, perhaps, greatest novel.

But before turning to an analysis of that novel it is necessary to say a few words about some other works of the Russian writer. There is, to begin with, his novel *The Youth* (1874–75) in which one of the principal characters, Versilov, bears a considerable resemblance to Schiller's Marquis Posa. Versilov reveals himself as a typical representative of the Russian intelligentsia, especially in his conviction that he has a social and political mission to fulfill on behalf of suffering mankind. In accordance with this conviction he does not live for himself but for the great and noble "idea of universal mankind." On one occasion, while commenting on Arkady Makarovich's dislike of women, he mentions the German poet by name :

My friend, that is almost something à la Schiller ! I have been wondering all the time—you are such a red-cheeked boy; you almost burst with health—and at the same time such a, should I say, antipathy for women.[38]

On another occasion, Versilov refers to Schiller's concept of the Beautiful and Sublime :

[36] Cp. Zenta Maurina, *Dostojewskij* (Memmingen, 1952), p. 135.
[37] Yarmolinsky, *Dostoevsky,* pp. 335–336.
[38] Dostoyevsky, *PSKP,* VIII, 27.

We did not know how to act for our profit and advantage. . . .
But, who knows, perhaps the demands of the Beautiful and Sublime
are in reality of such a nature—in this respect I have remained in
the dark throughout my life.[39]

Regarding Versilov's remark that dislike of women is "something à la Schiller," the objection can be raised that such an
assertion does not seem to be substantiated by the facts. In our
opinion, there is nothing, neither in Schiller's works nor in
Schiller's biography, that would lend support to the hypothesis of
his "antipathy for women." However, a possible explanation
would be that it is probably to Posa's warnings against Don
Carlos' involvement with Elizabeth that Dostoyevsky-Versilov
has reference here. Else it must be assumed that Dostoyevsky
invented this "antipathy" *ad hoc* for the purpose of disparaging
and ridiculing the quixotic and abstract aspects of an unhealthy
kind of Schillerean idealism.

After his Siberian experiences the conviction had taken root in
Dostoyevsky's mind that there are no people with perfect morality
as Schiller had depicted—at least not in real life or, at best, only
in the rarest of individuals. Arkady Makarovich voices this conviction in no uncertain terms. Being on the point of using black-
mail as a means of achieving his aims, Arkady justifies his act :

That I am going to exploit the "document,"—this does not mean
anything at all. This will not prevent me from being decent and
generous. *Schiller's ideal people do not exist in real life, they are
just fanciful inventions.* After all, this little bit of baseness will be
of no importance if only the goal is sublime.[40]

Dostoyevsky's struggle with Schiller's concept of the Beautiful
and Sublime which had begun during his penal servitude in
Siberia and which had found literary expression in his novel *The*

[39] Dostoyevsky, *PSKP*, VIII, 109.
[40] Dostoyevsky, *PSKP*, VIII, 380. [Italics mine.]

Injured and Oppressed, in his *Memoirs from the Underground,* and in *Crime and Punishment,* continues thus in the novel, *The Youth.* Arkady's revolt against Schiller's idealism amounts essentially to a revolt against that Schillerean concept with a view of justifying his own "little bit of baseness." Against Schiller's idea of the absolute identity of the Good and the Beautiful he sophistically sets his presumption that "baseness will be of no importance if only the goal is sublime." Arkady's views are presumably those of Dostoyevsky himself.

Nevertheless, Dostoyevsky must soon have felt that he had failed to win a decisive victory in his battle against Schiller's concept of the Good and the Beautiful for in *The Brothers Karamazov* the struggle breaks out with renewed violence. And it is highly characteristic of Dostoyevsky's relation to Schiller that —in the end—it is not the terrorist Verkhovensky or the sophist Arkady Makarovich who triumph but the saintly Alyosha Karamazov, who appears as the very embodiment of Schiller's "beautiful soul" and of his concept of the Good and the Beautiful.

In contrast to his critical and ironic attitude toward Schiller's ideal characters and concepts in his poetic works, Dostoyevsky's pronouncements on the German poet in his *letters* and *journalistic articles* are all characterized by a tone of high esteem and warm appreciation. This had become evident in his letters written to his brother Mikhail in the Forties and in his articles in *Vremya* and *Epokha* in the Sixties which show him as an impassioned advocate of Schiller's fame and poetic genius. This friendly attitude toward Schiller the man and Schiller the poet reaches a climax in the Seventies and continues without interruption to the very last days of his life. An important reference to Schiller can be found in Dostoyevsky's *Diary of a Writer* (1876). Affirming that every European philosopher and poet is more intimately appreciated

and understood in Russia than in any other country of the world,
except, perhaps, in the writer's native land, Dostoyevsky adduces
Schiller as the most striking example to prove and illustrate his
point :

Even though the French Convention of 1793, when sending the
certificate of citizenship *Au poète allemand Schiller, l'ami de
l'humanité,* did perpetrate a beautiful, stately and prophetic act,
nevertheless it did not suspect that at the other end of Europe, in
barbarous Russia, that same Schiller was much more national and
more akin to the barbarian Russians than to France—not only in
those days but even later, throughout our whole century where
Schiller, the French citizen and *l'ami de l'humanité,* was known,
and then but slightly—only by professors of literature, and not even
by all of them. Yet in Russia, together with Jukovsky, he soaked into
the Russian soul, left an impress upon it, and almost marked an
epoch in the history of our development.[41]

This is a crucial statement on the German poet. In its light all
preceding negative or ironical utterances on Schiller by the
various heroes of Dostoyevsky's novels lose much of their weight.
Furthermore, this statement serves to confirm the thesis that
Dostoyevsky's ironic attitude toward Schillerean enthusiasts did
not extend to Schiller himself. If any additional proof were
needed to establish Dostoyevsky's extraordinary esteem for the
German poet it can be found in his famous speech on Pushkin,
delivered on June 8,1880, at a meeting of the Society of Lovers
of Russian Literature. Here Schiller is placed on the same level
as Cervantes and Shakespeare : "In fact, in European belles-
lettres there were geniuses of immense creative magnitude—
Shakespeare, Cervantes, Schiller."[42] Dostoyevsky's high estimate
of Schiller's genius is no empty rhetoric, no accident. As a critic
has pointed out :

[41] Dostoyevsky, *The Diary of a Writer,* I, 343. [Italics Dostoyevsky's.]
[42] Dostoyevsky, *The Diary of a Writer,* "Pushkin," II, 977.

Dass diese hohe Bewertung Schillers [in the address on Pushkin] nicht nur eine rein-theoretische Anerkennung seiner geschichtlichen Bedeutung war, das zeigen die Schillerschen Motive in dem letzten grossen Werke Dostojewskijs—in den *Brüdern Karamasow.*[43]

The imprint Schiller has placed on *The Brothers Karamazov* is unmistakable. The very number of references to the German poet must be regarded as revealing:

Whereas Pushkin is mentioned six times, Shakespeare-five, Schiller is mentioned thirty two times, not counting those passages in which we can find allusions to ideas of Schiller (there are about ten such passages according to my [Chizhevsky's] calculation).[44]

All Karamazovs, with the exception of Smerdyakov, make reference to Schiller. Thus the old Karamazov, pointing to Ivan, exclaims during his visit to Father Zosima:

. . . that is my son, flesh of my flesh, the most beloved of my flesh! He is my most respectful Karl Moor, so to say, while this one who has just come in, Dmitry Fyodorovich, against whom I am seeking justice from you, is the unrespectful Franz Moor—they are both out of Schiller's *Die Räuber,* and so I am Regierender Graf von Moor. Judge and save us![45]

The old Karamazov apparently knew his Schiller well.—But did he really? Maxim Gorky, at any rate, reproaches him for not having read the dramas of Schiller with sufficient care and attention:

The older brothers Karamazov had their spiritual brothers among the German youth of the eighteenth century, and if father Karamazov had read attentively Schiller's dramas *Don Carlos* and *Die*

[43] D. I. Cyzevskyj, "Schiller und die Brüder Karamasow," *Zeitschrift für Slawische Philologie,* VI (Leipzig, 1929), 6. Woodhouse, however, denies that Dostoyevsky was "profoundly impressed by his [Schiller's] influence; rather the contrary." Cf. *op. cit.,* p. 19.

[44] Chizhevsky, "Schiller v Rossii," p. 123.

[45] Dostoyevsky, *PSKP,* IX, 73.

Räuber he would have been able to understand his children incomparably better than he actually did.[46]

Upon leaving the monastery, referring to the low bows of Father Zosima, Fyodor Pavlovich Karamazov remarks ironically : "We know these bows! 'Küsse auf den Lippen! Schwerter im Busen!' like in Schiller's *Die Räuber*."[47]

Significant references to Schiller are made during Dmitry's long conversation with Alyosha. It is not without surprise that one hears the half-drunk army officer quote verses from some of the philosophical poems of Schiller :

Lyosha, said Mitya,—you alone will not laugh! I would like to begin . . . my confession . . . with Schiller's hymn to joy : "An die Freude!" But I do not know German, I only know that it is "An die Freude." Don't think, either, that I am talking in a state of drunkenness. . . . He raised his head, thought for a moment, and suddenly began with enthusiasm :

Scheu in des Gebirges Klüften
Barg der Troglodyte sich,
Der Nomade liess die Triften
Wüste liegen, wo er strich,
Mit dem Wurfspiess, mit dem Bogen
Schritt der Jäger durch das Land,
Weh dem Fremdling, den die Wogen
Warfen an den Unglücksstrand!

Und auf ihrem Pfad begrüsste
Irrend nach des Kindes Spur
Ceres die verlassne Küste,
Ach, da grünte keine Flur!
Dass sie hier vertraulich weile,

---

[46] Maxim Gorky, *Sobranie Sochineniy* (Moskva, 1949–55), "Istoria molo-dogo cheloveka," XXVI, 167.

[47] Dostoyevsky, *PSKP,* IX, 91. Old Karamazov refers here to *Die Räuber,* I, 2.

Ist kein Obdach ihr gewährt,
Keines Tempels heitre Säule
Zeuget, dass man Götter ehrt.
Keine Frucht der süssen Ähren
Lädt zum reinen Mahl sie ein,
Nur auf grässlichen Altären
Dorret menschliches Gebein.
Ja, so weit sie wandernd kreiste,
Fand sie Elend überall,
Und in ihrem grossen Geiste
Jammert sie des Menschen Fall.

Mitya broke into sobs and took Alyosha's hand. "My dear, my dear, in dishonor, in dishonor also now. There is a terrible amount of suffering for man on earth, an awful lot of sorrow. . . . I scarcely think of anything but of that dishonored man. . . . I think of that man because I am that man myself.

Dass der Mensch zum Menschen werde,
Stift er einen ewgen Bund
Gläubig mit der frommen Erde,
Seinem mütterlichen Grund . . .

But the trouble is how should I enter into an eternal union with Mother Earth? I do not kiss her, I do not nestle to her breast. Should I transform into a peasant or a shepherd? I go on and I do not know if I am going to disgrace or to light and bliss. That is the trouble, because everything in the world is a puzzle! And whenever I have chanced to fall into the basest disgrace (and it has been occurring all the time) I always read this poem about Ceres and man. Has it made me better? Never! Because I am a Karamazov. For when I fall into the abyss, I fall headlong with my feet up, and I am pleased with that degrading way of falling and even am proud of it. But in the lowest depths of my shame I begin a hymn of praise. Let me be damned, let me be mean and vicious, but permit me to kiss the hem of the veil in which my God is hidden. Even though I

may be following the devil, I am your son, O Lord, and I do love
you, and I feel the joy without which the universe cannot exist.

> Freude trinken alle Wesen
> An den Brüsten der Natur,
> Alle Guten, alle Bösen
> Folgen ihrer Rosenspur.
> Küsse gab sie uns und Reben,
> Einen Freund, geprüft im Tod,
> Wollust ward dem Wurm gegeben,
> Und der Cherub steht vor Gott.

But enough poetry! I am in tears—let me cry. . . . I want to tell
you now about the worms to whom God has given sensual lust!
Wollust ward dem Wurm gegeben. I am that worm, brother, and
it is said of me personally.[48]

In the *Memoirs from the Underground* and in *Crime and
Punishment* the name of Schiller had been used as an ironic and
abusive epithet for every dreamer and idealist. But in his last
novel Dostoyevsky reverently bows his head before the German
poet. Through the mouth of Dmitry, passionately declaiming
"Das Eleusische Fest" and "An die Freude," Dostoyevsky, as it
were, wants to atone for the sin of his unjust apostasy from
Schiller. Dmitry is Karl Moor—contrary to the claim of Fyodor
Pavlovich who shows poor judgment and lack of psychological
insight into the character of his own children by comparing him
with the wicked and undutiful Franz Moor.

We may apply to Dmitry what the German poet said of Karl
Moor in his preface to *Die Räuber*: "Ein Geist, den das äusserste
Laster nur reizet um der Grösse willen, die ihm anhänget, um der
Kraft willen, die es erheischet, um der Gefahren willen, die es

---

[48] Dostoyevsky, *PSKP*, IX, 108–109. In Dostoyevsky the quotes are in
Russian (in Zhukovsky's free adaptation).

begleiten.'"⁴⁹ Schiller's verses sound strange in the mouth of this rough and reckless army officer. Schiller must speak for him and express what he himself, despite his arrogant and presumptuous behavior, is unable to put into words. Not for nothing does Dmitry-Dostoyevsky quote verses from "Das Eleusische Fest" and "An die Freude." These poems deal with ideas, concepts, and problems that have a fundamental importance in the philosophical and aesthetical works of the German poet: problems of the philosophy of history, the cultural evolution of the human race, and problems of ethics and beauty. In his conversation with Alyosha, Dmitry touches on these problems, too, when he exclaims:

Beauty is a dreadful and awe-inspiring thing! It is dreadful because it has not been unriddled and never can be unriddled, for God gives us nothing but mysteries. . . . Beauty! I cannot bear the idea that a man of exalted mind and heart starts with the ideal of the Madonna and ends with the ideal of Sodom. Yet even more shocking is that a man with the ideal of Sodom in his soul does not give up the ideal of the Madonna and his heart may be afire with that ideal, truly afire, just as in his days of childhood and innocence.⁵⁰

Once more, as in the *Memoirs from the Underground*, Dostoyevsky uses one of his heroes to give vent to the unbearable mental and spiritual pressures that had piled up in him during the years of his penal servitude in Siberia and in the years thereafter. In the conflict-laden heart of Dmitry there continues with unabated violence Dostoyevsky's struggle with the German poet's idealism and aestheticism; with his idea of the Good and the

⁴⁹ Schiller, *SW*, XVI, 16.
⁵⁰ Dostoyevsky, *PSKP*, IX, 108–109. Cf. H. Stammler: "Thus Schiller's . . . conceptions of the beautiful as the incarnation of the ideal . . . helped Dostoevsky formulate his aesthetics in religious terms." "Dostoevsky's Aesthetics and Schelling's Philosophy of Art," *Comparative Literature*, VII (1955), 319.

Beautiful in which the "underground" philosopher had already sought refuge after his regularly re-occurring periods of unbridled debauchery. Dmitry's last words are clearly reminiscent of certain passages in *Die Räuber,* especially of the scene at the Danube (III,2), where Karl Moor conjures the happy days of his childhood and innocence. Karl Moor also began with the ideal of the Madonna and ended with the ideal of Sodom—without abandoning the ideal of the Madonna. The heart of the great Robber, like Dmitry's heart, has remained on fire with the lofty ideas of justice, beauty, and all-embracing love. Although he is the chief of a gang of assassins, he feels that he has nothing in common with them : they are only "roguish thieves, miserable instruments of his greater intentions" (II, 3).

Dmitry, like Karl Moor, finds himself involved in a tormenting conflict with reality and society. Seeing the imperfections and downright defects of real life, both idealists aspire for a new and better and more beautiful world, for a reformed and ennobled humanity. Quoting "Das Eleusische Fest" and "An die Freude," Dmitry shows that his ideas and ideals are those of the German poet. But his agreement with Schiller is limited to the realm of dreams and poetry. Descending from the lofty heights of poetry into the degrading depths of his everyday existence, Dmitry finds himself again facing the unsolved problems of the discrepancy between life and ideal : "But the trouble is how should I enter into an eternal union with Mother Earth ?"

The parallel to Schiller is unmistakable and far-reaching, especially if one thinks of some of his other poems of a related nature such as "Sehnsucht" and "Der Pilgrim" which are fraught with a similar mood of frustration : "Und das Dort ist niemals hier !" Dmitry suffers intensely from this irreconcilable discrepancy between dream and reality, his shameful degradation and his inextinguishable yearning to "kiss the hem of the veil in which his God is hidden." What a critic has said of man in general might very well have been said of Dmitry Karamazov in particular :

Das Schöne ist nun nichts anderes als die verwirklicht, individuiert vorgestellte oder existierende Form dieser Ideale. Hierin stimmt Dostoyevsky weitgehend mit Schiller überein. Der Mensch kann nicht in einem ständigen Konflikt mit der Wirklichkeit leben, wenn er nicht eine Idee findet oder entwirft, die eine mögliche Lösung dieses Konfliktes bietet oder zu bieten scheint. Er will und braucht aber nicht nur die Idee, er will und braucht auch deren Realisierbarkeit und Realiserung.[51]

Thence Dmitry's tormenting doubts about the practicability of Schiller's sublime ideals and his quandry as to whether he should become a peasant or shepherd in order to achieve that higher degree of harmony and humanity envisaged by the German poet. But in his uncertainty and agony he sees no way out of his dilemma. All he professes to know is that "everything in the world is a puzzle." Moreover, Dmitry Karamazov reflects the views of the German poet, even in this attitude of bewilderment and awe before the unfathomable mysteries of the world.[52]

Though Dmitry, like the philosopher from the *underground,* sinks to the very depths of baseness and degradation, he is fully aware of his degradation. This consciousness of his own vileness gives him the strength of rising from the grimy abyss to the heights of magnanimity and religious inspiration; it gives him the strength of saying passionately "yes" to life and all its joys and sorrows. Dmitry cites Schiller's hymn "An die Freude" because there is music in his soul, the all-embracing music of love and a

[51] Lauth, *Die Philosophie Dostojewskis,* p. 360.
[52] Cp. Karl Berger, *Schiller* (München, 1909), II, 310: "Dass dem Menschen der Einblick in das Wesen der Dinge, in die übersinnliche Welt nicht vergönnt wird, ist eine der früh erworbenen Anschauungen Schillers." In this connection, cp. the poem "Die Worte des Wahns" (1799).

child-like humility in the face of the unfathomable mysteries of life. It is hardly an exaggeration to say that "An die Freude" is used as a kind of leitmotif in *The Brothers Karamazov,* and, again, within that poem a very special significance must be attached to the lines quoted by the exalted Dmitry : "Wollust ward dem Wurm gegeben,/Und der Cherub steht vor Gott." As will be remembered, Dmitry had applied these lines to his own person and life : "I am that worm and it is said of me personally." Yet not only he but also the old Karamazov is that "worm" whereas Alyosha represents the "cherub" who stands before the throne of God.

Dostoyevsky's distinction between the terms "joy" and "lust" is not at all accidental; on the contrary, it sheds a light on his ethical views and his conviction that true morality excludes any considerations of personal welfare or reward—in this life or beyond the veil. To both sentiments, exalted joy and sensual lust, Dmitry abandons himself with the full vehemence of his passionate temperament. All his chaotic existence is dominated by an all-embracing and indiscriminate love : "Seid umschlungen Millionen !/ Diesen Kuss der ganzen Welt !" "Let us love, Alyosha !" God and the devil are fighting and the battlefield is the fierce and passionate heart of this reckless army officer. Incidentally, Schiller has also left his imprint on Alyosha who is a reader and admirer of the German poet like the old Karamazov and Dmitry. In his conversation with the thirteen-year-old Kolya Krasotkin, Alyosha develops his theory of art which he conceives as play—"Spiel"—under the obvious influence of Schiller's *Briefe über die ästhetische Erziehung des Menschen* ("Der Mensch ist nur dann ganz Mensch, wenn er spielt.").

The picture of the Schiller-reading Karamazov family is completed by Ivan, who also has read his Schiller and has read him so well that he can quote him in the German original. Referring to the ballad "Der Handschuh" Ivan leaves Katerina Ivanovna with the words of the angry knight Delorges:

"I shall forgive you later, but now I do not want your hand! Den Dank, Dame, begehr ich nicht," he added, with a forced smile, showing nonetheless, that he could read Schiller, and had read him until he knew him by heart—something Alyosha would never have believed.[53]

Much more important in the economy of the novel is Ivan's impassioned rebellion against God which offers striking parallels to the rebellious "Storm and Stress" views of the German poet. In his conversation with Alyosha about the undeserved sufferings of innocent children, Ivan exclaims dramatically: "It is not God that I do not accept, Alyosha, only I most respectfully return to Him my claim ticket." In these words undoubtedly lies an allusion to Schiller's poem "Resignation," more specifically to its third stanza:

> Da steh ich schon auf deiner Schauerbrücke,
> Ehrwürdge Geistermutter—Ewigkeit.
> Empfange meinen Vollmachtsbrief zum Glücke,
> Ich bring ihn unerbrochen dir zurücke,
> Mein Lauf ist aus. Ich weiss von keiner Seligkeit.

Like young Schiller, Ivan rebels against the universe established by God ("Ewigkeit" in Schiller's poem) because "too high a price is asked for harmony." Like Schiller, Ivan returns to God his claim ticket ("Vollmachtsbrief") for he cannot be happy in this world created by an indifferent and pitiless Author of all things.

Ivan's contact with Schiller culminates in his legend "The

---

[53] Dostoyevsky, *PSKP*, IX, 190. About "... la brillante personnalité d'Ivan, son instruction et ses habitudes de savant," cf. R. Pletnev, "La légende chrétienne dans l'oeuvre de Dostoïevsky," *SEES*, VI (Montréal, Autumn–Winter 1961), 151.

Grand Inquisitor." Dostoyevsky took the figure of the Grand
Inquisitor from Schiller's drama *Don Carlos* which had fascinated
him to the point of obsession in the delirious days of his youth,
in the days of his friendship with Shidlovsky.

A comparison of Schiller's and Dostoyevsky's Inquisitor
reveals several interesting parallels. The figures of both Inquisitors
are shrouded in an atmosphere of icy and inhuman fanaticism,
with the difference that Dostoyevsky's Inquisitor, though characterized by the same fossilized monumentality of gesture, stands
on the pedestal of apocalyptic tragedy—a petrified monster,
reminding one of the incarnate Antichrist challenging his Creator
to the last and formidable battle of Armageddon. Christ, the
opponent of the Grand Inquisitor in *The Brothers Karamazov,* is
a more powerful adversary than the feeble King Philip in
Schiller's *Don Carlos* who, in the last scene of the drama, humbly
submits to the authority of the Cardinal. In *The Brothers
Karamazov* it is only the Grand Inquisitor who is speaking.
Christ himself remains silent throughout the long and bitter
tirade of the Inquisitor. But when he has finished, Christ silently
embraces and kisses him. The old man shudders. The kiss burns
in his heart. He opens the door of the prison and says: "Go, and
come no more! . . ." Terrible despair rings in his words and an
ominous threat. The kiss burns in his heart but it has not
changed his cold and power-thirsty mind.

The rigid attitude of the Grand Inquisitor results from his
conviction that freedom is not the highest good for humanity. In
his demoniacal arrogance and conceit he cannot believe that man
may value, and *does* value, freedom higher than life and happiness. Although he permits Christ to walk out of the prison it is
perfectly clear that his heart is not changed in the least. With
implacable consistency he will continue to devise plans for the
construction of an ideal ant-state where every one will be happy

—and an obedient weak-kneed slave. The Inquisitor's counterpart, the silent and yet powerfully eloquent figure of Christ, embodies the principle and ideal of invincible human freedom— invincible because implanted deeply and indestructibly by God himself in the immortal soul of every man. We find a similar concept of Christianity as a religion of freedom in Schiller's letter to Goethe of August 17, 1795 :

Ich finde in der christlichen Religion virtualiter die Anlage zu dem Höchsten und Edelsten, und die verschiedenen Erscheinungen derselben im Leben scheinen mir bloss deswegen so widrig und abgeschmackt, weil sie verfehlte Darstellung dieses Höchsten sind. Hält man sich an den eigentümlichen Charakterzug des Christentums, der es von allen monotheistischen Religionen unterscheidet, so liegt er in nichts anderm als in der *Aufhebung des Gesetzes* oder des Kantischen Imperativs, an dessen Stelle das Christentum eine freie Neigung gesetzt haben will.[54]

By replacing the figure of the King by the powerful figure of Christ, Dostoyevsky has attained a position of distinct superiority over the author of *Don Carlos*. It is an achievement which adds new dimensions to Schiller's ideological drama. Marquis Posa's appeal to the King, "Stellen Sie der Menschheit verlorenen Adel wieder her!" is immensely intensified, both deepened and heightened, by the introduction of the human, and yet simultaneously super-human, element personified in the figure of Christ.

The full significance of the many quotations from Schiller comes to light at the end of *The Brothers Karamazov* in the speeches of the prosecutor and Dmitry's lawyer Fetyukovich. In

[54] *Friedrich Schiller—Briefe*, ed. Reinhard Buchwald (Leipzig, n. d.), p.420. [Italics Schiller's.] Regarding Dostoyevsky's accusations of the Catholic Church, cp. W. Iwanow, *Dostojewskij* (Tübingen, 1932), p. 132: ". . . uraltes Vorurteil . . . würden einer besonderen kritischen Durchsicht bedürfen . . ." See also M. Karpovich, "Dostoyevsky, Belinsky, Schiller," *Novy Zhurnal*, XLV (New York, 1956), 280–283, and N. Lossky, *Dostoyevsky i yego khristianskoye miroponimanie* (New York, 1953), pp. 352–353.

his characterization of the defendant the prosecutor makes the following sarcastic remark :

Oh, he is impulsive, he is a wonderful mixture of good and evil, he is a lover of culture and Schiller, but he fights in the inns and tears out the beards of his boon companions.[55]

Fetyukovich skillfully exploits these remarks in his impassioned defense of the accused :

A moment ago, the gifted prosecutor ridiculed my client for loving Schiller—loving the sublime and the beautiful. In his place, I would not have ridiculed him for that. . . . This apparently rude and rough man seeks a new life, strives to reform himself, to be better, to become worthy and respectable, "sublime and beautiful," no matter how much this phrase has been ridiculed.[56]

Thereupon Fetyukovich proceeds to undermine the very foundations of the charges against Dmitry by challenging all supposedly irrefutable circumstances of the crime. "There was no money," he maintains, "there was no robbery, and there was no murder, either." In addition, Fetyukovich argues, the father of the accused does not deserve the name of a father :

Such a father as the old Karamazov cannot be called a father and does not merit this name. Filial love for an unworthy father is an absurd and impossible thing. . . . But as a man and as a citizen I make my appeal—*vivos voco*![57]

The sight of an unworthy father must inevitably stir up tormenting questions in the heart of a young man. But to these questions he will receive the usual unsatisfying reply : "He begot you, you are flesh from his flesh, and therefore you must love him." The young man will then ask himself : "Did he really love me when

[55] Dostoyevsky, *PSKP*, X, 361.

[56] Dostoyevsky, *PSKP*, X, 405.

[57] Dostoyevsky, *PSKP*, X, 406. Incidentally, the expression "vivos voco" is a reference to Schiller's poem "Das Lied von der Glocke." There is Schillerean pathos in the court scene but it borders on comedy.

he begot me? Did he beget me for my sake? He did not know me, nor did he know my sex at that moment, at the moment of passion, perhaps intensified by wine. . . ." Fetyukovich echoes here the reflections of Franz Moor in Schiller's *Die Räuber:* "Ich habe langes und breites von einer sogenannten Blutliebe schwatzen gehört. . . ." (I, 1), and, in another passage: "Den Vater, der vielleicht eine Bouteille Wein weiter getrunken hat, kommt der Kitzel an—und draus wird ein Mensch, und der Mensch war gewiss das letzte, woran bei der ganzen Herkules-arbeit gedacht wird." (IV, 2).

Another important link with Schiller is Dostoyevsky's concept of the "higher man" which constitutes one of the principal ideas of *The Brothers Karamazov.* The Russian continues and elaborates here (in the figure of Alyosha), Schiller's idea of the aesthetic man: "Der ästhetisch gestimmte Mensch wird allgemein gültig urteilen und allgemein gültig handeln, sobald er es wollen wird."[58] Dostoyevsky, it is true, does not agree with Schiller's belief in the superiority of the aesthetic man, but he rejects this idea only in a certain sense, namely as far as it is divested of the religious element. Thinking the idea of the aesthetic man to its end, Dostoyevsky arrived at the conclusion that it contained components dangerous to the idea of God and a moral world order—a conclusion that appears not unjustified in view of the later philosophy of Nietzsche and his concept of the "Übermensch." In contrast to Schiller, Dostoyevsky holds the opinion that aestheticism cannot create a stable equilibrium between the forces of good and evil struggling in the soul of man. What is more, he does not believe that aestheticism is

---

[58] Schiller, *SW*, XII, 88, "Über die ästhetische Erziehung des Menschen," 23. Brief. With reference to Alyosha, W. Iwanow observes: "Im Roman *Die Brüder Karamasow* ist Russland in der Gestalt der drei Brüder dargestellt, von denen der dritte, in seiner stillen Demut—ganz wie im Volksmärchen—der Erwählte des Schicksals ist." Cf. *Dostojewskij*, p. 121.

capable of reforming or redeeming suffering humanity.[59] His ideal
of the "higher man" is not the aesthetic man but the religious
man personified by the figures of Father Zosima and Alyosha.
The word "cherub" which Dostoyevsky uses so frequently when
speaking of Alyosha is the very same word that produces its
striking effect in Schiller's poem "An die Freude" : "Und der
Cherub steht vor Gott." Taken in connection with the preceding
line : "Wollust ward dem Wurm gegeben," the conclusion may
be drawn that Alyosha represents the antithetical elaboration of
the lowly "worms" Fyodor Pavlovich and Dmitry cringing in the
morass of moral degradation and sensual lust.

In conclusion, reviewing the long and tortuous path covered
by Dostoyevsky in the company of Schiller, we may say that he
owes more to the author of *Don Carlos* than to any other Russian or Western European writer. Schiller is the principal source
of his youthful exaltation, the poet about whom he raves and
dreams in his school days. For many years he is obsessed by the
idea of editing a complete translation of the works of Schiller.
Through Schiller's idealism he finds his way to the socialist
theories of Petrashevsky and Fourier, and it is Schiller who gives
him comfort and moral support in the difficult days of his imprisonment. The years of penal servitude and disillusionment in
Siberia deal a terrible blow to his Schillerean idealism but, in
spite of all, he remains faithful to Schiller the man and poet,

[59] Cp. the confession of the "underground" philosopher : "The more I
became conscious of the Good and of all that 'Beautiful and Sublime,' the
deeper I sank into my mud . . ." Dostoyevsky, *PSKP*, IV, 112; cp. also
Dmitry Karamazov's words : "And whenever I have chanced to fall into
the basest disgrace . . . I always read this poem about Ceres and man.
Has it made me better? Never !" Dostoyevsky *PSKP*, IX, 108–109. Again,
as in the case of the "underground" philosopher, a word of caution against
identifying Dmitry with Dostoyevsky. Also Ivan and Alyosha are exponents
of Dostoyevsky's complex personality. About Dostoyevsky's religious views
from an orthodox standpoint see P. Antoniy, *Slovar k tvoreniam Dostoyevskago* (Sofia, 1921).

defending him fervently against all attacks: "Yes, Schiller has really entered the very blood-stream of Russian society. . . ."

Dostoyevsky's novels from *The Injured and Oppressed* (1861) to *The Youth* (1874) are all characterized by a spirit of irony and sarcasm toward the quixotic representatives of Schillerean idealism, but in his last novel, *The Brothers Karamazov* (1880) and in his address on Pushkin (June 8, 1880), the climax of his glory and his public swan song, he pays again—as in the ecstatic days of his youth—glowing tribute to Schiller, ranking him with Cervantes and Shakespeare and hailing him as a "genius of immense creative magnitude." Schiller's idealism, despised and ridiculed by the champions of a dogmatic realism, reveals thus its remarkable vitality in the mind and works of the great Russian novelist.[60] What is more, through the works of Dostoyevsky Schiller's spirit continues to exercise a hidden influence—an indirect influence quite apart from the influence of his original works—upon contemporary humanity.

In his *Diary of a Writer* (1876) Dostoyevsky had declared that Schiller "almost marked an epoch in the history of our development." Looking at the life work of the author of *The Brothers Karamazov* we may say that Dostoyevsky, too, represents an "epoch," both in the spiritual development of Russia and of a large part of humanity. To be sure, his influence has been particularly strong and enduring in Western Europe which, strangely enough, has rarely realized that by imitating and praising the incomparable genius of the Russian it was unconsciously paying tribute to the genius of the "old-fashioned," disparaged, and oft-ridiculed author of *Don Carlos* who was the principal source of

[60] Yet there are many Western writers who see Dostoyevsky as completely outside the Western tradition. Cp. in this connection René Wellek: 'Dostoevsky's conscious attitudes toward Europe were often ambiguous; but as an artist and thinker he is part of the stream of Western thought and Western literary traditions." *Dostoevsky*, ed. R. Wellek (Englewood Cliffs, 1962), p. 7.

his inspiration. In the final analysis, Dostoyevsky's impact on the literature of the West may be regarded as a restitution to the West of those treasures which Russian art, Russian philosophy, and Russian literature had received from the West in the preceding centuries.[61] Seen from this correlative point of view, Schiller's aestheticism is bound to have an incalculable future of vibrant vitality through the mediation of Dostoyevsky. To be sure, correlated or not, the significance, the weight, and dynamic force of their artistic achievements guarantee a limitless number of echoes to these two representatives of mankind. Schiller and Dostoyevsky, "the heroes and saints of an idea,"[62] continue to challenge the unheroic and unholy reality of everyday life in their native countries and in the whole literate world.

[61] Cf. T. L. Motylev, "Dostoyevsky i mirovaya literatura," *Tvorchestvo F. M. Dostoyevskogo* (Moskva, 1959), pp. 15–44.

[62] Thomas Mann, "Goethe und Tolstoi," *op. cit.,* p. 203. In this connection, cf. also André von Gronicka, "Thomas Mann and Russia," *The Stature of Thomas Mann,* ed. Charles Neider (New York, 1947), pp. 310–311.

VIII

Ivanov

A MAN OF EXCEPTIONAL INTELLECTUAL AND SPIRITUAL STATURE, V. I. Ivanov (1866–1949) was the influential leader of St. Petersburg poets from 1905 until 1911. Equally versed as a poet, philosopher, and philologist, he envisioned a synthesis of the Dionysian spirit of ancient Greece and the syncretic ideas of Russian symbolism. Like Schiller and Stefan George, he had an exceedingly lofty conception of the vocation of the poet : "The poet is for Ivanov a priest, an oracle of truth which can be grasped only by intuition and expressed by symbols, that is, by myths. The poet is therefore a creator of myths, that is to say, a religious creator. . . ."[1] Leo Shestov gave Ivanov the epithet of "Vyacheslav the Magnificent," and "magnificent" is the only word that adequately describes the majestic and ornate structure of his style. Ivanov took great pride in the fact that it was necessary to read him "with a dictionary and with reference books."[2]

His masterpiece in the field of poetry is probably *Cor Ardens*, the *non plus ultra* of the ornate style in Russian literature. No less magnificent and elaborate is his flowery prose of which his *Correspondence between Two Corners*, a dialogue with the philosopher and critic Gershenzon, must be regarded as the most

[1] Ettore Lo Gatto, *Storia della Letteratura Russa* (Firenze, 1944), p. 482. Cf. also O. Deschartes, "V. Ivanov," *Oxford Slavonic Papers*, V (1954), 45, 49.
[2] Ivan Tkhorzhevsky, *Russkaya Literatura* (Paris, 1950), p. 473.

famous example. Ivanov was convinced that a renascence of the mythological production of the pious times of antiquity could be brought about even by modern man. "He [Ivanov] discovered in Dostoyevsky a great creator of myths, and he believed that the modern theater might become religious and choric like the Dionysian theater of Athens."[3]

It is from this point of view that the problem of Ivanov's attitude toward Schiller must be approached. Above all Ivanov valued in the German poet his contribution to the development of the dithyramb and the choric festivity. He doubtless did this under the influence of Dostoyevsky whose motto had been: "Seek for ecstasy and frenzy," and who could not find more ardent words in poetry for the celebration of these ecstatic and mystical experiences than the words of Schiller.[4] Seen in this mythologically and mystically oriented perspective, Schiller was bound to appear to Ivanov as a symbolist *sui generis* both in aesthetics and in poetry—a conception which sheds revealing light on the genealogy of modern symbolism.

Of crucial importance for the understanding of Ivanov's relationship to Schiller is his essay written on the occasion of the one hundredth anniversary of Schiller's death (May 9, 1805), and entitled "On Schiller."[5] In this essay Ivanov recalls the solemn funeral rites held by Baggesen in Denmark in 1791 upon the spurious report of Schiller's sudden death:

It is now one hundred years from the day of his [Schiller's] real apotheosis of which those glorious funeral rites on the shore of the sea had been but an inspired foreshadowing. His death was his

[3] D. S. Mirsky, *A History of Russian Literature* (New York, 1949), p. 451. Regarding Ivanov's alleged attempt to substitute Dionysius for Christ cf. Deschartes, *loc. cit.*, pp. 43–44.

[4] "K yubileyu Schillera," *Vesy*, VI (1905), 79. But note that Belinsky had profoundly influenced the Schiller image of both Dostoyevsky and Ivanov.

[5] Included in his collection of articles and treatises *Po zvezdam* (St. Petersburg, 1909).

mystical apotheosis. On May 9 (April 27), 1805, Schiller departed from this life to act as a "hero" and benefactor of humanity from the entrails of the earth or from those lofty heights whence the helmsmen of the spirit keep their vigil over us. In truth, it befits also the present generation to sing his "Song to Joy" during these days and to evoke with flute sounds of love and longing his departed but yet near and ever-present shadow.[6]

Ivanov, steeped in the tradition of Greek antiquity, sees in Schiller, after his "mystical apotheosis," a hero and demigod comparable to the laborer and sufferer, Heracles. On earth Schiller, like Heracles, completed the measure of earthly suffering. To substantiate this comparison, Ivanov quotes the two last stanzas from Schiller's philosophical poem "Das Ideal und das Leben":

Tief erniedrigt zu des Feigen Knechte
Ging in ewigem Gefechte
Einst Alcid des Lebens schwere Bahn,
Rang mit Hydern und umarmt' den Leuen,
Stürzte sich, die Freunde zu befreien,
Lebend in des Totenschiffers Kahn.
Alle Plagen, alle Erdenlasten
Wälzt der unversöhnten Göttin List
Auf die willgen Schultern des Verhassten.
Bis sein Lauf geendigt ist—

Bis der Gott, des Irdischen entkleidet,
Flammend sich vom Menschen scheidet
Und des Äthers leichte Lüfte trinkt.
Froh des neuen ungewohnten Schwebens
Fliesst er aufwärts, und des Erdenlebens
Schweres Traumbild sinkt und sinkt und sinkt.
Des Olympus Harmonien empfangen
Den Verklärten in Kronions Saal,

<hr/>

[6] Vyacheslav Ivanov, *Po zvezdam*, p. 71.

Und die Göttin mit den Rosenwangen
Reicht ihm lächelnd den Pokal.

Thus, in the heroic days of old, the inspired reciters of dithy-
rambs used to extoll the leader of their chorus. Later generations,
with the decline of the dithyrambic spirit, saw in Schiller merely
an exalted idealist.

Ivanov then conjures and epitomizes the sentiments and ideas
which the name of Schiller evokes in the mind of an educated
Russian and arrives at the conclusion that Schiller's name was,
and has remained to this day, the symbol of noble enthusiasm
for the ideals of the sublime and the beautiful :

The good and the beautiful conceived as an intrinsic identity;
the grandeur of the God-like body and spirit of man; the "dignity
of man" and the "dignity of woman," civic and social intrepidity;
sympathy, brotherhood, and equality in human relationships; an
untrammeled religiosity as the natural condition of the harmoniously
attuned and morally enlightened soul; the dynamism of a noble and
lofty struggle for truth and justice; finally, the great and sacred
motto "Freedom" as the pervasive form of all manifestations of
our rightful self-assertion,—this is the content of that cluster of
ideas and emotions that the name of Schiller stirs up in us. In truth,
he was the herald of all "that is human in man."[7]

But this lofty idealism of the German poet seems to Ivanov
tainted by a certain academic dogmatism and by dreamy, world-
detached abstractness. With apparent approval he adduces the
criticism of Heine who in Schiller's most sincere lyrical effusions
could not discern anything except "an orgy of logical notions
and a dance of incorporeal abstract ideas." Recalling Pushkin's
poem "October 19, 1825," he imagines that Pushkin, too, is
critical of Schiller's exalted abstractness when—"not without a
melancholy smile"[8]—he invites the friend of his youth, Küchel-

[7] Ivanov, *Po zvezdam,* p. 73.
[8] *Ibid.*

becker, to talk with him again : "Of the stormy Caucasian days, / Of Schiller, of glory, of love."

Schiller embodies for Ivanov the effervescence of youth. Maturity and bitter reality transform these youthful transports into sentimentally cherished but outworn memories. The preachings of Schiller (even when a child he used to preach playfully) have really turned out to be a "preachment,"—the proclaiming of dogmas which are indisputable but facile and infinitely naïve before the basilisk eye of life. The life of the nineteenth century, Ivanov contends, was too profound, intricate, and somber, to justify the starry-eyed enthusiasms of Schiller. Schiller's divine ardor was too pure : there was not enough of the salt of the earth in it. The basic antinomy in all things, so it seemed, had altogether escaped him. An apostle of beauty, he did not know the "beauty of Sodom" matching, according to Dostoyevsky, the "beauty of the Madonna" in our most abysmal aesthetic ecstasies.[9]

Schiller's idealism was introduced into the German schools as incontestable, as wholesome pedagogical material and thus was quickly turned into an insipidly sacharine message. As a result of the academic study of Schiller's works the majority of our contemporaries became, according to Ivanov, forever detached from living contact with that genius : "Wehe dir, Schiller, dass du ein Klassiker geworden !" Ivanov exclaims with heartfelt sadness.

As a disciple of Nietzsche, Ivanov was, of course, poignantly aware of the fact that to Nietzsche, Schiller was merely a trumpeter of morals ("Moraltrompeter"). And it almost appears to the Russian that nothing but the "pathos" has remained of what at one time, during the period of the "Storm and Stress," was the electrifying revolt of a genius :

[9] F. M. Dostoyevsky, *Polnoye sobranie khudozhestvennykh proizvedeniy* (Moskva–Leningrad, 1926), IX, 108–109.

The Robbers has almost been forgotten; Marquis Posa is still remembered. The victory of his principles, at one time revolutionary —not in life, it is true, but in the social consciousness—has mitigated all the poignancy of the experiences with which Schiller atoned for his glory as a prophet of lofty and exalted concepts and ideals.[10]

Despite his many good and partially perfect poetic works, posterity has failed even to notice in Schiller anything save "idealism" and "pathos." Ivanov, however, detects in Schiller something far more important, something living, immortal, indestructibly valuable, and he hails the German poet as one of the contributors to an ancient and labyrinthian movement destined to prepare an entirely novel phase of spiritual creation.

At this point it may seem fitting to turn the critical light on some of the judgments pronounced by Ivanov upon Schiller. These judgments, as can be seen, suffer from a certain onesidedness and partiality for the "lyrical effusions" of the German poet—an attitude which must evoke criticism in view of Schiller's much more relevant and valuable dramatic production. A German critic remarks in this connection :

Wir wollen uns heute, wo es mehr denn je für uns Deutsche darauf ankommt, das Bleibende vom Vergänglichen und sich mit Staub Bedeckenden zu scheiden, gleich zu Anfang unseres gemeinsamen Weges durch Schillers Leben darüber klar sein, dass es allein sein ungeheures dramatisches Lebenswerk ist, das ihm Unsterblichkeit sichert; dass seine Gedichte und seine prosaischen Schriften, soviel Wertvolles man darin auch findet, nur von dem grossen Dramatiker

[10] Ivanov, *Po zvezdam,* p. 74. As for Ivanov's debt to Nietzsche cf. J. Schor: "Von Nietzsche empfing er die Offenbarung des Dionysischen; aber aus dem dionysischen Geiste heraus überwand er Nietzsches Individualismus und erkannte in der 'Hellenischen Religion des leidenden Gottes' die Vorform des Christentums, das alte Testament der Heiden." W. Iwanow, *Die Russische Idee,* transl. J. Schor (Tübingen, 1930), p. VI. Cp. also Alexander Bakshy, *The Path of the Modern Russian Stage* (London, 1916), pp. 113–120.

mit in die Zukunft genommen werden und durch ihn immer wieder Leser finden.[11]

Obviously, the German critic is almost as much pro-drama as Ivanov is pro-lyric, but even though it may not necessarily be a balanced judgment it still sheds a light on the provocative one-sidedness of the Russian.

While it is true that Schiller, as a lyrical poet, represents the eighteenth rather than the nineteenth century, it is no less true that, as a dramatist, he was far ahead of his time. To reproach him with naïvety and fair-souledness seems unfounded in face of the works of his maturity. Already in *Don Carlos,* in the remarkable scene between King Philip and the Great Inquisitor (V, 10), the poet shows an insight into the "basic antinomy in all things" that is equally far removed both from naïvety and fair-souledness. As a German critic says:

Hier im *Carlos* spricht aus dem Munde des greisen Grossinquisitors zum erstenmal ein wirklich politischer Mensch, wird die wirkliche Grundlage aller Politik, die Macht, mit allen ihren Konsequenzen für Augenblicke blossgelegt. Der Idealist Schiller hat in dieser Szene zwischen dem König und dem greisen Träger des überpersönlichen kalten Willens zur Macht an sich über ein Jahrhundert vorgegriffen in die Welt Nietzsches und seiner Deduktion des Machtwillens als des letzten Lebensträgers.[12]

In the light of the development taken by mankind in the course of the last quarter century, Ivanov's words about the "victory of Marquis Posa's principles" acquire a peculiar timbre fraught with the irony of history. Nor has *Die Räuber,* contrary to his assumption, fallen into oblivion. As in the heyday of Schiller's glory this powerful drama continues to thunder across

[11] Wilhelm von Scholz, *Friedrich Schiller* (Hamburg, n. d.), p. 159.
[12] Paul Fechter, *Geschichte der Deutschen Literatur* (Gütersloh, 1957), p. 181.

the stages of many nations, electrifying its audiences and provoking storms of applause. What is more, with regard to some of his mature works—*Wallenstein* and *Wilhelm Tell*, for instance—the prediction can be ventured that their importance and fame will continue to grow in the future. Exception must also be taken to Ivanov's attempt to transfer Schiller into the sphere of mysticism despite the orginal and skillful way in which he brings forward his arguments. Since this attempt is of crucial importance for the elucidation of Ivanov's attitude toward Schiller it will be necessary to give a detailed description and analysis of this curious facet of Ivanov's Schiller-image.

Ivanov recalls an expression of the poet Afanasy A. Fet according to which Schiller was not only the poet of "what is human in man" but also one who looked "into the fiery heart of the world / With shining eyes." In addition, Ivanov refers in support of his position to Zhukovsky and Tyutchev who had heard something mysterious in his lyric poetry audible only "für feine Ohren"—a hushed and sibylline whisper. Ivanov concedes that it is difficult to notice this "whisper" amidst the tempestuous outbursts of Schiller's thundering and blazing oratory :

As a matter of fact, it was correctly observed that Schiller always addresses the crowd; that he always stands on a public square or in the limelight of the theater; that his pose matches the perspective, and that his voice is changed and amplified according to conditions. But he is not only an actor and orator : he is a priest and mystagogue who at times puts a finger to his lips in intimation of mystery and at times, amidst the silence of the assembled mystics petrified in sacred trepidation, obscurely prophesies secret things . . .

> Du musst glauben, du musst wagen,
> Denn die Götter leihn kein Pfand,
> Nur ein Wunder kann dich tragen
> In das schöne Wunderland . . . ("Sehnsucht")

Words so profoundly interpreted by Dostoyevsky . . . Thus, in the silence of the mysteries, resounded once the obscure revelations instilling grief, and terror, and disenchantment into the hearts of the novices so that later the flame of unexpected, purest hope might flash up for them all the brighter.[13]

Ivanov here surrounds Schiller's poem with a cloud of mysticism which obscures its original meaning. Written in 1801, the poem "Sehnsucht" reflects, in the main, Schiller's longing for the evergreen hills and balmy skies of sunlit Italy. Schiller's letter to the painter Reinhart of June 15, 1801, would seem to lend support to such an interpretation : ". . . unter meinen Wünschen und Plänen war längst auch eine Reise nach Italien, wozu ich vor der Hand keine Möglichkeit sehe." But even if there is no connection between Schiller's longing for Italy and the genesis of the poem, a more convincing interpretation than the one offered by Ivanov presents itself to the mind of the attentive reader. Schiller's "Sehnsucht," far from being directed at the sibylline sphere of mysticism, can be readily construed as his longing for a harmonious life, permeated by a heavenly tranquillity of the soul, to which he looks up with wistful eyes

> . . . aus dieses Tales Gründen,
> Die der kalte Nebel drückt . . .

To be sure, in the last stanza the poet says : "Du musst glauben, du musst wagen . . ." But the main stress in this line seems to rest upon the word *wagen* as one may infer from a preceding line in the same stanza : "Frisch hinein und ohne Wanken . . ." The *Wunderland* described by Schiller in the first three stanzas of the poem bears, at any rate, little or no resemblance to the

---

[13] Ivanov, *Po zvezdam,* p. 75. Cp. M. Bowra : "In Dostoyevsky he [Ivanov] saw someone akin to himself in his passionate devotion to the spiritual life and his vivid observation of the world around him." V. Ivanov, *Freedom and the Tragic Life* (New York, 1952), Foreword.

obscure sphere of mysticism constructed by Ivanov on apocryphal foundations.

From the poem "Sehnsucht" Ivanov turns to an examination of the poem "Der Pilgrim" which appears to him as a kind of "Pilgrim's Progress" :

> Noch in meines Lebens Lenze
> War ich und ich wandert aus . . .
> ....
> *Denn das Irdische wird dorten*
> *Himmlisch unvergänglich sein . . .*

True, his indefatigable journey over mountain peaks and precipices in pursuit of the eternally withdrawing "Unknown" is obviously hopeless :

> Ach kein Steg will dahin führen,
> Ach der Himmel über mir
> Will die Erde nie berühren,
> *Und das Dort ist niemals hier!*

But in spite of this, the traveler will continue his journey and the guide will remain loyal to the traveler. This *There,* unattainable in our earthly limits, is not just a dreamy *There,* nor the romantic *Dahin:* it belongs to the sphere of pure mysticism.[14]

But mysticism, it appears, presupposes a conviction that man is able to transcend the "earthly limits" whereas Schiller, in this poem and elsewhere, regretfully disavows such a possibility : "Dass dem Menschen der Einblick in das Wesen der Dinge, in die übersinnliche Welt nicht vergönnt wird, ist eine der früh erworbenen Anschauungen Schillers."[15]

Ivanov's reference to John Bunyan's *The Pilgrim's Progress* cannot be accepted without reservations. The analogy between

---

[14] Ivanov, *Po zvezdam,* p. 76. [Italics by Ivanov.]

[15] Karl Berger, *Schiller* (München, 1909), II, 310. Cp. especially Schiller's poem "Die Worte des Wahns."

Schiller's traveler and Bunyan's pilgrim rests solely on the poem's title and on Schiller's conception of human life as a pilgrimage. Beyond that there is nothing in Schiller's poem to justify such a comparison. Above all, the spirit of puritanism which pervades *The Pilgrim's Progress* is altogether absent in Schiller's work. Rather it is suggestive of Schiller's philosophical studies, particularly of his preoccupation with the philosophy of Kant. The lines:

> Und zu eines Stroms Gestaden
> Kam ich, der nach Morgen floss . . .

seem to suggest Schiller's contact with Kant whose home was in East Prussia, a land where a river (Alle) flows in an easterly direction ("nach Morgen") toward Königsberg, the city of the German philosopher. The poem in its entirety can best be characterized as an elegy in which the poet resigns himself to the thought that man will never be able to solve the last mysteries of the world: "Und das Dort ist niemals hier!"

In the course of his Schiller-analysis Ivanov examines the German poet's attitude toward nature. He finds that Schiller viewed the mystery of nature "with profound understanding characteristic of his 'sympathy for the universe.'" Recalling Vladimir Solovyev's saying that the kingdom of the plants represents "in a perceptible mystery the union of the earthly soul with the celestial world," and quoting an expression of the poet Afanasy A. Fet according to which the souls of the plants, equally kindred with earth and heaven, feel the "twofold life" of both "and thus are doubly inspired by it," Ivanov arrives at the conclusion that similar ideas moved also through the dreams of Schiller:

> Wenn der Stamm zum Himmel eilet,
> Sucht die Wurzel scheu die Nacht,

Gleich in ihre Pflege teilet
Sich des Styx, des Äthers Macht . . .
(Schiller, "Klage der Ceres").

To substantiate his view still further Ivanov turns to the kingdom of the animals which—like the plants—live in close union
with earth and heaven. As an example he quotes the last line
from Schiller's poem "Der Alpenjäger" in which the ancient
Spirit of the mountains gives a stern warning to the young and
reckless pursuer of the trembling gazelle: "Was verfolgst du
meine Herde?" From this poem Ivanov concludes that Schiller
viewed the animals described in the poem as "the sacred herd
of the Mother-Spirit," that ancient goddess of the earth whom
the Greeks venerated under the name of Mother Demeter. In
further substantiation of this far-fetched point of view Ivanov
quotes the four stanzas of Schiller's poem "Berglied":

And here, finally is an almost apocalyptic vision of the World
Soul the mysticism of which is not in the least impaired by its precise
concordance with the topography of the Alps:

Es öffnet sich schwarz ein schauriges Tor,
Du glaubst dich im Reiche der Schatten,
Da tut sich ein lachend Gelände hervor,
Wo der Herbst und der Frühling sich gatten,
Aus des Lebens Mühen und ewiger Qual
Möcht ich fliehen in dieses glückselige Tal.

Vier Ströme brausen hinab in das Feld,
Ihr Quell, der ist ewig verborgen,
Sie fliessen nach allen vier Strassen der Welt,
Nach Abend, Nord, Mittag und Morgen,
Und wie die Mutter sie rauschend geboren,
Fort fliehn sie und bleiben sich ewig verloren.

Zwei Zinken ragen ins Blaue der Luft,
Hoch über der Menschen Geschlechter,

Drauf tanzen, umschleiert mit goldenem Duft,
Die Wolken, die himmlischen Töchter.
Sie halten dort oben den einsamen Reihn,
Da stellt sich kein Zeuge, kein irdischer, ein.

Es sitzt die Königin hoch und klar
Auf unvergänglichem Throne,
Die Stirn umkränzt sie sich wunderbar
Mit diamantener Krone.
Drauf schiesst die Sonne die Pfeile von Licht,
Sie vergolden sie nur, und erwärmen sie nicht.

(Schiller, "Berglied")

The gate, the valley, the four torrents, all these are well-defined
factors in Christian symbolism—as is also the Queen herself. She is
the "Maiden from a Strange Country," she is the much-suffering
Mother–Demeter. . . .[16]

Ivanov's interpretation of the poem "Klage der Ceres"—if
not of the "Alpenjäger"—as well as the parallel he draws between Solovyev and Fet on the one hand and Schiller on the
other in their attitude toward the animal and plant kingdoms
seems to have some merit. Schiller's beautiful poetic image of the
grain buried in the earth which by its death gives rise to a new
life, thus bridging the gulf between night and light, world and
heaven, death and life, indubitably carries a highly symbolical
message of mystery and mysticism in the sense attributed to it by
Ivanov. A characteristic trait in Ivanov's view of Schiller's poetry
is his transformation of "der Geist, der Bergesalte" of the German poem into a feminine deity, a "Mother-Spirit," whom,
moreover, Ivanov identifies with the "much-suffering Mother–
Demeter," the blessing and protecting goddess of fertility.

As far as the "Berglied" is concerned, Goethe had already
conceded that it was "ein recht artiger Stieg auf den Gotthard,

[16] Ivanov, *Po zvezdam*, pp. 77–78.

dem man sonst noch allerlei Deutungen zufügen kann. . . ."
Goethe does not further define what he means by "allerlei
Deutungen," but his words show that he was conscious of the
profound implications and symbolism present behind the descriptive aspect of the poem. Ivanov's attempt at deciphering its
cryptic symbols by means of the syncretic key of pagan and
Christian mysticism may thus be regarded as an interesting and
original gloss enriching, though not exhausting, the interpreta-
tive possibilities of the "kleine poetische Aufgabe zum Dechiff-
rieren," as Schiller called the poem in a letter to Goethe of
January 26, 1804.

Deep in the poet's soul Ivanov senses an incurable grief for
paradise : "Auch ich bin in Arkadien geboren (Schiller, "Resignation") . . . ," a paradise which is forever lost. The contemplation of the pure Ideas has been disturbed by a mysterious fall of
man :

> Wollt ihr schon auf Erden Göttern gleichen,
> Frei sein in des Todes Reichen,
> Brechet nicht von seines Gartens Frucht.
> (Schiller, "Das Ideal und das Leben")

And yet, Ivanov continues, the turning of man's divine will
toward the mystic World is enough to accomplish the miracle of
freeing man from the thraldom of Chaos where all is "smoke
and vapor," and where "all earthly glories pass away" (Schiller,
"Das Siegesfest") :

> Aber flüchtet aus der Sinne Schranken
> In die Freiheit der Gedanken
> Und die Furchterscheinung ist entflohn,
> Und der ewge Abgrund wird sich füllen;
> Nehmt die Gottheit auf in euern Willen,

---

¹⁷ Schiller, *SW*, I, 299 (notes).

Und sie steigt von ihrem Weltenthron.
(Schiller, "Das Ideal und das Leben")

Ivanov then recalls Schiller's poem "Dithyrambe" where the poet, overwhelmed by the approaching throng of gods, ecstatically exclaims:

Sie nahen, sie kommen die Himmlischen alle,
Mit Göttern erfüllt sich die irdische Halle.
Sagt, wie bewirt ich, der Erdegeborne,
Himmlischen Chor?
Schenket mir euer unsterbliches Leben,
Götter! . . .

The benevolent gods reply:

Reich ihm die Schale! Schenke dem Dichter,
Hebe, nur ein.
Netz ihm die Augen mit himmlischem Taue. . . .

And his soul overflows with an ineffable tranquillity and lucidity of heavenly abundance:

Sie rauschet, sie perlet, die himmlische Quelle,
Der Busen wird ruhig, das Auge wird helle . . .

From his analysis of the above quotations Ivanov draws the following conclusions:

Thus, Schiller, in so far as a mystic was hidden in him, became with astonishing suddenness of inspirational buoyancy an ecstatic poet in the moments of his deepest experiences. It is from mystical ecstasy that the dithyramb is born as soon as the magical circuit of the choric dance is closed. And the poet, thyrsus-bearer and servant of Dionysus whom he "honored without knowing it," was, in fact, one of the first initiators of the choric festivities of the future:

Windet zum Kranze die goldenen Ähren,
Flechtet auch blaue Cyanen hinein,

Freude soll jedes Auge verklären!
(Schiller, "Das Eleusische Fest")

Schliesst den heilgen Zirkel dichter,
Schwört bei diesem goldnen Wein . . .
(Schiller, "An die Freude").[18]

As far as Schiller's "Dithyrambe" is concerned it must be remarked with critical sobriety that it was born not from "mystical ecstasy" but rather was sparked by the poet's joy at receiving twelve bottles of Rhine wine from Karl Theodor von Dalberg.[19] Furthermore, the last line of the poem ("Der Busen wird ruhig, das Auge wird helle") represents an outright disavowal of any ecstatic, bacchic or dithyrambic, spirit. Ivanov's reference to the title "Das Eleusische Fest" does not help to render his argumentation more convincing for its original title had been "Bürgerlied" and hardly suggestive of ecstatic mysticism. The weightiest argument versus Ivanov's interpretation, however, is the central message of the poem contained in its penultimate stanza, which is a lucid and emphatic statement of an ethical idea and not at all an ecstatic outburst of the Dionysian spirit:

Freiheit liebt das Tier der Wüste,
Frei im Äther herrscht der Gott,
Ihrer Brust gewalt'ge Lüste
Zähmet das Naturgebot;
Doch der Mensch, in ihrer Mitte,
Soll sich an den Menschen reihn,
Und allein durch seine Sitte
Kann er frei und mächtig sein.—
(Schiller, "Das Eleusische Fest")

Ivanov's quotation from the poem "An die Freude," in juxta-

[18] Ivanov, *Po zvezdam*, pp. 79–80.
[19] Schiller, *SW*, I, 289 (notes). Cf. also Wolfgang Kayser, "Dithyrambe," *Die deutsche Lyrik*, ed. B. von Wiese (Düsseldorf, 1956), I, 344.

position with the poem "Dithyrambe," instead of adding force and weight to his argument only serves to invalidate it completely. On close analysis these poems are found to contain a fundamental contradiction. In "Dithyrambe" the poet declares: "Die Freude, sie wohnt nur in Jupiters Saale" whereas in "An die Freude" he glorifies Joy as an omnipotent force pervading the whole universe:

> Freude heisst die starke Feder
> In der ewigen Natur.
> Freude, Freude treibt die Räder
> In der grossen Weltenuhr.
> (Schiller, "An die Freude")

But with that, Ivanov has not yet exhausted the arsenal of his arguments. To equip his arguments with an impregnable armor he conjures the shadows of two formidable witnesses—Beethoven and Dostoyevsky:

Two trustworthy witnesses, two chosen servants of Dionysus attest to the existence of the dithyrambic inspiration by which Schiller was dominated: Beethoven and Dostoyevsky. Beethoven chose the "Song to Joy" as the literary basis of his great and, in modern art, first musical dithyramb: the *Ninth Symphony*. Dostoyevsky revered and honored the memory of Schiller. He worshiped in the poet of humanity his love for the divine image of man, his faith in the God-likeness of man—a love and a faith not exhausted by the cultivation of positive "ideals" of life but deeply rooted in a mystical "touching of other worlds." Dmitry Karamazov knows only too well the bitterness experienced by Ceres descending from heaven when the good goddess found suffering everywhere no matter how far she wandered upon her weary rounds:

> Ja, so weit sie wandernd kreiste,
> Fand sie Elend überall . . .

But Dmitry also knows her prophetic testament:

Dass der Mensch zum Menschen werde,
Stift er einen ewgen Bund
Gläubig mit der frommen Erde,
Seinem mütterlichen Grund.

(Schiller, "Das Eleusische Fest")

Alas, Dmitry knows only too well this "misery" but he also knows this "covenant!" He suffered to the end from the antinomy of "worm" and "angel" in the dual nature of man :

Wollust ward dem Wurm gegeben,
Und der Cherub steht vor Gott.

(Schiller, "An die Freude")

However, he also experienced fully all the sacred emotions, all the pure ecstasies of the "covenant" :

Freude heisst die starke Feder
In der ewigen Natur.
Freude, Freude treibt die Räder
In der grossen Weltenuhr.
Blumen lockt sie aus den Keimen,
Sonnen aus dem Firmament,
Sphären rollt sie in den Räumen
Die des Sehers Rohr nicht kennt.

(Schiller, "An die Freude")

Thence, to "sing a hymn" signifies for Dmitry to recall the beloved songs of Schiller . . . Dostoyevsky who said : "seek ecstasy and frenzy,"—he who bade us kiss the earth and moisten it with our tears,—did not find in poetry more incandescent words expressing these ecstatic experiences than the words of Schiller.[20]

[20] Ivanov, *Po zvezdam,* pp. 81–82. What Ivanov here says of Dmitry he later says of Dostoyevsky himself : "Zwei Seelen wohnen in seiner Brust, und jede von ihnen weiss um die Bedingungen ihres Wachstums. Wenn der Stamm zum Himmel eilet, / Sucht die Wurzel scheu die Nacht . . ." W. Iwanow, *Dostojewskij* (Tübingen, 1932), p. 121. The quotation is from Schiller's "Klage der Ceres."

The witnesses invoked by Ivanov are formidable, indeed. But the fact that Beethoven incorporated part of the "Song to Joy" into his *Ninth Symphony* does not necessarily lead to the conclusion that Schiller was "dominated" by "dithyrambic inspiration." Ivanov seems also to have overlooked one very important factor : Beethoven's inclusion of Schiller's poem into the choral symphony was actually due to mere chance. A German critic says in this connection :

Das Chor-Finale sollte ursprünglich eingeleitet werden durch die Worte : "Heute ist ein feierlicher Tag—dieser sei gefeiert mit Gesang." Dann hatte Beethoven den barocken Einfall, dem Rezitativ die Worte zu unterlegen : "Lasst uns das Lied des unsterblichen Schiller singen !"[21]

Furthermore, Ivanov gives the "Song to Joy" an importance it did not have in the eyes of the poet himself who, on the contrary, expressed a very critical judgment about it at the height of his development as a lyric poet. In a letter of October 21, 1800, addressed to Körner, Schiller remarked :

Die "Freude" ["Song to Joy"] ist nach meinem jetzigen Gefühl durchaus fehlerhaft, und ob sie sich gleich durch ein gewisses Feuer der Empfindung empfiehlt, so ist sie doch ein schlechtes Gedicht und bezeichnet eine Stufe der Bildung, die ich durchaus hinter mir lassen musste, um etwas Ordentliches hervorzubringen. Weil sie aber einem fehlerhaften Geschmack der Zeit entgegenkam, so hat sie die Ehre erhalten, gewissermassen ein Volksgedicht zu werden. Deine Neigung zu diesem Gedicht mag sich auf die Epoche seiner Entstehung gründen; aber diese gibt ihm auch den einzigen Wert, den es hat, und auch nur für uns und nicht für die Welt noch für die Dichtkunst.[22]

Here is not the place to examine whether or not Dostoyevsky

[21] Hans Schnoor, *Oper, Operette, Konzert* (Gütersloh, 1956), p. 111.
[22] *Friedrich Schiller—Briefe*, ed. R. Buchwald (Leipzig, n. d.), pp. 736–37.

may be called a "chosen servant of Dionysus." The prevailing view seems to be that the Christian element predominates in most of his works. But even assuming that Dostoyevsky was a "servant of Dionysus"—and granting that he "did not find in poetry more incandescent words expressing these ecstatic experiences than the words of Schiller,"—is all this sufficient evidence to warrant the deduction that Schiller was a dithyrambic poet *par excellence?* Obviously not. Schiller's immortality, it appears to us, rests on his great dramatic achievements, and a time may come when all his lyric poems, including his ballads, will have sunk into oblivion. Finally, Ivanov's reference to the "dual nature of man" based on the verses:

> Wollust ward dem Wurm gegeben,
> Und der Cherub steht vor Gott.
> > (Schiller, "An die Freude")

reveals that he has misunderstood their actual meaning. Schiller does not speak here of the "dual nature of man" (man—half worm, half angel) but of his conviction that God has given Joy to all creatures without exception, to the lowest worm as well as to the most radiant angel. The verses preceding the quoted ones make this abundantly clear:

> Freude trinken alle Wesen
> An den Brüsten der Natur,
> Alle Guten, alle Bösen
> Folgen ihrer Rosenspur.
> Küsse gab sie uns und Reben,
> Einen Freund, geprüft im Tod,
> Wollust ward dem Wurm gegeben,
> Und der Cherub steht vor Gott.
> > (Schiller, "An die Freude")

To be sure, Ivanov himself must have felt that he had gone too far in proclaiming Schiller as a Dionysian poet "dominated" by "dithyrambic inspiration." At a later point of his Schiller-analysis he sounds a partial retreat from his original, imaginative but very vulnerable, position :

But it would be, nevertheless, a mistake to regard Schiller as the perfect representative of a dithyrambic poet. A real dithyramb (as it was postulated by the ancients) presupposes a certain continuous fullness and abundance of soul—in profound harmony with every joy and sorrow of the soul—at the bottom of which rests the great Yes to the world, in purple twilight, not accessible to the storms, like the golden ring of a mysterious betrothal. When, unable to contain the over-abundance, the golden brim of the fathomless bowl overflows with the foaming lymph of sentiment then the music of bacchic song is born *out of excess and superfluity*. The dithyramb is the least logical kind of poetry and the one most closely related to the element of music. In the dithyramb any *what* precipitates into the abyss of the soul's inebriation which has engendered it,—into the ineffable *how* of the spirit. From this nature of the dithyrambic muse Nietzsche obviously deduced his distinction between creation "from abundance" and creation "from hunger."[23]

Ivanov adopts this distinction made by Nietzsche and applies it *in toto* to his image of the German poet. Schiller, it seems to him, does not create "from fullness" but rather "from hunger." In this he sees the source of Schiller's *passion* [italics by Ivanov], and his dithyramb appears to him as a confirmation of this *passion*—an upward flight of yearning, but not the mighty surge of plenty and abundance.

Dionysus was not the father of Schiller's songs, but their god-father. Their real father, according to Ivanov, was Eros—the son of Want, or Poverty (Penia), as we know him in the myth in Plato's *Symposium*. These impetuous flights, these hungry ecs-

[23] Ivanov, *Po zvezdam*, p. 82. [Italics by Ivanov.] Cp. Maler Müller's "Dithyrambe" which is a "real dithyramb" as postulated by the ancients and by Ivanov.

tasies were carried by his universal love, but Schiller had to throw some *what* onto the bottom of his bowl to cause its instantaneous boiling; only then would the bowl bubble up and would pearly, golden, purple foam flow over its edge consummating an unearthly moment of ecstatic bliss . . . :

And we drink the foam and absorb with it the substance of a didactic intellect. Yet we crave only pure contagion through the ecstasy of a spirit that has lost itself and become oblivious of all limits; we crave that pregnant chaos should gush into us and give birth to its creative logos in our own self, in the depths of our unconsciousness. . . .[24]

There is no need to elaborate on Ivanov's considerations about the nature of dithyrambic poetry. What he says here of Schiller would seem to be more in keeping with the facts, especially his statement that it would be "a mistake to regard Schiller as the perfect representative of a dithyrambic poet." His allegation that Schiller created "from hunger" and that "want" was the real father of his songs appears to be justified in the light of Schiller's letter to Goethe (August 31, 1794) where the former warns his newly-won friend not to expect too much from him:

Erwarten Sie bei mir keinen grossen materialen Reichtum von Ideen; dies ist es, was ich bei Ihnen finden werde. Mein Bedürfnis und Streben ist, aus wenigem viel zu machen, und wenn Sie meine Armut an allem, was man erworbene Erkenntnis nennt, einmal näher kennen sollten, so finden Sie vielleicht, dass es mir in manchen Stücken damit mag gelungen sein.[25]

Of course, it might be objected that Schiller talks here a different language from Ivanov's, that Schiller here simply means the "want" and "lack" of erudition whereas Ivanov would seem to mean a poverty of inspiration, a lack of contact with the in-

[24] Ivanov, *Po zvezdam,* p. 83.
[25] *Friedrich Schiller — Briefe,* p. 355.

effable. But in another passage of the letter Schiller uses words which clearly imply a certain "poverty of inspiration" : "Noch jetzt begegnet es mir häufig genug . . . dass der kalte Verstand meine Dichtung stört . . . und so schwebe ich als eine Zwitter-art . . . zwischen dem technischen Kopf und dem Genie."

Contrasting Schiller with Goethe, Ivanov recognizes in the latter a poet who produced "from abundance" but who instinc-tively kept away from the spirit of Dionysus as if he were "frightened by dithyramb and tragedy." Ivanov then deplores that the pathos of the dithyramb "from abundance" has disap-peared with the ancient Hellenes. In the revival of the dithyramb he sees the principle task facing the poetry of the future. Even the ecstasies of that choric dithyramb of Joy, the *Ninth Symphony,* are to Ivanov only indicative of a profound dissatisfaction with his lot and a ravenous hunger in Beethoven for the ecstatic, not ecstasy itself. He associates this great "hunger of the spirit" with the rise of Christianity : "We are living and progressing in a Christianity of hunger that craves and thirsts for truth. We are waiting for a Christianity of abundance. . ."[26]

At this point, very significantly, Ivanov acknowledges that Schiller is a poet "profoundly Christian in his spirit notwith-standing his poetic longing for the 'gods of Hellas.' " To be sure, such a view harmonizes with Ivanov's concept that the pathos of Christianity is a great "hunger of the spirit" and also with his notion that Schiller, as a poet, created not "from abundance" but "from hunger;" but it hardly tallies with his earlier affirma-tion proclaiming Schiller a Dionysian poet "dominated" by "dithyrambic inspiration"—unless, of course, one is willing to accept Ivanov's syncretism collating Christ with Dionysus.

[26] Ivanov, *Po zvezdam,* p. 84. The question of Ivanov's "Christianity" is still an issue. In opposition to Deschartes, Ivanov's friend Makovsky main-tains that "Ivanov was not a Christian." Cf. "V. Ivanov v Rossii," *Novy Zhurnal,* XXX (New York, 1952), 145.

In support of his "diagnosis of Schiller's ecstatic nature" Ivanov adduces Schiller's self-definition as a "sentimental poet" in contrast to the type of the "naïve poet." In his opinion, Schiller's theory of "sentimental poetry" in essence reduces itself to the establishment of a certain irrevocable antithesis between the selfhood of a phenomenon and its perception and evaluation by the human spirit, between that which is given from without and that which is postulated from within. According to Ivanov, it is this antithesis which causes the melancholy of dissatisfaction characteristic of modern poetry in general. Thus, Ivanov continues, despite momentary ecstasies in blissful forgetfulness, the craving of the poet remains unappeasable and his Eros greedy for great accomplishment, reveals himself in reality as a son of Poverty. As can be seen, Ivanov reiterates here his previous formula of Schiller's creation "from hunger" with Eros as the "real father" of Schiller's songs, applying it to the special case of Schiller's theory of "sentimental poetry." It could be added that Schiller himself was well aware of the possibilities and limitations of the sentimental kind of poetry. In his letter of December 25, 1795, addressed to Wilhelm von Humboldt, the poet remarks:

Wir müssen also hier sorgfältig die Wirklichkeit von dem absoluten Begriffe scheiden. Dem Begriff nach ist die sentimentalische Dichtkunst freilich der Gipfel, und die naïve kann mit ihr nicht verglichen werden, aber sie kann ihren Begriff nie erfüllen, und erfüllte sie ihn, *so würde sie aufhören,* eine poetische Art zu sein. Der Wirklichkeit nach ist es aber ebenso gewiss, dass die sentimentalische Poesie qua Poesie die naïve nicht erreicht.[27]

There is no doubt in Ivanov's mind that Schiller's fame will be kept alive by the future poets of the dithyramb and the Dionysian festivity who will honor him as their prophetic precursor. A second characteristic of Schiller's poetic personality, related to

[27] *Friedrich Schiller—Briefe,* p. 463. [Italics by Schiller.]

the first, will also, in the opinion of Ivanov, endear him to those generations which will live to see "the orchestras of popular mysteries" :

> We mean the democratic spirit of his [Schiller's] poetry. We do not allude to the political "ideals" of Schiller, nor to his proclamation of "rights," nor to his wrath at injustice, nor to any *what* of his dreams no matter how defined. Something else is important : the pathos of choric art which is equally strong in Schiller's lyric poetry and in his dramas. Seldom is his lyric poetry, as it were, a personal confession under four eyes. More often it is the declamation of a religious teacher, or the tale of a rhapsodist, or—especially dear to us—the song of a leader of gorgeously-wreathed dancers. Everywhere Schiller is in the crowd and with the crowd; everywhere he is their herald and their voice. All his poetry is the constant communion of the poet, in priestly or tragical vestments, wreathed or masked, with his ideal community—the people. Schiller, the dramatist, had the picture of people's spectacles before his eyes; such was the inspiration which had prompted him to write his *Wilhelm Tell*. Thence his profound yearning for the restoration of the chorus of the classical tragedy : it was this yearning which led him to the conception of *The Bride of Messina.*[28]

It is true that Schiller's fame has been kept alive but not by the "future poets of the dithyramb and the Dionysian festivity" envisioned by Ivanov. In fact, such poets will be sought in vain in the literature of the past half century, unless one ranks the expressionists as "dithyrambic poets." These, however, failed to concern themselves with Schiller's fame.

Ivanov's statement regarding the "pathos of choric art which is equally strong in Schiller's lyric poetry and in his dramas" calls for a close scrutiny. To substantiate his viewpoint, Ivanov adduces quotations from about a dozen of Schiller's poems. Quite apart from the value of these quotations in Ivanov's argument,

[28] Ivanov, *Po zvezdam,* p. 85. [Italics by Ivanov.]

the limited number of the cited poems as compared with the several hundred poems actually written by Schiller makes them a most unreliable basis for the claim that Schiller was a Dionysian poet "dominated" by "dithyrambic inspiration," and that the "pathos of choric art" was "strong in Schiller's lyric poetry." Ivanov seeks further to buttress his thesis by reference to Schiller's dramatic production. Unfortunately, he fails entirely to elaborate on that point, giving little more than the titles of two of Schiller's dramas in which, according to his conviction, the "pathos of choric art" is "strong."

Perhaps he would have been able to make a case for the "pathos of choric art" in Schiller's *Wallenstein* and the subsequent dramas, especially in *Wilhelm Tell* which the German poet himself had characterized as uncommonly suitable for the theater thanks to its "Volksmässigkeit" (Schiller's letter to Wilhelm von Humboldt of August 18, 1803).[29]

As for *The Bride of Messina,* it goes without saying that this tragedy appealed to Ivanov primarily because of its classical form and the introduction of the chorus. However, apart from this, the drama contains certain religious (in the widest sense) elements which were bound to fascinate him in a particular way. Schiller's letter to Körner, dated March 10, 1803, gives us some indications in this respect :

Das Ideenkostüm, das ich mir erlaubte, hat dadurch seine Rechtfertigung, dass die Handlung nach Messina versetzt ist, wo sich Christentum, griechische Mythologie und Mahomedanismus wirklich begegnet und vermischt haben. Das Christentum war zwar die Basis und die herrschende Religion, aber das griechische Fabelwesen wirkte noch in der Sprache, in den alten Denkmälern, in dem Anblick der Städte selbst, welche von Griechen gegründet waren, lebendig fort, und der Märchenglaube sowie das Zauberwesen

[29] Cp. Walter Silz, "Chorus and Choral Function in Schiller," *Schiller 1759/1959,* ed. John R. Frey (Urbana, Illinois, 1959), pp. 147–170.

schloss sich an die maurische Religion an. Die Vermischung dieser drei Mythologieen, die sonst den Charakter aufheben würde, wird also hier selbst zum Charakter. Auch ist sie vorzüglich in den Chor gelegt, welcher einheimisch und ein lebendiges Gefäss der Tradition ist.[30]

There can be little doubt that it was this combination of mythological and syncretic elements in *The Bride of Messina* which greatly increased its poetic value in the eyes of Ivanov who, as we have seen, championed a syncretism linking Christ with Dionysus.

In conclusion, returning once more to the one hundredth anniversary of Schiller's death and its anticipation in Baggesen's funeral feast of 1791, Ivanov expresses his conviction that it would have been impossible to find a form of celebration more in keeping with the spirit of Schiller's poetic production than this choric funeral feast to the memory of the inspired "leader of the chorus,"—and it is not without regret that he exclaims:

Prematurely! Indeed, we are even now still far away (oh, now, perhaps, farther than ever!) from those ecstatic festivals which—we believe—one day, in rites welcome to his shadow, again will evoke the majestic image of the ivy-wreathed hero, the originator of folk festivals, with the music of flutes.[31]

Ivanov, as can be seen, has a very personal view of Schiller and holds him in the highest esteem. In another of his essays, "The Crisis of Individualism" (1905), he actually ranks the German poet on a level with Cervantes and Shakespeare:

For the first time in the history of the world they [Don Quixote and Hamlet] presented to the mind the questions of the new individualism and of the tragic antinomy hidden at its root. But two hundred years after them Schiller ceased being merely an individual

---

[30] *Friedrich Schiller — Briefe,* p. 803.
[31] Ivanov, *Po zvezdam,* p. 85.

in terms of our earthly way of perception. It is Schiller, the originator
of folk festivities, whose poetic production already marks the escape
(or return) from heroic isolation into a choric community of spiritual
freedom . . . Cervantes, Shakespeare, Schiller—this is the constella-
tion of stars on our horizon : let the astrologers of the spirit unriddle
the portent![32]

Although it cannot be denied that there are some Dionysian
and choric elements in the works of the German poet and that
the problem of the significance of the symbol for the purposes of
art held a lively interest for Schiller at the time when he
assimilated the philosophy of Kant (1787–97), the deduction
seems unavoidable that Ivanov interpreted Schiller in an extreme,
subjective, and arbitrary manner. On the inadequate basis of
a dozen poems and a few passing references to *Wilhelm Tell* and
The Bride of Messina Ivanov undertakes the Sisyphean task of
characterizing Schiller as "a Dionysian poet dominated by
dithyrambic inspiration." In view of Schiller's biography and the
prevailing rationalistic tendency of his poems and dramas the
question arises how a poet and scholar of the stature of Ivanov
could arrive at such a characterization of a spirit who was very
far from any kind of mysticism and ecstatic abandon :

Schiller ist kein Mensch der Mystik; hindurchgegangen durch
die medizinische Naturwissenschaft seiner Zeit und durch die
Anfänge der kritischen Philosophie, dazu noch ein direkter Erbe der
Aufklärung, hat er zum Transzendenten höchstens den Weg der
Abstraktion als Zugang offen.[33]

[32] Ivanov, *Po zvezdam*, p. 87. Ivanov here echoes Dostoyevsky : "In fact,
in European belles-lettres there were geniuses of immense creative magnitude—Shakespeare, Cervantes, Schiller." F. M. Dostoyevsky, *The Diary of a
Writer*, transl. B. Brasol (New York, 1949), II, 977. In this connection it
may be mentioned that Ivanov also ranked Dante and Goethe as "pioneers
and founders of tragic symbolism." Cf. Schor, *loc. cit.*, p. VII.
[33] Fechter, *op. cit.*, p. 182. Cf. also H. Rehder, "Zum Problem der
'Erschütterung' in Schillers Dichtung und Gedankenwelt," *Schiller 1759/*

The question why Ivanov looked at Schiller through the prism of symbolism and mysticism can perhaps be answered if we take into consideration that his view of Schiller represents a certain age, a certain school or rather style of thought. Viewing Schiller as a "forefather of modern symbolism" and a "Dionysian poet dominated by dithyrambic inspiration," tallied well with his own ideas and general philosophical and literary position and development. From this standpoint and seen in an imaginative historical perspective, Ivanov's peculiar attitude toward Schiller does not necessarily have to be "right" and based on solid philological "evidence." At any rate, to Ivanov, who attempts to claim him as a poet of mysticism and of Dionysian mysteries, as well as to all other mystics Schiller himself has apparently given an unequivocal reply in his "Tabulae Votivae":

> An die Mystiker
> Das ist eben das wahre Geheimnis, das allen vor Augen
> Liegt, euch ewig umgibt, aber von keinem gesehn.

1959, p. 106: "Aber er [Schiller] hatte . . . sein rationalistisches Erbe nie völlig aufgegeben."

IX

Conclusion : Retrospect and Prospect

IN THE PRECEDING CHAPTERS SCHILLER'S IMPACT ON RUSSIAN writers in the nineteenth century was traced and analyzed. The attempt was made to give a critical evaluation of Schiller's importance to each author and not a mere descriptive statement of that author's views of the German poet. Thus, at the beginning of this study, Schiller's great influence on Stankevich was thrown into relief and the contradictory nature of his relation to the German poet uncovered. It was shown that Stankevich the philosopher rejected Schiller's aestheticism on logical grounds, while Stankevich the romanticist accepted it on grounds of empathy. The analysis of Lermontov's relation to Schiller revealed his strong indebtedness to *Die Räuber* and *Kabale und Liebe* which left a distinct imprint on his entire dramatic production. In addition, an appraisal of Lermontov's far-reaching dependence in his plays on Schiller's philosophical and aesthetic writings was given.

Belinsky's attitude toward the German poet was found to be characterized by exalted admiration in his youth and by a scornful rejection of Schiller's aestheticism during the period of his "reconciliation with reality." Belinsky's instinctive recognition of Schiller's greatness was emphasized, as well as his re-conversion to the noble and impassioned "poet of humanity" during the period of his maturity. Schiller's uninterrupted and important role in the spiritual and ideological development of Bakunin was pointed out.

280

Bakunin's anarchical ideas, epitomized in his *Catechism of a Revolutionist,* were traced to the revolutionary spirit of Schiller's "Storm and Stress" dramas. The discussion of Herzen's life-long attachment to the author of *Don Carlos* gave occasion to analyze a writer, thinker, and a man of action who had dedicated his existence to the welfare of mankind and had never abandoned his "respect for the dreams of his youth" so largely inspired by Schiller. In his admiration of Schiller Herzen was joined by his friend and political ally, Ogarev, who remained a faithful admirer of the German poet to the last days of his life. A critic of society and a social revolutionary, Ogarev hailed Schiller as a "progressive poet" and as a "herald of a progressive Germany."

Reviewing the twists and turns of Dostoyevsky's relation to Schiller, we arrived at the conclusion that he owed more to the German than to any other Russian or Western European writer. Many of his works, including his last, and perhaps greatest, novel, *The Brothers Karamazov,* were interpreted as reflections of his tenacious struggle with Schiller's aestheticism.

Finally, the critical evaluation of V. Ivanov's views of Schiller led to the deduction that this famous poet and scholar had a very personal conception of the German. Ivanov's attempt to define Schiller as a dithyrambic poet *par excellence* was characterized as extreme, arbitrary and unconvincing.

It would be misleading indeed were we to convey the impression that the vogue of Schiller in Russia had come to an abrupt end with V. Ivanov and the symbolists. As a matter of fact, the fame of the author of *Don Carlos* continued to shine as brightly as ever in the hearts of the Russian people at the turn of the century, that is at the very time when in Germany itself his popularity was going into a serious decline :

Although in Germany, toward the end of the nineteenth century sharp and hostile voices were being heard frequently arguing that

Schiller's poetry had become antiquated, that it had outlived its time, and that it was rhetorical and far removed from real life—to us [the Russians] he continues to be an inspired poet whose noble verse,—speaking with the words of Lermontov,—"sounds, like the bell on the tower of the popular assembly, in days of national triumphs and defeats . . . for the citizens of future generations," calling from beyond the grave all nations, and therefore, also our nation to a new life and a bright future.[1]

These words were spoken in 1905, on the occasion of the one hundredth anniversary of Schiller's death, at a meeting of the Lovers of Russian Literature at the University of Moscow.

The outbreak of the First World War could only temporarily obscure the radiance of Schiller's image in a country in which he had "soaked into the Russian soul, left an impress upon it, and almost marked an epoch in the history of our development."[2] In the wake of the victorious revolution "the great German poet Friedrich Schiller" was triumphantly returned to the "first rank of the dramatic geniuses of world literature."[3] Once again Schiller became in truth a "national Russian poet," to repeat a turn of phrase used by Chernyshevsky, Dostoyevsky and others, with loving emphasis and proprietary pride. Schiller's ideas of human dignity and freedom, the heroic pathos of his struggle for the emancipation of the human spirit, the passionate fervor of his protest against tyranny and oppression swept like a storm through the ranks of the Russian masses who were then waging a desperate revolutionary war under the banner and in the name of very similar ideas:

Each upsurge of the revolutionary struggle of the Russian people was accompanied by a new enthusiasm for Schiller's poetry. It is

[1] Yury Veselovsky, "Schiller kak vdokhnovitel Russkikh Pisateley," *Russkaya Mysl*, II (Moskva, 1906), 15.
[2] F. M. Dostoyevsky, *The Diary of a Writer,* trans. Boris Brasol (New York, 1949), I, 343.
[3] F. P. Schiller, *Fridrikh Schiller* (Moskva, 1955), p. 5.

well known how warmly, in the years of the Civil War, the dramas
of Schiller were received by our revolutionary workers, the members
of the Young Communist League, and the soldiers of the heroic
Red Army. The novels by A. Tolstoy and K. Fedin, dedicated to
the theme of the Civil War, testify to this with sufficient eloquence.
Die Räuber, Kabale und Liebe, and *Don Carlos* occupied a place of
honor in the repertory of the Soviet theatre during the first years of
the great socialist October revolution. And they have preserved this
popularity down to our own times.[4]

One of the principal popularizers of Schiller in Russia after the
October revolution was the poet Aleksandr Blok. As stage director
of the Great Dramatic Theatre in St. Petersburg he wrote a number of speeches on Shakespeare, Schiller and other poets which
were read by the actors to the Red Army soldiers before the performances and which are veritable masterpieces of his magnificently simple and energetic style. In his speech on Schiller's *Don
Carlos* ("this colossal drama—colossal both in scope and in conception"), written in October 1919, Blok makes the following
interesting observation on the qualities of a great writer :

Great writers do not occupy themselves only with politics; they
have to touch upon it perforce but they are occupied with a far more
important matter—with art which, together with science, leads to
an understanding of the ultimate purpose of life. For this reason
great writers are not interested in depicting the kings as gloomy
rascals in whom there is nothing human; what interests them in man
above all is man as he was created by nature.[5]

The Russian poet here obviously refers to the figure of King
Philip in Schiller's *Don Carlos* for whose sufferings and sorrows,
often hidden behind the paraphernalia of his royal dignity and
power, he strives to arouse the sympathy of his audience com-

[4] *Fridrikh Schiller, Sobr. Soch.,* ed. Vilmont and Samarin (Moskva,
1955), I, 7.
[5] Blok, *Sobr. Soch* (Leningrad, 1936), XII, 210.

posed of revolutionary workers and peasants. To many of them it must have been a revelation that unhappiness could dwell also in a heart covered with royal purple and that the powerful ruler of half the world was powerless to free himself from unhappiness.

In his essay "The Downfall of Humanism" (1919), Blok hails Schiller as "the last great European humanist" and the last rhapsodist of mankind. Although Schiller died a premature death his humanistic ideas have not died with him : "The banner of humanism which Schiller had held intrepidly was convulsively seized by hundreds of anxious and nervous hands of the people of the nineteenth century—a century that was permeated with unceasing agitation."[6] His introductory speech on Schiller's *Die Räuber* was concluded by Blok with the following words :

Schiller's inspired drama, written one hundred forty years ago, will not lose its political significance as long as the spirit of struggle is alive in our hearts and as long as the battle-cry resounds : *In tyrannos!*[7]

Schiller was a "great name" and a "great and ardent poet" to Maxim Gorky also who ranked him together with Pushkin, Mickiewicz, Goethe, and Byron. It was the social aspect of Schiller's poetry which appealed to him in a particular way. In his article "Two Souls," written in December 1915 and published in the periodical *Letopis,* he speaks very highly of the social consciousness of the German poet : "The social romanticism of

---

[6] Blok, *Sochinenia* (Moskva, 1955), II, 308.

[7] Blok, *Sobr. Soch,* XII, 215. Cp. also K. Demtschenko and L. Genin: "Die Aufführungen von Schillers Trauerspielen in Petrograd während der Jahre der Revolution und des Bürgerkriegs sind eines der interessantesten und dabei am wenigsten erforschten Kapitel in der Geschichte der Erschliessung des Schillerschen Erbes in Russland. In dieser Epoche traten die charakteristischen Züge der Schillerschen Dramen, ihr heroisches Pathos, ihre politisch-agitatorische Wirkung und Schärfe, ihre Fähigkeit, die Massen zu packen und zu begeistern, besonders deutlich und eindrucksvoll in Erscheinung." "Schiller auf den Bühnen des revolutionären Petrograd," *Sinn und Form,* XI (Berlin, 1959), Heft 5/6, p. 927.

Schiller . . . is one of the most beautiful achievements of the West-European soul : it is the Holy Scripture of the genius of dynamic life."[8] Gorky thinks Schiller is at his best in those works in which he draws inspiration from the "well of national poetry which is infinitely deep, incalculably diverse, powerful, and full of wisdom."[9] In accordance with these views, Schiller's drama *Wilhelm Tell* takes a very high place in the esteem of the Russian writer since it springs forth from the "creative work of the people." Speaking of Pushkin's *History of the Revolt of Pugachev,*[10] Gorky parallels it to Schiller's *Geschichte des Dreissigjährigen Krieges:*

Pushkin also wrote a *History of the Revolt of Pugachev:* this is an attempt on the part of a poet to speak the language of a historian which Schiller spoke in his *Geschichte des Dreissigjährigen Krieges.*[11]

The rise of fascism in Germany filled Gorky with deep anguish and apprehension. His article "About Soldierly Ideas" (1932) reflects his bewilderment and angry indignation in the face of a whole series of frightening acts of terror committed by members of fascist organizations : "To see this delirious madness it was necessary to 'outlive' or 'get rid' of Goethe and Kant, Schiller and Fichte and a hundred of the greatest thinkers, poets, composers and painters."[12]

Schiller's fame in the Soviet Union outlasted the horrors of the Second World War. The Soviet-inspired World Peace Council resolved in 1955 to celebrate the 150th anniversary of the death of the "great Schiller" throughout the land. In the same year a Soviet biography of the German poet[13] and a seven-volume

[8] *M. Gorky—Materialy i issledovania,* ed. Balukhaty and Desnitsky (Moskva–Leningrad, 1936), II, 164.

[9] M. Gorky, *Sobr. Soch.* (Moskva, 1949–55), XXIV, 33.

[10] Introduction to the English edition of the works of Pushkin (1925).

[11] Gorky, *op. cit.,* XXIV, 257.

[12] Gorky, *Sobr. Soch.,* XXVI, 358.

[13] F. P. Schiller, *Fridrikh Schiller* (Moskva, 1955), pp. 430.

edition of his Collected Works (in Russian) were published by
the Government Publishing House in Moscow.[14] Schiller, the
author of the *Briefe über die ästhetische Erziehung des Menschen,*
appears here as a predecessor of communism and a herald of the
classless society : "He [Schiller] dreamed of a new government of
the people and of a 'harmonious society' without castes or
classes."[15] In the light of this peculiar "interpretation" of Schiller
it is not surprising to see his name imprinted on posters and
banners of the Soviet-directed "Camp of Peace and Democracy" :

The name of Schiller whose heart, according to words of another
great lover of mankind, Belinsky, always burned "with the most
passionate, ardent, and noble blood of love for man and mankind,
of hate for religious and national fanaticism, for prejudices, stakes,
and whips which divide people and force them to forget that they
are brothers to each other,"—this name will justly stand on the
banner of the peace-loving forces of all countries and all nations.[16]

Hand in hand with this "dialectic" interpretation of Schiller goes
the burning of incense before his "colossal" image. Soviet criticism
gives high praise to the poetic genius of Schiller and fully
recognizes the greatness of his contribution to German and world
literature :

His [Schiller's] contribution to literature—artistic, historical, and
philosophical—strikes us with the grandiosity of its dimensions;
especially if we consider how often serious illness interfered with his
intense labors.[17]

To adapt Schiller still more effectively to the needs of the Soviet
ideology, great stress is laid by the critics upon Schiller's concept
of work and his impassioned love of labor despite his feeble
constitution :

[14] *Fridrikh Schiller, Sobr. Soch.,* ed. Vilmont and Samarin (Moskva, 1955).
[15] *Fridrikh Schiller, Sobr. Soch.,* I, 6.
[16] *Fridrikh Schiller, Sobr. Soch.,* I, 76.
[17] *Fridrikh Schiller, Sobr. Soch.,* I, 5.

The motto of the great poet [Schiller] was his saying : "The main thing for man is love of work; for it gives him not only the means of subsistence but it, and it alone, gives value to his life." Schiller was always striving and always emphasized that work was the joy and fulness of life. . . ."[18]

Schiller's praise of indefatigable work is, of course, "adjusted" to fit into the framework of Soviet needs and Soviet ideology.

Since literature, according to the Marxist point of view, reflects but the forces and conditions of economic production, Schiller's poetry cannot be an exception. Thus Soviet criticism gives not an aesthetic but an ideological, a pragmatic interpretation of Schiller : seizing upon his concept and eulogy of work, this criticism parallels it to the Soviet society's concept of work (in the cause of a classless society, of the welfare of future generations, of a workers' and peasants' state, etc.). In the practice of the "construction of communism" this amounts to idolizing industrial and agricultural production which is set up as a kind of quasi-metaphysical ideal and quasi-mystical value in itself. Obviously, such a concept of work, to say nothing of the inhuman system of forced labor, has nothing in common with the free and creative "Spiel"—"play" eulogized by Schiller as "joy and fulness of life." Whereas God is excluded from the Soviet concept of work, no fruitful work is possible without God in the conception of Schiller :

> Von der Stirne heiss
> Rinnen muss der Schweiss,
> Soll das Werk den Meister loben;
> Doch der Segen kommt von oben.
> ("Das Lied von der Glocke")

In the meantime—regardless of any "official" or "dialectical" interpretation—Schiller continues to speak to the Russian people

[18] F. P. Schiller, *Fridrikh Schiller*, p. 12.

in his own challenging language capable of electrifying the hearts of the young generation. If the past may be regarded as an oracle foretelling things to come then there is every reason to believe that Schiller's influence on the Russia of tomorrow will not be less than the impact he had on the Russia of the past. It may well be that his great spirit will spark forces which will yet lead to new and unexpected developments.

Bibliography

This bibliography includes only works that were actually cited. For easy reference it was decided to list the items under the chapters in which they occur and to group them as primary and secondary sources. Within this grouping the items are arranged alphabetically by author.

INTRODUCTION

Primary Sources:

Belinsky, V. G. *Sochinenia V. G. Belinskogo.* 4 vols. Kiev, 1910–11.

Gertsen (Herzen), A. I. *Polnoye sobranie sochineniy i pisem,* ed. M. K. Lemke. 22 vols. St. Petersburg, 1919–25.

Vengerov, S. A. (ed.). *Schiller.* 4 vols. St. Petersburg, 1900.

Secondary Sources:

Braun, Maximilian. *Russische Dichtung im neunzehnten Jahrhundert.* Heidelberg, 1953.

Cyzevskyj, D. "Schiller und die Brüder Karamasow," *Zeitschrift für Slawische Philologie,* VI (Leipzig, 1929), 1–42.

Ehrhard, M. *Joukovski et le pré-romantisme Russe.* Paris, 1938.

Fischer, Rudolf. "Schillers Widerhall in der Russischen Literatur," *Berichte über die Verhandlungen der Sächsischen Akademie der Wissenschaften zu Leipzig* (Berlin, 1958), Bd. 103, Heft 5, 1–26.

———. "Schiller und Puschkin," *Wissenschaftliche Zeitschrift der Karl Marx-Universität Leipzig,* IX (Leipzig, 1959–1960), Heft 1, 73–76.

Gruzinsky, A. E. *Literaturnoye ocherki.* Moskva, 1902.

Lenin, V. I. *O literature i iskusstve.* Moskva, 1957.

Lotman, Ju. M. "Neue Materialien über die Anfänge der Beschäftigung mit Schiller in der Russischen Literatur," *Wissenschaftliche Zeitschrift der Ernst-Moritz-Arndt-Universität Greifswald* (Greifswald), VIII, 5/6, pp. 419–434.

Mirsky, D. S. *A History of Russian Literature.* London, 1927.

Nelidov, F. F. *Ocherki po istorii noveyshey Russkoy Literatury.* Moskva, 1907.

Passage, C. E. "The Influence of Schiller in Russia," *ASEER* (May, 1946), pp. 111–137.

Peterson, Otto P. *Schiller in Russland.* New York, 1934.

Tynyanov, Yu. *Pushkin v mirovoy literature.* Leningrad, 1926.

Veselovsky, Yury. "Schiller kak vdokhnovitel Russkikh Pisateley," *Russkaya Mysl,* II (Moskva, 1906), 1–15.

Volm, Matthew, *W. A. Zhukovskij als Übersetzer.* Ann Arbor, Michigan, 1945.

Zamotin, I. I. *Romantizm dvadtsatykh godov XIX stoletia v Russkoy Literature.* 2 vols. St. Petersburg–Moskva, 1913.

CHAPTER I

Primary Sources :

Bakunin, M. A. *Polnoye sobranie sochineniy,* ed. A. I. Bakunin. 2 vols. St. Petersburg [?], n.d.

Belinsky, V. G. *Pisma.* 3 vols. St. Petersburg, 1914.

———. *Sochinenia V. G. Belinskogo.* 4 vols. Kiev, 1910–11.

Gertsen (Herzen), A. I. *Polnoye sobranie sochineniy i pisem.* ed. M. K. Lemke. 22 vols. St. Petersburg, 1919–25.

Schiller, Friedrich. *Friedrich Schiller—Briefe.* Reinhard Buchwald, ed. Leipzig, n.d.

———. *Schillers Sämtliche Werke.* Säkular–Ausgabe, 16 vols. Stuttgart & Berlin, n.d.[1]

---

[1] Schiller's *Briefe* and *Sämtliche Werke* were used throughout the following Chapters.

Stankevich, N. V. *N. V. Stankevich–Perepiska.* Aleksey Stankevich, ed. Moskva, 1914.

Secondary Sources :

Astrov, V. A. *Ne nashli puti.* St. Petersburg, 1914.

Berger, Karl. *Schiller.* 2 vols. München, 1909–10.

Bowman, Herbert E. *Vissarion Belinski.* Cambridge, Mass. 1954.

Chizhevsky, D. I. *Gegel v Rossii.* Paris, 1939.

Cyzevskyj, D. I. "Schiller und die Brüder Karamasow," *Zeitschrift für Slawische Philologie,* VI (Leipzig, 1929), 1–42.

Gronicka, André von. "Friedrich Schiller's Marquis Posa," *GR,* XXVI (October, 1951), 196–214.

Heiseler, Bernt von. *Schiller.* Gütersloh, 1959.

Lossky, N. O. *History of Russian Philosophy.* New York, 1951.

L. I. "N. V. Stankevich," *Biblioteka dla chtenia* (St. Petersburg, March–April 1858), pp. 1–46.

Maykov, L. N. "Zapiska I. S. Turgeneva," *Vestnik Yevropy* (St. Petersburg, January 1899), pp. 5–18.

Mirsky, D. S. *A History of Russian Literature.* London, 1927.

Nelidov, F. F. *Ocherki po istorii noveyshey Russkoy Literatury.* Moskva, 1907.

Sakulin, P. "Istoriko-literaturnye besedy," *Vestnik Yevropy,* II (Petrograd, 1915), 246–265.

Sidorov, N. P. "N. V. Stankevich," *Golos Minuvshago,* IX (St. Petersburg, 1913), 1–6.

Tikhonravov, N. S. *Sochinenia.* 3 vols. Moskva, 1898.

Tolstoy, L. N. *Tolstovsky Muzey.* Obshchestvo Tolstovskogo Muzeya, ed. St. Petersburg, 1911.

Veselovsky, Aleksey N. *Zapadnoye vlianie v novoy Russkoy Literature.* Moskva, 1916.

Veselovsky, Yury. "Schiller kak vdokhnovitel Russkikh Pisateley," *Russkaya Mysl,* II (Moskva, 1906), 1–15.

Volynsky, A. L. *Russkie Kritiki.* St. Petersburg, 1896.

Yarmerstedt, V. K. "Mirosozertsanie kruzhka Stankevicha i poeziya Koltsova," *Voprosy Filosofii i Psikhologii* (Moskva,

March, 1894), pp. 162–181.

Zenkovsky, Vasily V. *A History of Russian Philosophy.* 2 vols. New York, 1953.

CHAPTER II

Primary Sources :

Belinsky, V. G. *Polnoye sobranie sochineniy.* 13 vols. Moskva, 1953–59.

Lermontov, M. Yu. *Polnoye sobranie sochineniy.* 4 vols. Moskva–Leningrad, 1947.

———. *Polnoye sobranie sochineniy.* 4 vols. Moskva–Leningrand, 1948.

Secondary Sources :

Klassiki Russkoy dramy. Leningrad–Moskva, 1940.

Kostka, Edmund. "The Influence of Schiller's Aesthetics on the Dramas of Lermontov," *PQ,* XXX (October, 1951), 393–402.

———. "Schiller's Influence on the Early Dramas of Lermontov," *PQ,* XXXII (October, 1953), 396–410.

———. "Schiller's influence on Lermontov's Drama *The Two Brothers,*" *PQ,* XXXV (April, 1956), 186–190.

Literaturnoye Nasledstvo. Vols. XLIII/XLIV. Moskva, 1941.

Manning, Clarence A. "The Dramas of Schiller and Lermontov," *PQ,* VIII (1929), 11–20.

Mirsky, D. S. *A History of Russian Literature.* New York, 1949.

Troyat, Henri. *L'étrange destin de Lermontov.* Paris, 1952.

Zamotin, I. I. *M. Yu. Lermontov.* Varshava, 1914.

CHAPTER III

Primary Sources :

Belinsky, V. G. *Dmitry Kalinin, Sbornik obshchestva lubiteley rossiyskoy slovesnosti na 1891 god,* pp. 437–533. Moskva, 1891.

———. *Polnoye sobranie sochineniy V. G. Belinskogo,* ed. S. A.

Vengerov, 12 vols. St. Petersburg, 1900.

――――. *Sochinenia V. G. Belinskogo.* 4 vols. Kiev, 1910–11.

――――. *Pisma.* 3 vols. St. Petersburg, 1914.

――――. *Stati i materialy.* Leningrad, 1949.

Vengerov, S. A. (ed.). *Schiller.* 4 vols. St. Petersburg, 1900.

Secondary Sources :

Annenkov, P. V. *Literaturnye vospominania.* Leningrad, 1928.

Bowman, H. E. *Vissarion Belinski.* Cambridge, Mass., 1954.

Chizhevsky, D. "Schiller v Rossii," *Novy Zhurnal,* XLV (New York, 1956), 109–135.

Karpovich, M. "Dostoyevsky, Belinsky, Schiller," *Novy Zhurnal,* XLV (New York, 1956), 280–283.

Lavretsky, A. *Estetika Belinskogo.* Moskva, 1959.

Literaturnoye Nasledstvo. Vols. LV, LVI. Moskva, 1948–50.

Lo Gatto, Ettore. *Storia della Letteratura Russa.* Firenze, 1944.

Malia, Martin E. "Schiller and the Early Russian Left," *Harvard Slavic Studies,* IV (Cambridge, Mass., 1957), 169–200.

Malnick, Bertha. "V. G. Belinsky," *SEER* (London, May, 1949), pp. 363–380.

Masaryk, Thomas G. *The Spirit of Russia.* 2 vols. New York, 1955.

Mirsky, D. S. *A History of Russian Literature.* London, 1927.

Nelidov, F. F. *Ocherki po istorii noveyshey Russkoy Literatury.* Moskva, 1907.

Panayev, I. I. *Literaturnye vospominania.* Leningrad, 1950.

Peterson, Otto P. *Schiller in Russland.* New York, 1934.

Pypin, A. N. *Belinsky.* St. Petersburg, 1908.

Schiller, F. P. *Fridrikh Schiller.* Moskva, 1955.

Schultze, Bernhard. *W. G. Belinskij.* München, 1958.

Silberstein, Leopold. "Belinskij und Cernysevskij," *Jahrbücher für Kultur und Geschichte der Slaven,* N. F. VII, Heft II (Breslau, 1931), 163–189.

Struve, Gleb. "A Belinsky Centenary Bibliography," *SEER* (London, May, 1949), pp. 546–562.

Veselovsky, Aleksey. *Zapadnoye vlianie v novoy Russkoy Literature.* Moskva, 1906.

Veselovsky, Yury. "Schiller kak vdokhnovitel Russkikh Pisateley," *Russkaya Mysl,* II (Moskva, 1906), 1–15.

Wellek, René. "Social and Aesthetic Values in Russian Nineteenth-Century Literary Criticism," *Continuity and Change in Russian and Soviet Thought,* E. J. Simmons, ed. Cambridge, Mass., 1955. pp. 381–397.

Yengalychev, N. N. "V. G. Belinsky," *Russkaya Starina,* XV (St. Petersburg, January, 1876), 61–87.

Zenkovsky, Vasily V. *A History of Russian Philosophy.* 2 vols. New York, 1953.

CHAPTER IV

Primary Sources :
Bakunin, M. A. *Sobranie sochineniy i pisem.* 4 vols. Moskva, 1934–35.
———— *Polnoye sobranie sochineniy,* A. I. Bakunin, ed. 2 vols. St. Petersburg [?], n.d.

Secondary Sources :
Annenkov, P. V. *Literaturnye vospominania.* Leningrad, 1928.
Mikhail Bakunin, Sbornik. Moskva, 1926.
Carr, E. H. *Michael Bakunin.* London, 1937.
Chizhevsky, D. I. *Gegel v Rossii.* Paris, 1939.
Iswolsky, Hélène. *La vie de Bakounine. Paris,* 1930.
————. *Soul of Russia.* New York, 1943.
Kornilov, A. A. *Molodye gody Mikhaila Bakunina.* Moskva, 1915.
Masaryk, Thomas G. *The Spirit of Russia. 2 vols.* New York, 1955.
Nomad, Max. *Apostles of Revolution.* Boston, 1939.
Pfitzner, Josef. "Michael Bakunin und Preussen im Jahre 1848," *Jahrbücher für Kultur und Geschichte der Slaven,* N. F. VII, Heft III (Breslau, 1931), 231–284.

Steklov, Yu. *M. A. Bakunin.* 4 vols. Moskva–Leningrad, 1926–27.

Weiant, E. T. *Sources of Modern Mass Atheism in Russia.* Basel, 1950.

Wilson, Edmund. *To the Finland Station.* New York, 1940.

CHAPTER V

Primary Sources :

Gertsen (Herzen), A. I. *Polnoye sobranie sochineniy i pisem,* ed. M. K. Lemke. 22 vols. St. Petersburg, 1919–25.

"Neizdannye pisma A. I. Gertsena k N. I. i T. A. Astrakovym," ed. L. L. Dogmer, *Novy Zhurnal,* XLVI (New York, 1956), 1–48; XLVII (1956), 49–80; XLVIII (1957), 81–112; XLIX (1957), 113–144 (Prilozhenie).

Ogarev, N. P. *Izbrannye proizvedenia.* 2 vols. Moskva, 1956.

Stankevich, N. V. *N. V. Stankevich—Perepiska,* ed. Aleksey Stankevich. Moskva, 1914.

Secondary Sources :

Annenkov, P. V. *Literaturnye vospominania.* Leningrad, 1928.

Bogucharsky, V. Ya. *Aleksandr Ivanovich Gertsen.* St. Petersburg, 1912.

Derzhavin, N. S. *A. I. Gertsen.* Moskva–Leningrad, 1947.

Elsberg, Ya. *Gertsen.* Moskva, 1956.

Gertsen v vospominaniakh sovremennikov. Moskva, 1956.

Huch, Ricarda. *Michael Bakunin und die Anarchie.* Leipzig, 1923.

Kostka, Edmund. "Grillparzer and the East," *Monatshefte* October, 1955), pp. 273–284.

Literaturnoye Nasledstvo. Vols. XXXIX/XL (1941), and LXI (1953), Moskva.

Malia, Martin E. "Schiller and the Early Russian Left," *Harvard Slavic Studies,* IV, 169–200. Cambridge, Mass., 1957.

———. *Alexander Herzen and the Birth of Russian Socialism.* Cambridge, Mass., 1961.

Martini, Fritz. *Deutsche Literaturgeschichte.* Stuttgart, 1952.

Masaryk, Thomas G. *The Spirit of Russia.* 2 vols. New York, 1919.

Milioukov, P. N. *Le Mouvement Intellectuel Russe.* Paris, 1918.

Mirsky, D. S. *A History of Russian Literature.* New York, 1949.

Peterson, Otto P. *Schiller in Russland.* New York, 1934.

Schaible, K. H. *Geschichte der Deutschen in England.* Strassburg, 1885.

Setschkareff, Wsewolod. *Schellings Einfluss in der Russischen Literatur der 20–er und 30–er Jahre des XIX Jahrhunderts.* Leipzig, 1939.

Tkhorzhevsky, Ivan. *Russkaya Literatura.* Paris, 1950.

CHAPTER VI

Primary Sources :

Anonymous. "Correspondance de Michel Bakounine," Lettre d'Ogareff à Bakounine, *La Société Nouvelle,* II (Paris, 1895), 595.

Gertsen (Herzen), A. I. *Polnoye sobranie sochineniy i pisem,* ed. M. K. Lemke. 22 vols. St. Petersburg, 1919–25.

"Neizdannye pisma A. I. Gertsena k N. I. i T. A. Astrakovym," ed. L. L. Dogmer, *Novy Zhurnal,* XLVII (New York, 1956), 49–80 and XLIX (1957), 113–144 (Prilozhenie).

Mendelson, N. M. "Iz proshlogo," Pisma N. P. Ogareva, *Novy Mir,* V (Moskva, 1931), 170–194.

Ogarev, N. P. *Izbrannye sotsialno-politicheskie i filosofskie proizvedenia.* 2 vols. Moskva, 1952–56.

———. *Izbrannye proizvedenia.* 2 vols. Moskva, 1956.

"N. P. Ogarev," Pisma k T. N. Granovskomu, A. I. Gertsenu i M. F. Korsh, ed. N. M. Mendelson, *Zvenya,* I (Moskva, 1932), 96–154.

Secondary Sources :

Altshuller, A. & Tsinkovich, V. "Schiller v Rossii," *Teatr,* V

(Moskva, 1955), 143–145.

Anikst, A. "O kharaktere realizma Schillera," *Teatr,* V (Moskva, 1955), 53–67.

Annenkov, P. V. *Literaturnye vospominania.* Leningrad, 1928.

Arkhiv N. A. i N. P. Ogarevykh. Moskva, 1930.

Berger, Karl. *Schiller.* 2 vols. München, 1909.

Chizhevsky, D. "Schiller v Rossii," *Novy Zhurnal,* XLV (New York, 1956), 109–135.

————. *Gegel v Rossii.* Paris, 1939.

Eichenbaum, B. M. "Tragedii Schillera v svete yego teorii tragicheskogo," *Iskusstvo staroye i novoye,* Sbornik, St. Petersburg, 1921, pp. 113–127.

Gershenzon, M. *Obrazy proshlogo.* Moskva, 1912.

————. *Istoria Molodoy Rossii.* Moskva, 1908.

————. *Zhizn V. S. Pecherina.* Moskva, 1910.

Iovchuk, M. T. *Filosofskie i sotsiologicheskie vzglyady Ogareva.* Moskva, 1957.

Jzjumov, A. "Der Briefwechsel V. S. Pecerins mit A. I. Herzen," *Jahrbücher für Kultur und Geschichte der Slaven,* N. F. IX, Heft IV (Breslau, 1933), 493–517.

Kropotkin, P. *Ideals and Realities in Russian Literature.* New York, 1925.

Literaturnoye Nasledstvo. Vols. XXXIX–XL (1941), LXI (1953). Moskva.

Malia, Martin E. *Alexander Herzen and the Birth of Russian Socialism.* Cambridge, Mass., 1961.

————. "Schiller and the Early Russian Left," *Harvard Slavic Studies* IV, (Cambridge, Mass., 1957), 169–200.

Milioukov, P. N. *Le Mouvement Intellectuel Russe.* Paris, 1918.

Mirsky, D. S. *A History of Russian Literature.* New York, 1949.

Nelidov, F. F. *Ocherki po istorii noveyshey Russkoy Literatury.* Moskva, 1907.

Opisanie rukopisey N. P. Ogareva. ed. A. Z. Chernyak. Moskva, 1952.

Passek, T. P. *Iz dalnikh let*. Moskva–Leningrad, 1931.

Peterson, Otto P. *Schiller in Russland*. New York, 1934.

Piper, L. *Mirovozzrenie Gertsena*. Moskva-Leningrad, 1935.

Putintsev, V. *N. Ogarev*. Moskva, 1959.

Sakulin, P. N. *Iz istorii Russkago idealizma*. Moskva, 1913.

Tkorzhevsky, Ivan, *Russkaya Literatura*. Paris, 1950.

Yakovenko, Boris V. "Aus dem Briefwechsel vor kurzem tätiger Personen," *Der Russische Gedanke*, IX (1889), 161 (Notes).

CHAPTER VII

Primary Sources :

Dostoyevsky, F. M. *Polnoye sobranie sochineniy*. 14 vols. St. Petersburg, 1883–1904.

———. *Polnoye sobranie khudozhestvennykh proizvedeniy*. 10 vols. Moskva–Leningrad, 1926–28.

———. "Nechto o Schillere," *Vremya*, I (St. Petersburg, 1861), 113–114.

———. *The Diary of a Writer*. trans. by Boris Brasol. 2 vols. New York, 1949.

———. *Pisma*. ed. A. S. Dolinin. 4 vols. Moskva–Leningrad, 1928–59.

Secondary Sources :

Antoniy, Preosvyashchenny. *Slovar k tvoreniam Dostoyevskago*. Sofia, 1921.

Berger, Karl *Schiller*. 2 vols. München, 1909.

Chizhevsky, D. "Schiller v Rossii," *Novy Zhurnal*, XLV (New York, 1956), 109–135.

Cyzevskyj, D. "Schiller und die Brüder Karamasow," *Zeitschrift für Slawische Philologie*, VI (Leipzig, 1929), 1–42.

Dostoevsky. ed. René Wellek. Englewood Cliffs, N. J., 1962.

Fischer, Rudolf. "Schiller und Puschkin," *Weimarer Beiträge*, III (1960), 603–611.

Gorky, Maxim. *Sobranie Sochineniy*. 30 vols. Moskva, 1949–55.

Gronicka, André von. "Thomas Mann and Russia," *The Stature of Thomas Mann,* ed. Charles Neider. New York, 1947.

Grossman, Leonid. *Tvorchestvo Dostoyevskogo.* Moskva, 1928.

Ivanov, Vyacheslav. *Po zvezdam.* St. Petersburg, 1909.

Iwanow, Wjatscheslaw. *Dostojewskij.* Tübingen, 1932.

Karpovich, M. "Dostoyevsky, Belinsky, Schiller," *Novy Zhurnal,* XLV (New York, 1956), 280–283.

Kirpotin, V. Ya. *F. M. Dostoyevsky.* Moskva, 1960.

Lauth, R. *Die Philosophie Dostojewskis.* München, 1950.

Lloyd, J. A. T. *Fyodor Dostoevsky.* New York, 1947.

Lossky, Nikolay. *Dostoyevsky i yego khristianskoye miroponimanie.* New York ,1953.

Mann, Thomas. "Dostojewski—mit Massen," and "Goethe und Tolstoi," *Gesammelte Werke.* 10 vols. Berlin, 1955 (X, 617–635, 157–273).

Maurina, Zenta. *Dostojewskij.* Memmingen, 1952.

Meier–Graefe, Julius. *Dostojewski.* Berlin, 1926.

Michelis, Eurialo de. *Dostojevskij,* Firenze, 1950.

Motylev, T. L. "Dostoyevsky i mirovaya literatura," *Tvorchestvo F. M. Dostoyevskogo.* Moskva, 1959.

Parker, Fan. "The Revival of Dostoevskij on the Soviet Stage," *SEEJ,* XVI (Spring, 1958, No. 1), 33–41.

Pletnev, Rostislav. "La légende chrétienne dans l'oeuvre de Dostoïevsky," *SEES,* VI (Montréal, Autumn–Winter, 1961), 131–157.

Russkie pisateli o literature. 3 vols. Leningrad, 1939.

Stammler, Heinrich. "Dostoevsky's Aesthetics and Schelling's Philosophy of Art," *Comparative Literature,* VII (1955), 313–323.

Tkhorzhevsky, Ivan. *Russkaya Literatura.* Paris, 1950.

Vengerov, S. A., (ed.). *Schiller.* 4 vols. St. Petersburg, 1900.

Wasiolek, Edward. "AUT CAESAR, AUT NIHIL : A Study of Dostoevsky's Moral Dialectic," *PMLA,* LXXVIII (March, 1963), 89–97.

Woodhouse, C. M. *Dostoievsky.* New York, 1951.

Yarmolinsky, Avrahm. *Dostoevsky.* New York, 1934.

CHAPTER VIII

Primary Sources :

Dostoyevsky, F. M. *Polnoye sobranie khudozhestvennykh proiz-vedeniy.* 10 vols. Moskva–Leningrad, 1926–28.

―――. *The Diary of a Writer,* trans. by B. Brasol. 2 vols. New York, 1949.

Ivanov, Vyacheslav. *Po zvezdam.* St. Petersburg, 1909.

―――. *Freedom and the Tragic Life,* Foreword by Sir Maurice Bowra. New York, 1952.

Iwanow, Wiatscheslaw, *Die Russische Idee,* trans. by J. Schor. Tübingen, 1930.

Iwanow Wjatscheslaw. *Dostojewskij,* trans. by Alexander Kresling. Tübingen, 1932.

Secondary Sources :

Anonymous. "K yubileyu Schillera," *Vesy,* VI (1905), 78–79.

Bakshy, Alexander. *The Path of the Modern Russian Stage and Other Essays.* London, 1916.

Berger, Karl. *Schiller.* 2 vols. München, 1909.

Deschartes, O. "V. Ivanov," *Oxford Slavonic Papers,* V (1954), 41–58.

Fechter, Paul. *Geschichte der Deutschen Literatur.* Gütersloh, 1957.

Kayser, Wolfgang. "Dithyrambe," *Die Deutsche Lyrik,* ed. Benno von Wiese. 2 vols. Düsseldorf, 1956.

Lo Gatto, Ettore. *Storia della Letteratura Russa.* Firenze, 1944.

Makovsky, Sergey. "Vyacheslav Ivanov v Rossii," *Novy Zhurnal,* XXX (New York, 1952), 135–151.

Mirsky, D. S. *A History of Russian Literature.* New York, 1949.

Rehder, Helmut. "Zum Problem der 'Erschütterung' in Schillers Dichtung und Gedankenwelt," *Schiller 1759/1959,* ed. John R. Frey. Urbana, Illinois, 1959. pp. 104–128.

Schnoor, Hans. *Oper, Operette, Konzert.* Gütersloh, 1956.

Scholz, Wilhelm von. *Friedrich Schiller.* Hamburg, n.d.

Silz, Walter. "Chorus and Choral Function in Schiller," *Schiller 1759/1959,* pp. 147–170.

Tkhorzhevsky, Ivan. *Russkaya Literatura.* Paris, 1950.

CHAPTER IX

Primary Sources :

Blok, Alexander. *Sobranie sochineniy.* 12 vols. Leningrad, 1936.
———. *Sochinenia.* 2 vols. Moskva, 1955.

Dostoyevsky, F. M. *The Diary of a Writer,* trans. by Boris Brasol. 2 vols. New York, 1949.

Gorky, Maxim. *Sobranie sochineniy.* 30 vols. Moskva, 1949-55.

Schiller, Friedrich. *Fridrikh Schiller—Sobranie sochineniy,* ed. Vilmont & Samarin. 7 vols. Moskva, 1955.

Secondary Sources :

Demtschenko, K. & Genin, L. "Schiller auf den Bühnen des revolutionären Petrograd," *Sinn und Form,* XI (Berlin, 1959), Heft 5/6, pp. 927–935.

Gorky, Maxim. *M. Gorky—Materialy i issledovania,* ed. Balukhaty & Desnitsky. 4 vols. Moskva-Leningrad, 1936-41.

Schiller, Franz Petrovich. *Fridrikh Schiller.* Moskva, 1955.

Veselovsky, Yury. "Schiller kak vdokhnovitel Russkikh Pisateley," *Russkaya Mysl,* II (Moskva, 1906), 1–15.

Index

Achilles, 137

Aeschylus, 77

Aesthetics, 14, 15, 20, 21, 25, 32, 39, 40, 45–48, 61, 67, 68, 70–72, 78, 86, 91, 95, 99, 113, 120, 123, 124, 133, 139, 142, 156, 160, 165, 166, 179, 184, 217, 221, 227, 228, 239, 247, 248, 250, 252, 255, 280, 281, 287

Aksakov, Konstantin S., 25, 98, 103, 105

Alba, Duke, 102

Alexander I, 14, 139

Aller (Ogarev's tutor), 185

Altshuller, A., 190

America, 58, 214

Anarchism, 116, 130, 159, 195, 281

Anikst, A., 212

Annenkov, Pavel V., 91, 122, 138, 182

Antiquity, 110, 111, 136, 162, 165, 251–253, 256, 262, 271

Antoniy, P., 248

Arminius, 110

Arnim, Bettina von, 119

Art, 25, 26, 46, 47, 67, 68, 70, 72, 85, 91–94, 96, 102, 104, 107, 109, 112, 124, 168, 186, 217, 221, 222, 227, 242, 249, 250, 267, 278, 283, 286

Astrov, V. A., 24, 25

Atheism, 54, 61, 118, 130, 133, 230

Augustenburg, Prince of, 200

Avrora, 14

Babeuf, Francois N., 177, 178

Baggesen, J., 252, 277

Bakshy, Alexander, 256

Bakunin, Mikhail A., 18, 22, 25, 30, 41, 45, 87, 91, 92, 95–97, 101, 102, 105, 106, 109, 110, 113, 116–134, 159, 192, 205, 209, 280, 281; *Catechism of a Revolutionist,* 130, 131, 134, 281; *State and Anarchy,* 131, 134

Bakunin, Nikolay, 105, 123, 124

Bakunina, Alexandra, 129

Bakunina, Lubov, 37, 39, 42

Bakunina, Tatyana, 126

Bakunina, Varvara, 118, 119, 125

Balukhaty, S. D., 285

Beer family, The, 30, 129

Beethoven, Ludwig van, 267, 269, 273

Belinsky, Vissarion G., 15, 16, 18, 20, 22, 24–27, 41, 45–47, 49, 81–115, 116, 118, 119, 122–125, 126, 154, 158, 196, 199, 200, 212, 219, 245, 252, 280, 286; "Anniversary of Borodino," 94; "Derzhavin," 200; *Dmitry Kalinin,* 81–84, 111; "Griboyedov's *Woe from Wit,*" 94; "Hamlet," 94; "Literary Reveries," 86, 95, 111; "Menzel, the Critic of Goethe," 94; "Pushkin," 112, 114

Bell, The, see *Kolokol*

Bely, Andrey, 19

Béranger, Pierre J. de, 110